Roman Nottinghamshire

Mark Patterson

For Christian

Roman Nottinghamshire

Mark Patterson

Five Leaves Publications
www.fiveleaves.co.uk

http://romannottinghamshire.wordpress.com/

Roman Nottinghamshire
by Mark Patterson

Published and reprinted in 2011
by Five Leaves Publications,
PO Box 8786, Nottingham NG1 9AW
www.fiveleaves.co.uk

Reprinted with a new Afterword 2012

ISBN: 9781907869129

Five Leaves acknowledges
financial support from
Arts Council England

Five Leaves is represented by Turnaround,
and distributed to the booktrade by Central Books

Front cover photograph courtesy of
Newark and Sherwood District Council,
back cover photograph by Mark Patterson

Other photograph credits
are listed on pages 282-285

Typeset and designed by
Four Sheets Design and Print

Printed in Exeter by Imprint Digital.

Contents

Introduction 7

Chapter 1 11
Margidunum: the last remains of Roman Nottinghamshire

Chapter 2 14
Roman invasion and the fate of the Corieltauvi
History of the Corieltauvi; Romanisation; recent excavations at Besthorpe; rebellion in the new province

Chapter 3 53
Margidunum II: the excavations of Oswald and Todd

Chapter 4 68
Life's essentials in Roman Nottinghamshire: food, work, art and belief
Named Roman people in the region; Redhill curse tablets; cult of Attis; cult of Toutatis; Christianity; art; industry; diet

Chapter 5 109
Following the Fosse Way: Ivan Margary's road 5f
Route of the Fosse Way; Vernemetum, Ad Pontem, Newark, Crococolana; Tracing the Fosse Way today; the dualling of the A46

Chapter 6 158
To the ford at Littleborough and the temple at Redhill
The road to Littleborough; Scaftworth fortlet; Other Roman roads; The road to and from Ad Pontem; Bawtry to Ollerton; Derby to Redhill

Chapter 7 182
Forts and other military sites
The fort at Broxtowe; Osmanthorpe; temporary camps at Calverton, Farnsfield, Gleadthorpe and Holme; Dorket Head

Chapter 8 206
Villas: lives of the rich and famous
Mansfield Woodhouse; Southwell; live archaeology in Southwell; Barton-in-Fabis; Oldcotes; Flawford; Car Colston; Thurgarton and Epperstone; Cromwell

Chapter 9 248
Hidden wealth: the coin hoards

Bibliography 260

Illustrations 282

Index 286

Afterword 298

Introduction

This book is an attempt to bring together in accessible narrative form some of the large amount of research, writing and thinking concerning life in a small part of the Roman Empire now called Nottinghamshire. Many other counties have their Roman histories; by contrast, Nottinghamshire's has hitherto been told in fragmented form via references in books and scores of scholarly articles published in specialist historical and archaeological journals. Some of these articles can be found relatively easily. For example, the excellent annual reports of Nottinghamshire's principal historical and archaeological society, the Thoroton Society of Nottinghamshire (hereafter referred to as the Thoroton Society), can be found in several local libraries. Many other articles, though, are in specialist journals accessible only via expensive subscriptions or through university libraries. Meanwhile, background material relevant to Nottinghamshire and the East Midlands in the Roman period is scattered across hundreds of books concerning the Roman province *Britannia*, which form a fraction of the vast quantity of volumes written about every conceivable aspect of Roman history and culture. The result is that the bulk of the detailed material about Nottinghamshire's Roman past has been practically inaccessible to the casual reader.

One arguable consequence of this is that there is a general low level of awareness among people in Nottinghamshire of their Roman heritage, a knowledge problem exacerbated by Nottinghamshire's reputation as a county of meagre archaeological interest. This issue was raised in print in 1954 when Thoroton Society member R.M. Butler described Nottinghamshire as an 'archaeological blackspot' and sought reasons for its 'backwardness' in the matter. He was talking about archaeology from all periods, not just Roman. But he continued: 'The first and most weighty reason is the absence of any large visible monuments of the past. Nottinghamshire has no Stonehenge, no Devil's Dyke, no Roman Wall. Such important sites are a principal factor in the growth of archaeological science.' Yet, while only two ancient sites meant anything to scholars beyond the county borders, both of these were Roman — *Margidunum* and the villa near Mansfield Woodhouse. The problem was that other counties, including the four neighbouring Nottinghamshire, just did things better.

Butler's point about the lack of 'large visible monuments' cannot be denied. No Roman structures are thought to remain intact except for a well that was recently discovered near *Margidunum* and a puzzling length of wall found near the villa at Southwell. But this apparently unpromising fact has to be placed beside the many treasures of Roman art and design that have been found in the county and the expectation that more remain to be discovered. Recent findings in south Nottinghamshire at *Margidunum*, for example, suggest that perceptions about the wealth and status of the long-buried Roman town may have to be upgraded. In Southwell, the discovery of the neatly constructed Roman wall has generated new debate and controversy about the future of the town's large villa and made the conservation of Roman heritage a live issue in the Minster town. At Oldcotes in Bassetlaw, north Nottinghamshire, a villa floor mosaic with an image of Theseus in the Minotaur's labyrinth probably still lies intact under a church and will, hopefully, one day see daylight again. Besides this, anybody with healthy curiosity should feel a sense of wonder at the influence that the ghosts of ancient Romans continue to exert on the Nottinghamshire landscape. If you drive along the A46 Fosse Way, or follow the road from Littleborough to Bawtry, or the road from Derby to Long Eaton, you are following routes laid out by Roman army road surveyors. If that sense of wonder is absent, then I hope this book will help change your mind, because generating a sense of awe and wonder about the living ancient past is one of this book's goals.

It needs be said only once that there was no such entity as 'Nottinghamshire' in the period AD 43–410 covered by this book. Modern county boundaries did not exist then. Neither was there a region called the East Midlands, although those words are used for the sake of clarity in this book to describe a recognised area of England. As far as anybody can tell, Nottinghamshire and most of the modern political entity called the East Midlands fell within an administrative area called the *Civitas Corieltauvorum* which had its capital at Leicester and took its name from the Iron Age tribe that occupied the region. The regional nature of the tribe and the civil administration over it means it is impossible to discuss 'Roman Nottinghamshire' without a regional context.

What was it that drove Rome to invade and colonise Britain — and Nottinghamshire — in the first place? Julius Caesar's two brief forays into southern England in 55 and 54 BC were, officially, part of his greater campaign to conquer Gaul in the name of the Roman Republic. His stated reasons for invasion were to prevent the Britons from assisting rebellious Gauls, and to gather information about the islands. In the Imperial era of the early 1st century AD, the Emperor Caligula organised, and then abandoned, an expedition to Britain. With these precedents, the Emperor Claudius launched a major invasion in 43 that was to have a permanent impact on the islands that, according to Pliny the Elder, its natives called Albion. The decision to invade may have been connected with Claudius' desire for both Imperial plunder and personal prestige, believing that Britain would give him quick military honours and shore up his claim as Emperor. His reign had begun inauspiciously, to say the least. According to the biographer Suetonius, Claudius hid, trembling, behind a pair of curtains on a balcony in the Emperor's Palace when he heard that Caligula, his nephew, had been assassinated. A soldier searching the Palace saw a pair of feet beneath the curtains and pulled Claudius out, at which Claudius clasped the soldier's knees, only to find himself proclaimed Emperor. Claudius' modern reputation for being a stammering, ungainly old fool — a 'doddering half-wit' in the words of the historian Guy de la Bédoyère — seems forever sealed by the 1970s TV series *I, Claudius* based on Robert Graves' novel. But, on reading Suetonius, Claudius also appeared to be a strange mix of traits to his contemporaries: a learned man immersed in history who wrote 28 volumes in Greek, yet such a figure of fun that he had olive stones thrown at him by guests when he feel asleep after dinner. But whatever his achievements or failings in Rome, he seems to have seriously underestimated British resistance to his invasion army. Claudius visited Britain only once, bringing war elephants to assist in the early stages of the invasion, and was back in Rome six months later. A triumphal procession was held in Rome and Claudius renamed one of his sons Britannicus. But it took 40 years for the Roman army to reach northern Scotland and, ultimately, all of the island north of Hadrian's Wall was to remain out of Roman control for the duration of the Roman occupation, which ended in 410. Claudius' triumphal procession now appears as premature as President George W. Bush's proclamation of 'Mission Accomplished' after the 2003 invasion of Iraq.

My thanks go to: Peter Allen and Bingham Heritage Trails Association; Geoff Bethel and Dennis Sutera at the Highways Agency; Mike Bishop, former principal archaeologist at Nottinghamshire County Council; Dr Will Bowden of the University of Nottingham, for reading part of the manuscript; Ross Bradshaw, of Five Leaves Publications, for giving me the opportunity; Richard J. Buckley at the University of Leicester; Keith Challis and the Thoroton Society of Nottinghamshire; Adam Daubney of the Portable Antiquities Scheme in Lincolnshire; Mark Dorrington at Nottinghamshire Archives; Sam Glasswell and Katarzyna Wosiak of Bassetlaw Museum; Dr Fiona Haarer at the Society for the Promotion of Roman Studies (the Roman Society); Glyn Hughes and Kevin Winter at Newark and Sherwood District Council; City of Lincoln archaeologist Mick Jones; David Knight of Trent and Peak Archaeology; Ruth Leary; Andy Meloy at Scott Wilson; Nottingham Local Studies Library; Clare Pickersgill at the University of Nottingham Museum; Christine Shaw of Butser Ancient Farm; Southwell Community Archaeology Group; Ursilla Spence, senior archaeological officer at Nottinghamshire County Council; Adam Thompson of Salford University; the University of Nottingham Department of Maps and Special Collections; Nottingham City archaeologist Gordon Young and Ann Inscker, collections manager archaeology, history and natural sciences; and last but not least Virginia Baddeley, Historic Environment Record officer at Nottinghamshire County Council, who generously answered many questions, created a map and made room for me in her office.

Chapter 1

Margidunum: the last remains of Roman Nottinghamshire

Carving of a 'warrior god' believed to come from *Margidunum*.

The last standing remains of Roman Nottinghamshire appear to be a bump in a farmer's field next to the road from hell. They are the most obvious surviving defences of *Margidunum*, the sprawling Roman town that was a living, working roadside community for the 367 years that Britain was part of the Roman Empire. The town is clearly marked on the standard Ordnance Survey Explorer map of Nottingham and the Vale of Belvoir, no. 260. There, in the bold black capitals that the Ordnance Survey reserve specifically for Roman sites, on farmland about a thumb's length south of East Bridgford in Rushcliffe, you can see 'Margidvnvm Roman Town'. The road from hell, of course, is the A46 Fosse Way, the old Roman highway that swoops up from Leicester carrying up to 25,300 fast vehicles a day and has been ranked as one of the most dangerous trunk roads in Britain. And the bump? We should really be calling it a 'low mound' since these are the two words used by Professor Roger Wilson in his *Guide to the Roman Remains in Britain*, first published in 1975 and much reprinted since. Nottinghamshire is referenced only once in the whole book, and that's in an appendix. And the words relate to the last visible remains of *Margidunum*. The exact words are: 'Part of E defences of Margidvnvm visible as low mound.' But which low mound is it? Inconspicuous piles of earth can look pretty similar after all.

After tramping through mud on the *eastern* side of the A46 using a schematic map of *Margidunum*'s once broad ditch and rampart defences, I tracked Prof. Wilson's low mound down to the low mound that lies parallel to the road, near the entrance to a large field. It sits more or less over the place the map shows as being a location of the defences. And it is the only low mound that makes sense. So here are the last standing remains of the Roman Empire's presence in Nottinghamshire. No other Roman structures survive above ground in the county.

Margidunum itself has been slowly sinking back into the earth for 1,600 years — stolen stone by stone, ploughed over, and then rather more drastically flattened by the roundabout that was built here in the late 1960s and which takes its name from the Roman settlement without any intended irony. As the great architectural writer Nikolaus Pevsner noted of East Bridgford, with characteristic brevity: 'Its greatest archaeological treasure is not visible to the eye.'

At the time of my last visit, the ambient traffic noise around *Margidunum* was notched up a few more decibels by the growl of excavators and dumper trucks constructing a bridge to carry the new A46 dual carriageway on a route just west of the line of the ancient defences. A strange way to treat a Scheduled Ancient Monument, you might think, and especially one that was on English Heritage's 'Heritage At Risk' list in 2010. Yet for all this, *Margidunum* — or at least the idea of it — remains at the heart of the modern idea of *Roman Nottinghamshire.*

As far as anybody knows, *Margidunum* was among the largest Roman settlements in the county. Partly because of this, and partly because of its strategic location on the main Roman road midway between the regional administrative capital at Leicester and the Roman military fortress and army veterans' *colonia* at Lincoln, it is usually one of the few Roman sites in Nottinghamshire placed on maps showing the main road networks of Roman Britain. Yet in so many ways *Margidunum* is a puzzle that defies neat categorisation. The task of interpreting the site over its own 350-year existence is made all the harder because of perceived shortcomings in the two major excavations that took place at the site in the 20th century. As one modern archaeologist says of *Margidunum*: 'It's a nightmare.' Until recent decades the place was judged to have been the site of a Roman fort. Although the fields in which it stood go by the collective name of Burrow Fields, part of the area close to the site is called Castle Hill, an apparent reference to the remains of stone wall defences which could be seen at least until the middle of the 19th century. Then, in the 1960s, new archaeological analysis redefined *Margidunum* primarily as a somewhat untidy and sprawling civilian roadside settlement. Yes, it had been defended by a substantial network of ditches and ramparts and later a stone wall — but defences were not at all unusual for small Roman towns. Yet the signs of Roman military presence at *Margidunum* early in its history also suggested that there probably *had* been a fort close by — which nobody has found yet.

Subsequently, in 2003, as a result of geophysical surveys, fieldwalking and the recovery of Roman building rubble, a substantial villa building was found in a field to the south west of the defences, near the entrance to RAF Newton. Featuring what appeared to be a large walled courtyard, the villa's complex of core rooms has been estimated to measure around 100 by 60 metres (328 by 197ft), placing the building among the largest villas of its type in the region. The discovery of this villa, and at least two others nearby, suggests that *Margidunum* had at least a handful of well-off residents and neighbours and was connected to several productive villa estates in the Romano-British countryside.

More recently, part of another previously unknown substantial building and other structures at the site came to light when soil was stripped off beside the Fosse as part of the archaeological survey which took place prior to the A46 dualling scheme. Most of what is left of this building remains unexcavated and unseen. But with at least three villas known to be close to *Margidunum*, and new roads, tracks and field marks also discovered, the evidence is building that the accepted interpretation of this Roman town may have to change. In brief, the town seems to have been both larger and wealthier than previously thought. Clearly, the *Margidunum* story is still far from complete, and unravelling that story may have become harder with a new dual carriageway skimming the edge of the ancient defences.

Chapter 2

Roman invasion and the fate of the *Corieltauvi*

Educated Romans in Italy and the rest of the Empire must have heard about the land in distant Britain that would later be called Nottinghamshire. The polymath Ptolemy, writing in Greek in 2nd century Alexandria, identified the tribal people of England's eastern Midlands region, the *Corieltauvi*, in his guide to the places of the known world, the *Geographia*. As well as locating the *Corieltauvi* in the section devoted to the British Isles, Ptolemy's book also named *Ratae* (Leicester) and *Lindum* (Lincoln) as the tribe's two towns, and gave reasonably accurate mileage distances for both from *Londinium*. Yet Ptolemy almost certainly never visited Britain, never mind Leicester. For him, as for perhaps most other citizens of the Roman Empire who gave it a thought, Britain was probably regarded as a distant, isolated, wet and cold land whose wild people were still only partly pacified a century after the Emperor Claudius had invaded with four legions in AD 43. A century before then a Republican army under the ambitious general and politician Julius Caesar had invaded Britain two years running, in 55 and 54 BC, and had both times returned to Gaul after scoring victories over southern British tribes. Caesar's advance didn't penetrate much further north than the Thames and so he may have had scant knowledge of the *Corieltauvi* people who occupied present-day Nottinghamshire, Lincolnshire, Leicestershire and perhaps northern Northamptonshire. Nevertheless, in his third-person account of his wars in Britain and Gaul, Caesar gave the first eye-witness description of the lifestyles of Britain's Iron Age people:

> *Most of the tribes in the interior do not grow corn but live on milk and meat, and wear skins. All the Britons dye their bodies with woad, which produces a blue colour, and this gives them a more terrifying appearance in battle. They wear their hair long, and*

> *shave the whole of their bodies except the head and the upper lip. Wives are shared between groups of ten or twelve men, especially between brothers and between fathers and sons; but the offspring of these unions are counted as the children of the man with whom a particular woman cohabited first.* [1]

Later writers such as the 1st century historian Tacitus emphasised the bravery and hardihood of British people, but still felt compelled to stress that Rome was dealing with people who were beyond real understanding:

> *Who the first inhabitants of Britain were, whether natives or immigrants, remains obscure; one must remember we are dealing with barbarians.*[2]

Caesar returned to Gaul at the end of summer in 54 BC, taking British hostages with him and arranging for subdued tribal kings to pay a regular financial tribute to Rome. Although the experience had been acutely hostile for the Britons, the brush with Caesar's army encouraged greater communication and exchange between Roman and British cultures, or at least the culture of the people living in the southern areas facing Roman Gaul. Continental-made goods such as pottery had long found their way into Britain and exports to Rome now included silver, gold, iron, cattle, hides, hunting dogs — and slaves. Yet almost a century later, in 43, an Imperial army of perhaps 40,000 soldiers under the fourth Emperor, Claudius, landed in Kent, with the intention of colonising the entire island. Directed by the province's first soldier-governor, Aulus Plautius, four legions began the process of subduing the disunited regional patchwork of tribes. The drive north and into western and eastern England seems to have been the responsibility of Legion IX *Hispana* and Legion XIV *Gemina*. The occupation of the East Midlands was probably completed by 47 when a new governor, Ostorius Scapula, took over the direction of the campaign. It is not known which of the two legions had responsibility for the region, but it was Legion IX that was subsequently stationed at Lincoln, where a legionary fortress was constructed.

Roman army engineers had initially built two roads to aid the army's penetration and consolidation in the East Midlands. One was the main road north from London to Lincoln, called Ermine Street; the other was a branch off it called King Street, which went north from *Durobrivae* (Water Newton in north

Cambridgeshire) to rejoin Ermine Street at Ancaster in Lincolnshire. However, perhaps just slightly later in this invasion period, a remarkable third road, the Fosse Way, was also constructed between Devon and Lincoln, cutting across south east Nottinghamshire on the way. Many of the early main Roman roads were radial routes spreading across the province from the administrative capital at *Londinium*; the Fosse Way stands out as a road alone and its exact purpose has been debated for many decades. One belief among archaeologists was that the Fosse Way marked a frontier of the Roman advance, with the territory conquered by 47 lying south and east of the road while land west and north — Wales, northern England and Scotland — remained unpacified. Although this frontier idea has been largely discounted now, a string of small towns developed along the route of the road in Nottinghamshire. From south to north these were: *Vernemetum*, near Willoughby-on-the-Wolds; *Margidunum*, near East Bridgford; *Ad Pontem*, at Thorpe, near East Stoke; Newark; and *Crococolana*, at Brough. *Margidunum* may have been established as a small Roman fort within the first ten to fifteen years after the invasion but later became a civilian settlement. An early garrison was also present at *Ad Pontem*. While no evidence of a garrison has been found at *Crococolana*, one of Nottinghamshire's loveliest pieces of Roman metalwork, a copper cheek-piece from a ceremonial cavalry helmet, was discovered here in the early 20th century. *Vernemetum*'s nature remains vague although its name suggests it had a temple or shrine. Newark, for which no Roman name is known, may have developed as a settlement because of its location around a junction of the Fosse Way and the pre-Roman trackway now called Sewstern Lane. Some or all of these Fosse Way settlements surely acted as staging posts for Imperial messengers and important travellers, providing accommodation and changes of horse for the *cursus publicus*, the Imperial mail and courier service, for example. However, only *Margidunum*, with its large and centrally heated buildings, has so far produced physical evidence that it had the means to support this role.

Meanwhile, away from the Fosse Way, forts were established in Nottinghamshire and surrounding areas to give the army an early defensive presence in the territory of the *Corieltauvi*. Forts are known from Broxtowe in north Nottingham, Dorket Head at

Arnold and Osmanthorpe, near Southwell. Several temporary camps were also constructed during the period of active campaigning at Holme, Calverton, Farnsfield and Gleadthorpe. Four more such camps have been provisionally identified at Hayton, Collingham, Misterton and Ollerton. Later in the Roman period a small fortlet was also established near Bawtry to cover a crossing of the river Idle by the road from Lincoln to York via Doncaster. A little further to the east this road crossed the Trent, watched over by the small town of *Segelocum*, Littleborough. The river crossing, apparently via a paved ford, appears to have been guarded by a small fort on the Lincolnshire side of the river.

To the south, the fort at Broxtowe in particular has been regarded by some as part of the chain of defences that were, supposedly, established along or near the Fosse Way frontier. But while the frontier idea has an appealing logic to it, if the road was a frontier it didn't last long and neither did it help establish peace within the ostensibly pacified areas. The *Iceni* people of modern East Anglia soon rebelled against their forced disarmament, being quelled only by force.

Over the next decade Roman military efforts concentrated on suppressing resistance in Wales. Then, in 60 or 61, the *Iceni* revolted again, this time led by Queen Boudica. This serious uprising deep inside the occupied zone was suppressed with considerable brutality and not before three major Roman towns, including *Londinium*, were burned by the insurgents. Campaigning then continued for another 20 years before governor Julius Agricola had completed the military exploration of most of north eastern Scotland by 84. The military campaign in this period has been likened to the early fighting in modern Afghanistan; rather than facing a unified enemy, the Romans, like NATO forces, were dealing with a patchwork of warlords and individual tribes of fluctuating loyalties. All told, it took an army of 20,000 regular legionary soldiers and an equal number of non-Roman *auxilia* troops some 40 years to complete the primary subjugation of *Britannia*, the northernmost province of the Roman Empire. Even then, Scotland was soon abandoned, this being followed by the Emperor Hadrian's decision in around 122 to create a permanent northern frontier in the form of a wall running between the Tyne and the Solway Firth.

NEW NOTTINGHAM DISCOVERIES

Striking Roman Finds on the Broxtowe Estate

COINS, BRONZE PINS, KNIVES, BUTTONS, DICE—AND 2,000-YEAR-OLD OYSTER SHELLS

REMARKABLE finds of Roman pottery, trinkets and coins have been made on the Broxtowe estate, and now have a place at the Nottingham headquarters of the excavating section of the Thoroton Society, of which Mr. W. H. Goddard is hon. secretary and treasurer.

Search is still being made for further articles, the belief being that much is still buried in the locality of considerable historical interest.

The first find by the excavators was

The find led the members to continue investigations. For six weeks they explored the area at Broxtowe, and were rewarded by finding

Roman coins of the first century.
Several brooches (fibulae).
Rings.
Bronze pins.
A silver spoon.
Knives.
Buttons.
A Roman dice of wood.

The dice is marked with neat circles and is of dainty workmanship, much like a 20th century dice.

An unusually large quantity of Roman

Newspaper article announcing the Broxtowe fort discovery in the 1930s — from the *Nottingham Journal.*

Many of the tribal chieftains in England had readily made peace with the Romans soon after the invasion. Others, such as Boudica of the *Iceni*, delivered bloody revenge on the invaders while another insurgent leader, Caratacus, waged guerrilla war from south Wales before being handed over to the invaders by the Queen of the *Brigantes* and paraded in Rome. But the story of the Roman military campaign against the *Corieltauvi* in Nottinghamshire and surrounding counties is a blank. Accounts of the invasion of Britain by writers in antiquity tended to concentrate on people and events in south east England, northern England, Wales and Scotland or on specific and notable dramas such as the Boudican revolt. Reference is not made to any resistance to the Roman invaders by the *Corieltauvi*, whether battles were fought or whether local chieftains made a peace agreement. And since the *Corieltauvi* themselves left no written evidence of their fate, one conclusion has to be that the *Corieltauvi* quickly made peace with the invaders and that armed resistance was minimal. Had matters been different, classical historians of the invasion period such as Dio Cassius and Agricola's son-in-law Tacitus might have mentioned them. But while the narrative detail of this period of local history is lacking, one must avoid drawing specific and colourful conclusions about it using slim archaeological evidence as props, as was done in the early 20th century when archaeology was in the hands of passionate amateurs.

One guilty party was a key figure in Nottinghamshire's archaeological history, Dr Felix Oswald, who excavated *Margidunum* almost single-handedly for more than 20 years. Oswald, whose day job was District Probate Registrar for Nottingham, found evidence of fire damage at *Margidunum* and built up a story around this that the fort had been burned by Britons chasing Legion IX up the Fosse Way as they fled Boudica's savage rebellion. Oswald's son, Adrian, who was also an archaeologist active in Nottinghamshire, may have fallen into the same trap when he excavated a Roman villa at Norton Disney, near *Crococolana*, in the 1930s. Based on evidence of fire and human destruction he told a newspaper reporter that 'the last inhabitants were massacred in 367 AD by the Picts, and their remains litter the upper floors'. Then again, one of the three skeletons Oswald found in the villa ruins had a knife in its ribs, so perhaps he had good reason to go for a dramatic reconstruction of events. Alas, professional archaeologists

The cavalry helmet cheek-piece found at *Crococolana*. The human figure is believed to represent Castor or Pollux.

today tend to be much more circumspect in their published conclusions, making cautious suggestions based only on the evidence of their excavations, supported by a broad foundation of peer-written research and references. Modern archaeology is consequently rarely as much fun to read as the Oswalds' colourful reports.

Who were the *Corieltauvi*? It is only since the 1960s that some measure of identity of the people whom the Roman invaders conquered in ancient Nottinghamshire has begun to emerge. Previously, the *Corieltauvi* were regarded as one of several peripheral peoples surrounding a core of considerably better-known tribes in south east England such as the *Catuvellauni*, *Atrebates* and *Durotriges*, who were thought to be most exposed to cultural influence from the continent in the 150 years or so leading up to the Claudian invasion in 43. These influences stemmed from two sources: the Romans expanding into Gaul and the coming of Gallo-Belgic settlers, who crossed from northern France and whose lifestyles came to dominate tribal culture in south east England by the time Claudius invaded. These continental cultural influences percolated as far as the *Corieltauvi* and were visibly expressed in the design of coins, which were direct derivatives of northern Gaulish coins. Indeed, G.F. Allen, whose analysis of tribal coinage in the early 1960s helped give the *Corieltauvi* a firmer identity, suggested that the tribe itself was primarily Gallo-Belgic in origin, the colonisers having first penetrated into Lincolnshire via the Humber in the first half of the first century BC. If so, these may have been just the latest wave of immigrants from areas such as the Somme and Marne valleys to penetrate into the area and a suggestion has been made that the ancient hill fort at Breedon Hill in Leicestershire, built at least by the 3rd century BC, had its defences strengthened to deal with such incomers. Felix Oswald went further in his speculations, suggesting that the *Corieltauvi* people had ultimately originated in Bavaria, where there was a tribe called the *Caritani* which had migrated west to the Marne region of Gaul, and then to Lincolnshire.

As well as coins and pottery, archaeologists have discovered a significant number of late Iron Age settlements across the region over the past 40 years. Some 14 or 15 larger settlements are known across Nottinghamshire, Lincolnshire and Leicestershire. Plotted on a map, they appear to be regularly spaced 20–30km (20 miles) apart. However, more than a hundred settlements of all sizes have been cautiously identified in Nottinghamshire (compared with 220 in Leicestershire and Rutland) including alleged hill forts, small farmsteads and large settlements covering several acres. Although a tribal capital has yet to be firmly identified in the region (if indeed one existed), relatively large and 'nucleated' settlements have been identified at Old Sleaford and Dragonby in Lincolnshire. Dragonby, excavated between 1964 and 1973, covered 7.6 hectares and yielded evidence of rudimentary streets and roundhouses. But it is Old Sleaford, which included a strong pallisade defence, granaries, a possible shrine and a coin-making mint, that is the main contender for the Corieltauvian capital. Covering at least 32 hectares, the community was one of the largest pre-Roman settlements in Britain. At Old Sleaford and Dragonby, as at Iron Age communities in Nottinghamshire, the common domestic house form was the roundhouse. Although reconstructed Iron Age roundhouses can be seen dotted around Britain today, a fine example in

Iron Age roundhouse built by archaeology student and farmer Grahame Watson at his farm in Calverton. "Every man needs a shed," says Grahame. The roundhouse, which required around 80 local oak and ash trees plus five tons of water reed for the roof, is open for school and group visits. This photograph was taken in July 2010 when it was open for the Festival of British Archaeology.

Nottinghamshire is the one built by farmer and archaeology student Grahame Watson at Calverton.

Although the tribal heartland has been placed by some in the Lindsey area of Lincolnshire, several Iron Age settlements have been excavated in Nottinghamshire since the 1960s, many in advance of gravel quarrying near the Trent. In many cases these Iron Age communities were succeeded by Roman settlements. An exception to this general rule was one excavated in 2004 at Whatton in Rushcliffe; the settlement appeared to have been abandoned perhaps 150 years before the Roman invasion and left only faint traces of its existence to interpret: ditches, post-holes, pottery fragments and pieces of clay in which impressions of daub (from 'wattle and daub' walls) were made. A small number of communities, leaving better evidence of their existence, have been excavated at locations as geographically spread as Gonalston, Worksop, Aslockton, Rampton, Scratta Wood, Holme Pierrepont and Gamston, near West Bridgford. Settlement density was highest along the Trent Valley and in the south of the county. A small number of communities well outside this area included one at Raymoth Lane, Gateford, Worksop, which appears to have been established in the 'transition' period of the Roman invasion and was occupied until the 4th century. The skeletons of six stillborn or prematurely born babies were found here during excavations. A more extensive settlement at Gamston, which was also occupied well into the Roman period, produced evidence of trade between the original Iron Age inhabitants and their contemporaries in Charnwood Forest and Lincolnshire. An even larger settlement, covering 20 hectares (49 acres), was excavated at Aslockton in 1992 and had the apparently unique layout of two oval-shaped areas with a small open space at the centre.

A site that visibly juxtaposes Iron Age and Roman cultures is at Cromwell, where a Roman villa and farm were imposed on top of Iron Age farmland. At Lockington in Leicestershire, just over the county border from Long Eaton, a 40 metre long (130ft) Roman villa was built adjacent to the site of a cluster of around 20 native roundhouses which were between eight and eleven metres (26–36ft) in diameter. An unanswered question is whether the villa and the roundhouses, representing invading and native cultures, existed at the same time, and if so, for how long.

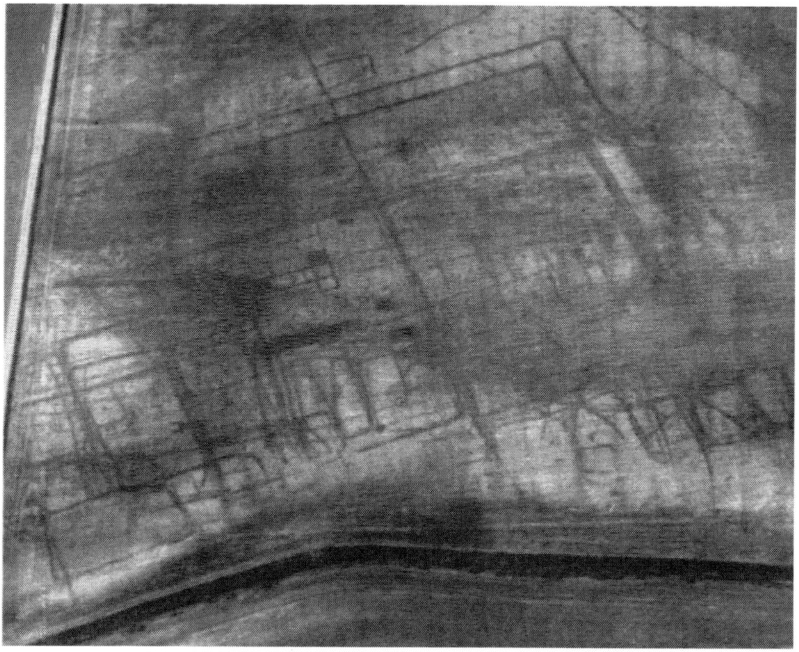

Aerial photograph showing cropmarks of the Cromwell villa, the regular shape seen at middle left within the larger rectangle. This is a close-up view of the same image seen in the chapter on villas.

Although most of the Iron Age settlements in the region are on low-lying land, several hill forts are known. The best known are in Leicestershire and include Breedon Hill, which had defences of pallisades and ramparts made of huge boulders. Finds at this site included a miniature bronze shield, just 72mm long and 36mm wide, which is believed to have had a religious significance. Around ten allegedly Iron Age occupied hill sites are known in Nottinghamshire including a noted cluster between Farnsfield and Burton Joyce. Perhaps the best candidate for a 'hill fort' is the elevated defended settlement at Combs Farm, near Farnsfield, where a partial excavation in 1960–61 by Sherwood Archaeological Society unearthed a ditch with both Iron Age and Roman features. However, doubt has been cast on the validity of other sites which are claimed to be hill forts. The site near Oxton usually known as Old Ox, with its well-defined ramparts, ditches and entrance, is visibly not on a hill. And, as has been pointed out by Nottinghamshire's former principal archaeologist Mike Bishop, it is probably not Iron Age either. Other alleged sites include Crow Wood, Styrrup; Camp Hill, near Kirklington; Fox Wood, Woodborough; and Lodge Farm, Burton Joyce. Another elevated site is Dorket Head, near Arnold in north Nottingham, where a Roman fort seems to have succeeded some kind of Iron Age occupation from which a large and significant collection of pottery has been recovered.

Coins, pottery, settlements — yet even archaeologist Malcolm Todd, who in 1973 wrote the only book-length analysis of the tribe, *The Coritani*, might have been forced to admit that the tribal people who lived mostly across Nottinghamshire, Lincolnshire and Leicestershire still lacked a shaping narrative of the kind that the southern English tribes have possessed since Caesar and Tacitus described them. However, an aside is needed here. Was the tribal name *Coritani* or *Corieltauvi*? The traditional name *Coritani* is derived from the mention by Ptolemy in the 2nd century and this was widely used until recently. The name change originated in the early 1980s, when four lines of Latin grafitti on a piece of Roman roofing tile found at *Tripontium* (Churchover, Warwickshire), about 24km from Leicester, were re-analysed by an archaeologist called R.S.O. Tomlin.[3] The lines appeared to include a garbled version of the tribal name, from which Tomlin deduced that the correct name for the tribe was in fact *Corieltauvi*, not *Coritani*. Despite Todd's rejection of the new name, *Corieltauvi* stuck and this has now been widely adopted as the tribal title. However, it has now undergone further modification, with scholar Andrew Breeze claiming that the correct name is Coriel*tavi*, with the *v* pronounced like a *w*.[4] Breeze argued that the name meant 'host of (or the region of) many rivers'. In this book, we are sticking with the more widely accepted *Corieltauvi*.

Todd tried to work out where the tribal territory had been and suggested two sets of borders: one enclosed the natural land of the *Corieltauvi* before the Roman invasion, the other marked out the official administrative zone imposed by the invaders which had *Ratae Corieltauvorum*, Leicester, as its capital. He suggested that the natural pre-invasion territory extended south to the land between the Nene and Welland, ending in a border zone that mingled with the lands of the powerful *Catuvellauni* tribe; the north west tribal border was vague but settlement west of the Trent was scarce; north, the border perhaps came up against the powerful *Brigantian* confederacy north of the Trent; to the north east the border was marked by the Humber, above which were the *Parisi* people. That left the eastern border. Although the tribal land extended across modern Lincolnshire to the sea, evidence of higher sea levels in the late Iron Age period suggests that the Fenland coastline was further west than it is now, seawater inundating an area as far inland as Boston.

Todd's rough pre-invasion borders were largely based on the distribution of tribal coins and it is the coinage, only fully assigned to the *Corieltauvi* since the 1960s, that has helped to give the tribe a degree of identity among the patchwork of Iron Age tribes that faced the Roman army in 43. The evidence of the coins is ironically two-sided, revealing as much about the *Corieltauvi* by what they don't say as by what they do. The tribe initially issued uninscribed silver and gold coins bearing convoluted and aesthetically pleasing 'Celtic' designs. These were perhaps produced in the late 1st century BC. Then, in the early 1st century AD, a new generation of coins were issued bearing crude images such as horses and boars on one side and double sets of letters on the other.

Images from mythology, such as Apollo's laurel wreath, could also be included. The most extensively used of the sets of letters was VEP C ORF. Later still, gold and silver coins stamped with full names such as
VOLISIOS and DVMNOCOVEROS,
VOLISIOS and DVMNOVELLAVNVS,
VOLISIOS and CARTIVEL,
were issued. The names on these latter types, the most fully developed of the *Corieltauvi* coins before the Roman invasion, have been interpreted in several ways: as the names of two chieftains ruling linked factions of the tribe; as the names of two rulers with filial connections (king and heir?); or as the names of two magistrates, although this word is meant in the Roman sense of elected officials wielding high authority, as opposed to the contemporary meaning of middle-aged men and women punishing burglars with community service orders. Caesar described the tribes in Gaul as having men of 'great prestige' in power to have the final say on tribal matters, so the idea has sound precedent in antiquity.

Whatever the final meaning of the words, the coinage at least seems to give us the names of some prominent people in the tribe as well as effectively providing the *Corieltauvi*'s only written records. Perhaps it was Volisios and a co-ruler who led the tribe when the Roman army marched in (and perhaps it was not, since this is utter speculation). However, the coinage differs significantly from those issued by the 'core' tribes of England's south east, which were latterly heavily influenced by Roman design in their use of imagery, profiles of tribal leaders (imitating the profiles of Emperors on Roman coinage) and use of Latin words such as REX. By contrast, *Corieltauvi* craftspeople may have consciously omitted, or had dim knowledge of, such signs of recognition of Roman influence when they designed their currency.

Unlike British tribes of the south east who had had close contact with the Roman world since Caesar's brief invasions in 55 and 54 BC, and some of whose chieftains had visited Rome, the *Corieltauvi* leadership may have lacked any sense of compulsion to display what were essentially prestige signs of Roman influence on their currency. This suggests a definite cultural and physical distance from Roman influence and the tribes in south east England that were closest to it. This point was not lost on G.F. Allen, who wrote the first full-scale analysis of *Corieltauvi* coinage in 1963. 'The style of the coins shows conservatism carried to excess,' he said. 'But the superficial impression of primitive incompetence is belied by the full mastery shown of the techniques of engraving, striking, and even of forgery.' He continued: 'The coinage points to a people, at least as far as the coin-using class was concerned, lacking the more imaginative Celtic gifts, avoiding any temptation to flirt with Rome, and fully endowed with the technical skills of the time and place, and pursuing its own self-contained, conservative course.' The finding of over 4,000 fragments of coin-making moulds at Old Sleaford in 1960 and 1961 suggested that a tribal mint had been located there. Some additional evidence of coin-making has also been found in Leicester.

Allen's view of tribal conservatism can be seen as a somewhat back-handed compliment, and his opinion was opposed by experts such as the University of Nottingham's Jeffrey May, excavator of Dragonby. Far from being backwards, said May, the *Corieltauvi* ran a well-organised, stable and modern wealthy state, with settlements developed on urban lines as well as anywhere in Britain. He added: 'It was probably factors such as these that attracted the Romans to their land and led to their apparently rapid subjugation.' Indeed, the absence of coinage produced by tribes to the north and west of the East Midlands suggests that the *Corieltauvi* take the prize as being the most northerly Iron Age people in the Roman world to make coins.

It was Allen, incidentally, who first fully identified the tribe with its coinage. The earlier failure in identification was partly due to the fact that two major coin hoards were found in Yorkshire. Most of the tribal coins have been found in Lincolnshire, Leicestershire, Rutland and Northamptonshire (relatively few *Corieltauvi* coins have been reported from Nottinghamshire) and the Yorkshire hoards, which included many 1st century Roman *denarii*, have been interpreted as the wealth of tribal people who fled north to escape the Roman occupation.

Is there anything that can be said about the tribal people's physical attributes, and their language? Tacitus gave some physical descriptions of people in Britain, including the tribes of Caledonia (red hair, large limbs) and south Wales (swarthy, curly hair). Both he and Caesar also agreed that the people of the south east who lived closest to Gaul looked like the Gauls. Alas, neither author mentioned the *Corieltauvi*. Regarding language, however, modern linguists suggest that the Iron Age tribes spoke Brithonic, from which the existing 'Celtic' languages of Welsh, Cornish and Breton are derived. With studies also suggesting that regional variations in spoken Brithonic probably existed, the way is clearly left open to claim that the *Corieltauvi* people of the East Midlands spoke with a distinct, regional accent.

Despite this, and the excavations of so many Iron Age settlements, the East Midlands people who were to fall under Roman rule remain hazy and essentially unknowable. Lacking knowledge of individuals and names, descriptions have to be general. Yet the old-fashioned idea that Iron Age peoples such as the *Corieltauvi* were little more than woad-covered bumpkins who almost deserved to be subjugated by Roman civilisation has long since been discredited: the people of the eastern Midlands lived in organised settlements and felled woodland for agriculture, growing crops and keeping animals such as sheep and cattle;

some of their farms were perhaps organised with close-knit regular field systems of the kind now seen as cropmarks in parts of north Nottinghamshire and south Yorkshire; they made their own distinctively patterned fine pottery, produced metalwork, ornate weapons and horse gear and possibly had an industry trading salt made by evaporating seawater on the Lincolnshire coast; they had cultural connections with the wider world, perhaps also selling wool and importing goods from Europe such as pottery that reached them via the region's rivers. And they (or at least a small elite among them) also had the ability to read and write with Latin lettering, inscribing the names of their leaders on high value coins. Furthermore, as the finding of the plaited gold alloy necklace now known as the Newark Torc in 2005 suggests, some among them had status and wealth enough to possess beautiful jewellery.

Gold *stater* coin of the *Corieltauvi*, dated c.70–50 BC, found during metal detecting in a field south of Bawtry in 1994. The design is that of a horse. It is now in the possession of Bassetlaw Museum, Retford.

This attempt to summarise some knowledge about the *Corieltauvi* would, in an ideal world, act as the prologue to the drama that was next to unfold: the physical invasion of the East Midlands by the Roman army soon after the invasion in 43. Unfortunately, it is a story without a denouement since the ancient written accounts of the immediate post-invasion campaign do not mention the fate of the *Corieltauvi*. We are therefore left to make suggestions based on what was happening elsewhere in Britain at the time. And one plausible scenario is that the *Corieltauvi* leadership rolled over and surrendered. Having seen an apparently superior Roman military machine quickly defeat the tribes of south east England, capturing and occupying *Camulodunum* (Colchester) with the help of the war elephants brought over by Claudius, the chieftains of the East Midlands may have decided that peace was a better policy than death and destruction had they resisted. If so, perhaps an alliance was agreed with the invaders whereby the *Corieltauvi* region became a nominally independent but loyal client kingdom of the Romans. Such client kingdoms had existed since Caesar's invasions and, in the Claudian era, some form of agreement or even alliance with the invaders was initially agreed by several tribes including the *Brigantes*, *Iceni* and *Regni*. Relations between some chieftains and Rome were so close that Claudius had even loaned money to some of them, although attempts to recover the debt from the *Iceni* were later to inspire Boudica to rebel.

In his book *The Coritani*, Malcolm Todd suggested that the Roman invasion may even have been welcomed by the *Corieltauvi* leaders. Sandwiched between the aggressively expansionist *Catuvellauni* to the south and the powerful *Brigantes* to the north, the chieftains of the East Midlands could have regarded the invasion at least as a way of nullifying two potent rivals. There was certainly little unity between the tribes of Iron Age Britain facing the Roman army, a situation which was to the army's advantage. In Caesar's time 90-odd years earlier, tribes had fought tribes and one tribal prince had even fled to the continent seeking Roman protection after his father had been killed by the chieftain of another tribe. Inter-tribal rivalry existed when Claudius' army came over (the treacherous handing over of Caratacus being one example of this) and so feelings of *schaudenfreude* may have been running high among the *Corieltauvi* when the Romans occupied the lands of other more powerful tribes. 'Once they owed obedience to kings; now they are distracted by the jarring factions of rival chiefs,' wrote Tacitus of the Britons. 'Indeed nothing has helped us more in war with their strongest nations than their inability to co-operate. It is but seldom that two or three states unite to repel a common danger; fighting in detail they are conquered wholesale. The climate is objectionable...'

Whether the tribe offered resistance or peace terms, one important hint that the Roman army had overrun the East Midlands region soon after the invasion comes from the patchy account of the period found in Tacitus' *Annals*. Tacitus, who had yet to be born at the time of the invasion, said that when governor Aulus Plautius was succeeded by Publius Ostorius Scapula in 47, four years into the invasion, the native tribes saw this as an opportunity to attack. The new governor's reaction to these latest hostilities was to defeat the Britons and then prevent them from re-grouping. His method of achieving this was to 'disarm the suspected tribes, and establish forts to hold in check all the country between the Trent and the Severn'. The implication of this is that all territory south and east of a line drawn between the Severn and Trent was already occupied by the Roman army within four years of the legions coming ashore. Although Tacitus' text is vague, a line traced on a map from the Severn estuary to the Trent's northern course towards the Humber has almost all of modern Nottinghamshire in the occupied zone.

Worn coin of the Emperor Claudius, who launched the Roman invasion of Britain in 43, found in Nottinghamshire.

An additional clue that the region was quickly occupied, and quickly accepted Roman rule, is that Roman military installations in Nottinghamshire seem to have been abandoned relatively quickly. The founding of the fort at Broxtowe has been dated to around 50 or 60 and it was perhaps abandoned by the very early 70s; a military presence at *Margidunum*, preceding the civilian town, may have ended in the 70s. Other settlements along the Fosse Way such as *Ad Pontem* had small garrisons which became civilianised in the early 2nd century. The impression is that the Roman army felt sufficiently secure that their forts could be abandoned at some point in the 70s, that is, within 30–35 years of the invasion. If so, this would not have been unusual; as the military front line moved northwards new forts were required and older forts in conquered territory could be abandoned to release troops. Although there is a good deal of guesswork involved in the dating of the few known Nottinghamshire forts, their abandonment would fit in with the beginning of a new campaign, led by the governor Petillius Cerialis in 69, to quell the rebellious *Brigantes,* whose territory began somewhere north of the Trent. The handful of camps at Calverton, Farnsfield, Gleadthorpe and Holme (see Chapter 7 for more on these camps) seem to have been temporary bases set up by troops on the march and these, along with the large and apparently semi-permanent fort at Osmanthorpe, have been linked by some to the march of troops on their way north to deal with an earlier disturbance among the same tribe.

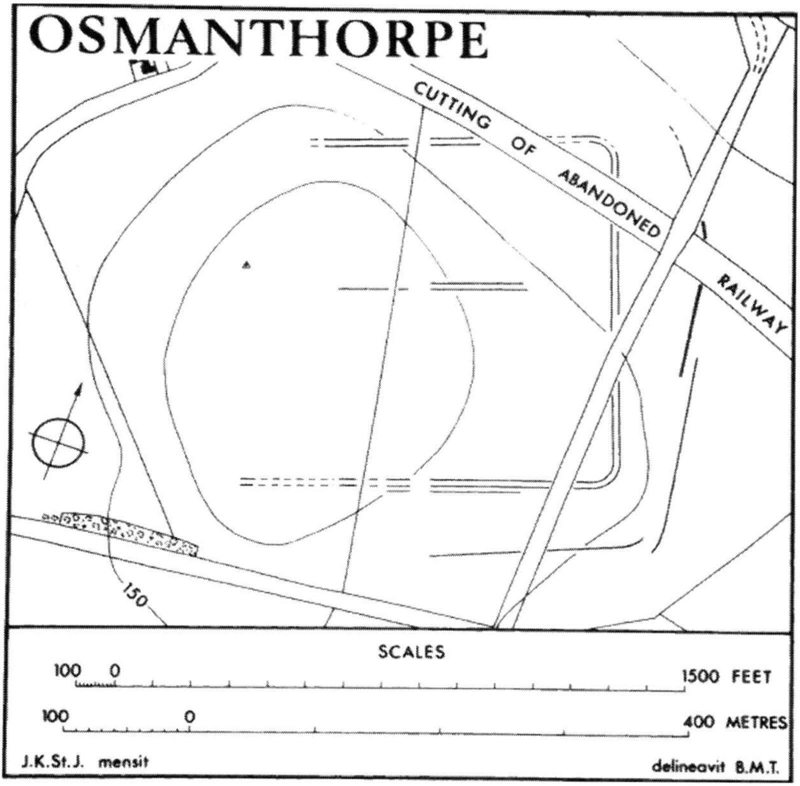

Plan of the large rectangular fortress on the hill at Osmanthorpe, near Southwell. This is a different plan from the one that appears in chapter 7 on forts.

Yet there cannot have been an invasion in history which did not meet resistance and it is unthinkable that some warriors among the *Corieltauvi* would not have come into conflict with the invaders. If so, the fighting in an age of swords, spears, arrows and stone and catapult projectiles would have been a grim and bloody business of hacking, stabbing and bludgeoning. In the aftermath of Agricola's great victory at Mons Graupius in Scotland in the 80s the scene was described with these words: 'arms, bodies, severed limbs lay all around and the earth reeked of blood'. Hundreds of miles to the south, a mass grave of British defenders from the siege of Maiden Castle hill fort in Dorset includes the skeleton of a man with a ballista bolt — a catapult-fired supersized arrowhead — lodged in his spine; at *Vindolanda* Roman fort, near Hadrian's Wall, the decapitated and discarded skull of a man was recovered from a rubbish ditch, his head having been pierced and shattered by a sharp object, and then bludgeoned. At the Roman settlement at Redhill in Nottinghamshire, at the confluence of the Trent and the Soar, the skeleton of a man who had suffered 'a thrust with a pointed weapon through the left jaw' was found.

But while the Roman state had no hesitation in using the sword to assert its dominance, the Britons could also take savage revenge on their would-be colonisers. In 60 or 61, Queen Boudica of the *Iceni*, enraged by her treatment at Roman hands, including the 'severe measures' used to recover money loaned to tribal leaders, whipped her followers into an armed rebellion which allegedly caused the deaths of 80,000 Romans and their allies. According to the 2nd century Greek historian Dio Cassius, the uprising was so successful that 'the island was lost to Rome'. Taking advantage of the absence of the Roman governor Suetonius Paulinus, who was campaigning in Anglesey, the Britons sacked *Londinium*, *Verulamium* (St Albans) and *Camulodunum*, hunting down Roman troops in forts and outposts. Grisly revenge was taken on 'the noblest and most distinguished women' among the Romans (or allied Britons), who were hung upside down and had their breasts cut off, which were then sewn to their mouths. The women were later impaled on stakes. An army unit from Legion IX hurried out from a fort now identified as Longthorpe, near Peterborough, and had its infantry wiped out by the rebels, only the cavalry escaping back to its base. Eventually Paulinus rallied the army and led Legion XIV *Gemina* to defeat Boudica's army in battle. She killed herself or 'fell sick and died', and so the greatest crisis in the initial subjugation of Britain passed.

By this point the Emperor Nero was in power in Rome, having succeeded Claudius in 54. Yet regardless of who ruled in Rome, it is impossible to imagine that the *Corieltauvi* people of the time were not affected, or inspired, by the great rebellion to their immediate south and east which almost regained Britain's independence. Although no instances of armed resistance are recorded in the eastern Midlands, an idea of *Corieltauvi* martial potential comes from a small number of recovered Iron Age military items. These include an ornate 1.12 metre high bronze shield, a sword and a scabbard mounting all recovered from the river Witham in Lincolnshire. In Nottinghamshire, a decorated shield boss has been found in the Trent at Redhill and a sword scabbard plate was recovered from Sutton-on-Trent. Several items of horse equipment such as part of a bridle bit, found in Leicester, are thought to have been used with a war chariot.

Roman writers tended to express admiration for the Britons as warriors, including their skill in use of chariots, their martial fervour, their courage and their hatred of enslavement. Although there was a self-regarding element to this (the brave enemy vanquished by the even braver Roman victors), as well as an intriguing early hint of the 'noble savage' idea that would excite 18th century philosophers, the Roman historians speak unequivocally of occasional battle victories by the Britons. However, despite local successes against Roman units in guerrilla warfare, the Britons were repeatedly defeated in open battle by the disciplined legions and auxiliaries, even when the Britons were fighting from behind defensive positions. Hill forts certainly offered no safe haven from attacks of Roman infantry clad in their bands of *lorica segmentata* armour, and who were trained to use the *testudo* formation — shields held flat over their heads — to protect them from aerial missiles, as they did when assaulting and defeating Caratacus' final army on a hilltop. Retreating to a town didn't offer any safety either. The Roman historian Suetonius records that the commander of Legion II *Augusta*, Vespasian, the future Emperor who ultimately succeeded Nero, had 'fought thirty battles, subjugated two war-like tribes, and captured more than twenty towns' — and all in the first four years of the invasion. He also captured the Isle of Wight in the same period.

But while the Britons knew that the Roman army was not invincible, and Boudica's uprising must have given soldiers every reason to be watchful over the population, the active front line in the conquest of Britain had moved on from Nottinghamshire and the East Midlands at some point in the 70s. After a spell of civil war among the *Brigantes*, the northern tribe finally broke out into open rebellion against the Romans in

69 and governor Petillius Cerialis was forced to invade the territory using two legions. The battle front thus moved north, with the Nottinghamshire territory perhaps being initially used as a buffer zone between the war zone and the uneasily pacified land to the south. By this point a fort may already have been established at Lincoln, with a new road, to become known as the Fosse Way centuries later, being driven up to it through Nottinghamshire. The fort was enlarged as a full legionary fortress before Lincoln became a *colonia* for the retirement of Roman army veterans after completing their 25-year term of duty. There was undoubtedly a strategic controlling purpose in siting the *colonia* here. As Tacitus said of another *colonia* at *Camulodunum*: 'This would serve as a defensive force against rebellion and inculcate respect for the laws in the allies.'

After invasion and war came a guarded peace and the spread of Roman laws, language and customs that were to change the patterns of life in Britain. In Nottinghamshire, the conquerors built networks of durable, metalled roads of which the Fosse Way is only the best known; military installations became civilian settlements, although sometimes still with defensive features; in some of the settlements, all being villages or small towns such as *Margidunum*, rectangular buildings began ousting the roundhouse as the preferred form and industries such as metal-working and pottery-making began to grow, perhaps to help supply Britain's huge occupying army. Beyond the towns, new kinds of well-appointed farmhouses began to appear in the early part of the 2nd century and, at locations such as Southwell and Mansfield Woodhouse, these villas were to develop into luxury residences with opulent décor of a kind that wealthy Romans would have been familiar with in Italy. Central heating and regular bathing were just two of the novelties brought to Nottinghamshire from Rome. Many other villas, some clustering around towns, others apparently isolated in the country, were built across Nottinghamshire but seem to have been most common near the Trent and in the south of the modern county. Farming both along the Trent Valley and on the less fertile sandy soils of north Nottinghamshire also seems to have became better organised and therefore probably more productive — perhaps in order to feed a growing population, perhaps also to produce a surplus that could be sold to the army. Meanwhile, the old *Corieltauvi* currency was replaced by Roman money, creating a cash economy which made the acquisition of new home-made and imported goods a possibility for anybody who had the means.

The background to these profound changes was the Romans' creation of new regional administrative areas called *civitates*, based on the old tribal areas. The East Midlands region was thus called the *civitas Corieltauvorum*. The *civitas* allowed the old tribal aristocracy to remain in day-to-day control of the region, although these arrangements were probably not in place until direct military rule had been lifted from across the region. As Ptolemy noted in Alexandria, the two major towns that developed in this *civitas* were *Lindum* and *Ratae* and it is *Ratae*, modern Leicester, which has been usually identified as the regional capital. A regular grid layout of streets had been laid down in Leicester by 120 and subsequent developments included large public spaces and buildings such as a forum and basilica, temples and market as well as shops and wealthy private town houses boasting ornate floor mosaics and wall frescoes. Leicester's celebrated floor mosaics, such as the Peacock mosaic, Cyparissus mosaic and Blackfriars pavement, are an indication that the Iron Age settlement next to the river Soar had developed into a wealthy Roman town by the middle of the 2nd century. A large gymnasium and public baths were also built, which remain today as the Jewry Wall. Agricola, who became governor of Britain in 78, had already attempted to spread Roman customs by encouraging public building and inspiring the sons of the tribal chieftains to learn the new language, Latin. This was accompanied by the adoption of Roman styles of dress by the Britons, and perhaps it was in *Ratae* that the new toga-wearing, Latin-speaking Britons of the *Corieltauvi* could be seen soonest.

Colonialism

In mid-October 2010 the archaeologist, historian and occasional *Time Team* expert Neil Faulkner told a small archaeology conference at the University of Nottingham: "I am sorry if some people think that the Roman Empire was a cross between the United Nations and the National Trust. It was not: it was about robbery and exploitation." A few people laughed. But nobody gasped in surprise since this approach to the Roman mission has become the orthodoxy in British academic archaeological thinking. Yes, the Roman infrastructure of roads, sewers, villas and so on provides the ready answer to the question 'what did the Romans do for us?' Yet the rosy old wisdom that the Roman conquest was morally and materially beneficial to Britain, and probably inevitable anyway, has given way to a harder analysis of events from 43 onwards as a process of naked colonisation necessitating the subjugation and exploitation of most of the native population. With Britain's own Empire now almost gone, and historians no longer required to justify British colonisation by looking to the example of the Roman Empire, a new 'post-colonial' perspective has taken shape which is regionally represented by, among others, University of Leicester archaeology professor David Mattingly. In Mattingly's analysis, the Roman Empire's occupation of Britain was not a Good Thing at all; in fact, from the point of view of the vast majority of ancient Britons, Roman occupation was actually a Very Bad Thing Indeed. In this view a few native tribal rulers benefited from cosying up to the Roman powers, this being a deliberate mechanism of Rome's model of imperialism. But for almost everyone else, the Roman presence brought ruthless exploitation and subjugation. 'For the majority of Britons, it is clear that in the short term the Romans were very bad news and, even in the medium and long term, Britain in the Roman Empire was a colonized and exploited territory,' writes Mattingly.[5] 'This was not a Golden Age, though the opportunities provided by the empire were golden for some individuals among the British elite and assorted immigrants into the province.' This is a perspective which speaks much of status, elites and unequal power relationships: the ultimate antidote, if you wish, to the gentle Ladybird Book view of history which saw the Romans as ultimately benign rulers (dig out the 1959 Ladybird *Julius Caesar and Roman Britain* to confirm this: one page shows soldier-governor Agricola — a 'hammer of the Scots' centuries before Edward I — getting cosy with the Brits around a night-time camp fire). Separated by half a century from the end of the British Empire, other writers have provided a differently weighted but still sobering picture of the reality of the Roman mission in Britain. As the Roman historian Guy de la Bédoyère said: 'It was an oppressive and rapacious culture that did nothing to discourage people from accepting its comforts and security.'

Part of the new post-colonial analysis, which involves taking a 'bottom up' view of events from the British perspective, also assumes the idea that our visual and mental mapping of Roman Britain is badly skewed by the apparent absence of the native population itself. You can see this for yourself by looking at the most recent Ordnance Survey map of Roman Britain, which includes the expected infrastructure of Roman roads, villas, cities, towns, forts, aqueducts and even lighthouses. Where exactly did the natives — Iron Age Britons, later the 'Romano-British' — live among all this? They are absent. As has been said by others, this traditional method of mapping the province, which is essentially the archaeological footprint of the invaders but not the invaded population, should properly be called 'the Roman Empire in Britain' or 'Romanised Britain' rather than Roman Britain.

Fortunately, the settlement map of Nottinghamshire during the Roman period has been fleshed out in increasing detail by archaeologists over the past five or six decades. Since 1945 aerial photography has been the most useful tool in the identification of sites in British archaeology, with depth of knowledge of Romano-British landscapes and lifestyles greatly increased by the analysis of ancient animal bones, plant seeds and spores. In Nottinghamshire, developer-funded excavations of several significant Iron Age/Romano-British settlements have taken place over the past 40 years. Many of these settlements have been exposed ahead of gravel extraction adjacent to the Trent, funding of the work being a legal obligation imposed on the quarrying companies by national planning legislation. Although *Margidunum* and the Fosse Way are still the best-known reminders of the Roman period in Nottinghamshire, the county's Historic Environment Record now lists 78 'Roman settlements' and 16 'Roman farmsteads' and it has been suggested that the peak population may have exceeded the population during William the Conqueror's reign almost a thousand years later.

Settlement pattern

In *The Making of the English Landscape*, published in 1955, W.G. Hoskins estimated that the entire British population on the eve of the Roman invasion was no more than 400,000, or 'about the size of modern Bristol'. Hoskins then quoted figures that the population under the occupation grew to between half a million and one and a half million people. Mattingly puts the population at around two million, with 80 per cent living in rural areas.[6] With its lack of large towns to match the likes of Lincoln and Leicester, Nottinghamshire's rural population may well have exceeded this proportion, suggesting that the lives of the vast majority of local people revolved around agriculture. Excavations indicate that other communities of people, perhaps including shopkeepers and artisans such as bakers and metal-workers, clustered around Romanised settlements such as *Margidunum* along the main transport and communication route through the county. Some must have worked on the farm estates of the villa owners. A few of the tribal nobles may themselves have lived in villas as part of the peace agreement with the invaders. But we can speculate that most people must have based their lives and work around farming and small rural settlements whose names have long been swallowed up by the centuries.

As in the Iron Age, farming and settlement were particularly dense on the fertile soils of the Trent Valley, a matter which has been officially noted since 1960 when the former Royal Commission on the Historical Monuments of England flagged up the importance of the area's archaeology in a report titled *A Matter of Time*. Roman-period systems of rectangular fields, first revealed as cropmarks from the air, have been studied at Lamb's Close, Kelham and at South Muskham, the latter area having also been excavated in 1968 when there was some evidence of industry such as iron smelting. South Muskham was subsequently designated as an Area of Major Archaeological Importance in local plans. But an accumulation of aerial photographs of the area taken since 1945 has revealed that these settlements lie within a larger, 15km long densely occupied strip of land along the Trent stretching at least from Newark to Normanton-on-Trent.

Most of the settlements were on the western bank of the river: Kelham, South Muskham, North Muskham, Cromwell, Carlton-on-Trent, Sutton-on-Trent and Normanton-on-Trent. On the eastern bank, cropmarks have revealed settlements near Winthorpe and Holme, Collingham and Besthorpe. And it is at Besthorpe gravel quarry that recent excavations have revealed the existence of an extensive Romano-British agricultural settlement composed of two probably related communities. One dig has focused on the land next to Ferry Lane Farm while the latest excavation, visited by the author in summer 2010 and expected to be completed in 2012, has looked at an adjacent settlement on a raised sand dune near a quarry called Mons Pool, which is part of the Besthorpe nature reserve. This is one of the few on-going excavations of a Roman-period settlement in Nottinghamshire at the time of writing. The evidence suggests that the lives of people here were impoverished and perhaps as culturally far from the Imperial splendour of 'the Glory that is Rome' as can be imagined. Both settlements — the word 'village' implies a density of building which is absent — had Iron Age habitation before the Roman period and the Mons Pool settlement has evidence of occupation stretching back to the Neolithic. Finds of artefacts at both settlements have been prolific. At Ferry Lane Farm, one field alone yielded 1,512 artefacts on the surface, 38 per cent of which were Romano-British pottery sherds. The pottery suggests that the settlement was mostly occupied from the 2nd to the 4th century. Most of the other settlement is now believed to lie under water at the bottom of the Mons Pool quarry, from where divers recovered pottery in 1973. What is being excavated now is believed to be the edge of the settlement. Nevertheless, archaeologists from the University of Salford have recovered a considerable amount of pottery, jewellery and coins and found evidence for three buildings, one Bronze Age and two from the Roman period. Ten human burials have also been found, only the nails remaining of their long disintegrated coffins.

Excavation director Adam Thompson with a small selection of pottery, and a quernstone for grinding cereal seeds to flour, found at Mons Pool.

What kind of people lived here in the Roman era? One theory is that this land was the home of labourers who worked on the estates of the nearby villa at Cromwell, on the other side of the Trent. If so, there would have to have been a river crossing to allow them to reach their work. The people here, cultivating dense systems of rectangular fields divided by boundary ditches, were poor but had enough money to trade and buy small amounts of imported pottery from Gaul, Spain and Italy. The stamp of a Gaulish pottery-maker called Masvetvs, active from 150 to 180, was found on a fragment of glossy red *samian* pottery. Other pottery came from Dorset and Oxfordshire, the Nene Valley, Derbyshire and Lincolnshire. The finding of a kiln at the Mons Pool settlement suggests that the people here also made their own pottery. They also worked with leather. "My feeling is that this was the Roman working class living here, perhaps with the estate manager living with them as overseer," says the Mons Pool excavation director, Adam Thompson. "They were probably creating a surplus from the land to sell to the Roman army." One possible indication of the relative lack of wealth at the site is that people were buried in wooden coffins. By contrast, at nearby *Crococolana* on the Fosse Way, some of the dead were

A representative selection of small finds from Mons Pool including a piece of decorated *samian* pottery, an unwashed brooch still showing its coloured enamel and a small bright silver coin showing Faustina, the deified wife of the 2nd century Emperor Antoninus Pius, successor to Hadrian.

buried in everlasting lead coffins. "I think there was a practice here of burying people in the corners of fields so that you wouldn't plough up grandad when you were working the fields," says Thompson. When the Roman administration in Britain ended in the early 5th century, and the army left forever, the local economy went bust. He adds: "As soon as the Romans disappeared from the region, this site disappeared. With the end of the economic boom, it closed down." Wind-blown sand from the dunes must have quickly helped cover the Mons Pool settlement when the people wandered off; a well was used as a rubbish dump; buildings would have fallen down, the holes for the supporting posts filling with sand. The same is happening now. Thompson says the excavation is difficult because blown sand can obliterate newly exposed features in an hour. He's inherited the task of writing the final archaeological report on the settlement and expects to see it published in 2013. But by that time the sand may well have covered this marginal and nameless community over once again.

Other rural Trentside settlements have also been excavated south of Newark at Gamston, Gonalston and Holme Pierrepont where, in 1968, three Iron Age–Roman flat-bottomed oak dugout canoes and a 12-spoke Roman wooden wheel were found during gravel quarrying. Their location up to 85 metres (280ft) south of the Trent suggested that all the objects had been inundated by water in an ancient flood. The wheel, considered a rarity because of its completeness and lack of wear, is just over 80cm

Stray piece of broken flue tile lying in the sand at Mons Pool. They were placed in walls to distribute heat from central heating systems and usually indicate the presence of a wealthy villa-type house. But excavation director Adam Thompson says he needs more evidence to prove the existence of a villa here.

(33 inches) in diameter and had an iron rim which has eroded away.

The extensive settlement at Gamston, excavated in the early 1990s by David Knight of Trent and Peak Archaeology prior to a housing development, had evolved out of an Iron Age

Roman wheel found at Holme Pierrepont.

community. Amid the thousands of pottery sherds found here was half a glass ring bead, coloured opaque yellow. Chemical analysis showed that it had originated in continental Europe in the Roman period, a small reminder of how ancient Nottinghamshire was connected to the wider Empire. The Gamston settlement now lies under houses close to Morrison's superstore.

Like Gamston and Holme Pierrepont, the community at Gonalston also began before the Romans arrived. Excavated in the mid-1990s, this two hectare (five acre) site was in the path of Tarmac's Hoveringham Quarry and revealed a complex evolution of paths, tracks, enclosures, ditches, pits and paddocks that were being used until the later Roman period. This settlement also provided a good reason why people should pay more attention to that threatened and neglected feature of the landscape, ponds. Archaeologists uncovered a pond at Gonalston which seemed to have been used as a rubbish dump, except the rubbish comprised 2,000 pottery sherds including large fragments of a fine vessel decorated with images of leaping lions, trees, leaves and buds. The vessel was later dated to 130–160 and was the product of a workshop of one Maccius of Lezoux in Gaul.

An additional point about the Gonalston settlement is that it seems to have been eventually abandoned as a result of rising water levels in the Trent. Other low-lying Roman settlements possibly affected by this include those at Rampton and Littleborough, the latter showing clear evidence of flooding and rebuilding. The underlying trend behind this was that the Roman period coincided with a wetter climate. According to David Knight, who has produced an excellent study of the evidence for landscape change in this period, this increasing wetness was accompanied by 'significant population growth' which led to more agricultural production and woodland clearance.[7] Rather than having to hack their way through ancient wildwood, the palaeobiological evidence of pollen samples suggests that Nottinghamshire's Romano-British people lived in a landscape that was mostly cleared for pasture and arable farming. The Trent Valley changed from a heavily wooded landscape to grassland suitable for animal husbandry and cereal crops. Some surviving woodlands seem to have been managed by coppicing and there is evidence for this from an enclosed settlement at Menagerie Wood, near Worksop, where coppice poles were found during excavations in the 1980s. But areas of wildwood still existed in places. Evidence for this comes from an oak-lined Roman well found at *Margidunum*, where the wooden planks showed signs of slow growth, suggesting they came from trees that had grown in competition with each other in old, unmanaged woodland. By contrast, a later 3rd century Roman well excavated at Lound in the mid-1990s was lined with planks from fast-growing trees, suggesting they grew in open woodland with reduced competition. Pollen recovered from the well also indicated that the 3rd century landscape here was one of grassland and few trees: hallmarks of a landscape managed for farming. And with a booming population, Roman Nottinghamshire will have needed increasingly productive farms.

David Knight is among those who believe that the population in the 2nd and 3rd centuries may have equalled or exceeded Nottinghamshire's population at the time of the Domesday survey in 1086. And the population then was...? In *The Making of the English Landscape*, W.G. Hoskins quoted a figure of 20,000 people for Nottinghamshire at the time of Domesday. However, the 1086 figure has been put at around 23,500 to 30,000 at its highest by the former principal archaeologist of

Nottinghamshire County Council, Mike Bishop.[8] Bishop says that the 1086 totals are based on accepted extrapolations from figures in the Domesday survey. In both the Roman period and the 11th and 12th centuries population distributions were densest in the Trent Valley and on fertile land north and south of the river. But a difference between the two periods is that the Idle Valley and Sherwood sandstone country in the north, plus the extreme west of the county, all appear to have been 'well occupied' in the Roman period. In 1086, these areas were sparsely populated. "Evidence of Roman settlement is widely present, across the whole county and all of its terrains," Bishop adds.

One result of population growth may have been a move by people on to relatively poor land, such as the sand dunes at Besthorpe. Another consequence would have been a need for more intensive use of land, evidence of which perhaps exists across an area around 40km long by 14km wide (25 by 8.5 miles) between Ollerton in north Nottinghamshire and the river Don in south Yorkshire. The importance of this area was first recognised in 1973 by a former RAF bomber pilot called Derrick Riley who specialised in using aerial photography to identify archaeological sites. Riley, who was employed by Sheffield University, added a great deal to the knowledge of Nottinghamshire's Roman landscape over many years and photographs of some of the forts and camps he identified can be seen elsewhere in this book. But it was the ghost of an ancient and organised farmed landscape, not a military site, that Riley saw across a wide swathe of the north Nottinghamshire countryside.

Here, cropmarks revealed the former existence of a dense system of rectangular fields with ditched enclosures. Riley said the fields resembled bricks in a wall and the pattern has since been known as the 'brickwork-plan' field system. The pattern revealed a coherent and consistent approach towards agricultural production in an area of infertile soils. The organisation extended to the orientation of the fields, which tended to run consistently at right angles to the rivers of the area, the Idle, Maun and Meden. The ditched enclosures which connected the fields were interpreted as the small farmsteads where the ancient farmers had lived. Although parts of the field system appeared to date to the late Iron Age shortly before the Roman invasion, excavations supported Riley's thinking that the landscape was mostly Roman and had origins in the 1st century. The land continued to be farmed in this way until at least the 3rd century and when one of the small farmsteads, at Dunston's Clump, Babworth, was excavated in 1981, evidence of occupation spanning 150–200 years was found. Signs of a rectangular farmhouse were also found here, this being interpreted as possible evidence of Roman influence on native building design.

Although the largest concentration of brickwork fields was seen in the area between Retford and Worksop, especially around Babworth, the Roman landscape also touched on land near Bawtry, Harworth, Mattersey, Ranskill, Blyth, Hodsock Priory, Barnby Moor and the Dukeries estates of Welbeck, Clumber and Thoresby. 'This was a planned system of land use, covering large tracts of country,' said Riley, who photographed the whole area using hand-held cameras from small Cessna aircraft, his pilots flying in circles around areas of land to give him the best angles.

However, admitting that it is difficult for some people to get excited about Roman field systems, it seems appropriate to ask what light this landscape sheds on life among the Romano-British of ancient Nottinghamshire. One question that has been asked is why the land was organised in this distinctive way and who owned it. Was it part of the estate of a local private villa? Was it part of a large Roman Imperial estate? Answer: nobody knows. Villas are scarce in this part of the country and there is no specific evidence suggesting that it may have been owned by the Roman state. Whoever owned these fields, they would have been poor for arable production. As Riley pointed out, the acidic soil, lying on top of the Bunter sandstone, made it unsuitable for most crops including wheat. The alternative is that the fields, with their separating ditches, could have been used for stock grazing. Archaeologist Ruth Leary, who helped analyse the results of a massive fieldwalking exercise over the brickwork landscape between Ollerton and Bawtry, has tentatively suggested that the economy here was based on sheep.

But whether the land was owned by one person or many, the individuals who actually worked the land here were perhaps living not far above a subsistence level. Although there were people in this area who had the means to buy pottery from outside the immediate area, the Dunston's Clump archaeologists remarked that the farmers there do not seem to have been rich folk. Far from it. Indeed, remarks about the general poverty of Nottinghamshire's Romano-British farms crop up several times in the reports. Although the settlement at Raymoth Lane, Worksop (where the skeletons of the stillborn and premature babies were found) was described as 'neither perceptibly wealthy nor humble', the evidence for the settlement at Rampton left an impression of the 'parochial and relatively impoverished nature of the economy.' Further south, the Romano-British settlements at Gonalston and Aslockton were both regarded as 'low status'. This general impression of poverty among the rural population has to be contrasted with the great wealth demonstrated by several of Nottinghamshire's villa owners and perhaps some of the people who lived in and around towns such as *Margidunum*. Poverty aside, the dense brickwork landscape suggests a requirement for high food production, perhaps reflecting a growing population. Other Romano-British settlements excavated in the county include Staunton in the Vale of Belvoir and several sites in the north of the county such as Mattersey, Menagerie Wood and Chainbridge Lane, Lound, as well as the recently excavated communities at Besthorpe in the east. These have also helped fill in the picture of life among the Romano-British that is missing from the maps of roads, villas and forts.

With little evidence of an abrupt cultural change in these small communities, the day-to-day business of life for the many people tied to the land may not have changed overnight with the coming of the Roman invaders. But life did change and perhaps initially not for the better. Land, which was the basis of wealth in the Roman economy, was no doubt taken from the natives and parcelled out to new Roman landowners and their tribal allies. Malcolm Todd, who excavated the four-acre site at Staunton in the mid-1970s, found so little evidence of material wealth there that he thought the farm must have been worked by slaves and owned by an absentee landlord in the veterans' *colonia* at Lincoln.

As well as land seizure, new taxes were imposed on agriculture including a tax on the production of grains. Tacitus described how the people had to shoulder the burden of profiteers, who humiliated the Britons by taking their grain and then made them wait at public granaries where they were forced to buy back their own grain at high prices. The Britons were also ordered to transport their grain over long distances to remote and inaccessible places. Although Tacitus said that Agricola reformed this situation, the description gives a taste of the exploitation that the invaders brought.

Impressions of general Roman high-handedness and cultural arrogance can be found in other ancient sources, some well known, others relatively new. The causes of Boudica's revolt among the *Iceni* and *Trinovantes* tribes were recorded by the Roman historians and included the humiliation of her household and her nobles: Boudica was raped, her daughters flogged, royal relatives were treated like slaves and the Icenian chieftains had their land taken away. Meanwhile, at the new *colonia* at the Trinovantian capital *Camulodunum*, Britons had been driven from their homes and their land handed over to Roman army veterans; adding insult to material injury, a large temple to the Deified Emperor Claudius was set up here. It was these accumulated humiliations that led Boudica and her insurgent army to seek such terrible revenge on the invaders. Centuries later, and hundreds of miles away, a thin Roman wooden writing tablet, apparently a memorandum concerning British military tactics at the end of the 1st century, was unearthed at *Vindolanda* Roman fort near Hadrian's Wall in Northumberland. A unique reminder of the invaders' condescension towards the natives, the tablet bore the previously unseen word *Brittunculi*, a derogatory term translated as 'wretched Britons'.

There was, however, a form of control available that was more invidious than tax, land seizure and the sword; and it was control from the *inside* via the slavish copying of Roman lifestyle by the Britons. As Tacitus famously wrote: 'And so the Britons were gradually led on to the amenities that make vice agreeable — arcades, baths and sumptuous banquets. They spoke of such novelties as "civilisation", when really they were only a feature of enslavement.' There are no records specifying that the people of the East Midlands had to put up with the extreme outrages that the *Iceni* of East Anglia were forced to endure; but, equally, it would very surprising if the *Corieltauvi* were for any reason spared the theft of land, imposition of taxes and cultural arrogance that the Romans brought to other parts of the country in the early stages of the occupation.

Another aside is needed here: where was Nottingham in all this? Although it is now believed that the county capital was founded by the Saxons, or the Danes, in the 8th or 9th centuries, antiquarians and historians of the 18th and 19th centuries took it as read that the city had Roman origins. Charles Deering's *History of Nottingham*, published in 1751, devoted considerable space to speculation over whether Nottingham, or even West Bridgford, could have been the Roman *Causennae,* which is today usually associated with Sapperton in Lincolnshire. By 1834, the writer of *Dearden's Directory of Nottingham* considered that there was 'indubitable' evidence of occupation even before the Romans but that this period of history would forever remain a mystery. The archaeological evidence for any susbstantial Roman occupation is, however, scarce. As Prof. John Beckett wrote in *A Centenary History of Nottingham*: 'When one considers that the discovery of Roman sherds is the single most common experience of any gardener in almost any part of England, the silence of the evidence from Nottingham is remarkable.' Yet people were in the area during the Roman period: a Roman coin hoard was unearthed in Forest Fields in the early part of the 20th century; pottery and evidence of Romano-British ditches, pits and fields were seen in early 2007 at Grove Farm, Clifton, prior to the building of the current retirement village there; more pottery was found in Plumptre Street during construction work; and the early Roman fort was excavated at Broxtowe in the 1930s prior to the building of the housing estate.

Faced with a complete absence of references to the East Midlands region in classical texts, building up a detailed chronology of life in Nottinghamshire over the next 300 years of the Roman presence is a difficult task. However, some trends have been identified. For example, around 20 villas and villa sites are officially known in Nottinghamshire and many of those that have been excavated show that construction took place in the early part of the 2nd century, with occupation continuing until the middle or late 4th century. These were country homes, in other words, that were lived in for around 250 years or more. Over this long lifespan, the villas tended to become more complex and elaborate, with various corridors, rooms and extensions being added. New building phases were sometimes motivated by destruction of the old phase by fire. Some villas, like the large example at Mansfield Woodhouse which was first excavated in the late 18th century by the Nottinghamshire antiquarian Major Hayman Rooke, seem to have started life in the late 1st century as humble timber structures. But like the other large villa at Southwell, the Mansfield Woodhouse villa developed into a large structure of many rooms complete with bathing suite, central heating and interior décor including large complex floor mosaics and brightly patterned walls. The recent discovery of a skilfully constructed wall at the Southwell villa, 50 years after the villa was excavated, has raised many further questions about a building that was one of the largest of its type in the region. None of the Nottinghamshire villas, however, appears to have survived much beyond the mid-300s. This is in keeping with a pattern seen throughout Britain, where villas seem to have enjoyed a golden age in terms of wealth, design complexity and sheer quantity in the last part of the 3rd century and first half of the 4th. Yet this heyday was followed by an apparently quick decline. The end of villas at Mansfield Woodhouse, Flawford, Thurgarton and Norton Disney, the last just over the county border in Lincolnshire but linked to the small Fosse Way town at *Crococolana*, have all been dated to between 350 and 380. Similar dates have been given for the end of occupation at the villas at Southwell, Barton-in-Fabis and Epperstone. Explanations for this decline have included radical changes in land ownership and the end of the economic upswing that had supported the villa golden age in the first place. But banditry and lack of safety in the countryside may have been a more compelling reason for villa owners to abandon their homes. As has already been noted, Adrian Oswald believed that the end of the Norton Disney villa was down to the murder of the occupants by rampaging northern barbarians.

Between the initial building of villas and their golden age, there was a lull in villa construction during the 3rd century. And it was also in this period that some Roman towns in Nottinghamshire and the surrounding area had their defences strengthened. At Thorpe, on the Fosse Way, a small 1st century fortlet was succeeded by a civilian settlement surrounded by a ditch, which was in turn replaced by a much larger enclosure surrounded by a stone wall, 2.6 metres thick, surrounded by more ditches. Adding new fortifications like this seems to have been a common development feature of several towns and villages in the province at this time. At Great Casterton, in Rutland, a town wall and bastions, plus wide, deep ditches were also added at the end of the 2nd century or beginning of the 3rd.

Why new defences were felt to be necessary at this time is not clear. One argument is that strong fortifications were required in a troubled period when Roman civil society was starting to crumble as the costs of paying for the army began to divert money away from public services. War also came back to *Britannia* at the start of the 3rd century as the north African-born Emperor Severus began campaigning in Scotland again; there were numerous barbarian invasions on the continent; and on two occasions later in the 3rd century rebel Emperors broke away from Rome and set up mini-Empires which included *Britannia*. How all this played out in the tiny part of the Roman world now called Nottinghamshire is not recorded, but one sensible response to this period of uncertainty may have been to build bigger walls and ditches around your towns. "The frontiers were becoming porous and I think the countryside was becoming insecure and dangerous," said Roman historian Neil Faulkner, speaking in Nottingham in 2010. "The countryside was increasingly infested by bandits."

Indeed, this is a good place to speculate as to how the people of Roman Nottinghamshire could have been affected by some of the other larger events of the Empire. Even before the first invasion of Scotland by Agricola in the 80s began there was an epic struggle for power following the suicide of Claudius' successor Nero in 68. Although former legionary commander Vespasian emerged as eventual victor in the so-called 'Year of the Four Emperors', bringing an end to the Julio-Claudian dynasty that had run the Empire since the accession of Caesar's great nephew and adopted son Octavian in 27 BC, the new civil war tested the loyalties of the four legions stationed in Britain. One entire legion, XIV *Gemina*, plus selected detachments from the three others in the province (including Legion IX *Hispana*, stationed at Lincoln) were summoned to fight on the continent. The governor of Britain at the time fled the country, leaving the province to be briefly ruled by the legionary commanders. And it was during this chaotic period, when a quick succession of four Emperors in Rome split the army's loyalties, that civil war broke out among the *Brigantes*, to the immediate north of conquered *Corieltauvi* territory.

However, it is after this drama, which culminated in Vespasian's founding of the short-lived Flavian dynasty, that one enters even vaguer historical territory so far as Nottinghamshire itself is concerned. The difficulty lies in relating the known datable events in the narrative of Roman Britain to life within the small area addressed by this book. We can only speculate, for example, as to how a peasant farmer at Babworth or a skilled metal-worker in the Trent Valley may have felt about the division in 212 of the entire British province into two sub-provinces called *Britannia Superior* and *Britannia Inferior*. The latter comprised northern Britain, including the ancient lands of the *Corieltauvi*, and had its capital at *Eboracum*, York. That same year the Emperor Caracalla granted Roman citizenship to all free people throughout the Empire, a status previously available only to born Romans and certain groups who had earned the privilege. The extension of citizenship was suspected as being a way of increasing the Emperor's tax base.

By 312, a century later, the province had been subdivided again into four regions with the part known as *Flavia Caesariensis* possibly covering the East Midlands, with Lincoln as its capital. A large villa at Greetwell in Lincolnshire, the remains of which were recorded and demolished in the 1880s, has been put forward as the possible residence of the local Roman governor. In the following year the Emperor Constantine

Modern statue of the first Christian Emperor, Constantine, outside York Minster.

— proclaimed Emperor in York by the British legions, later founder of Constantinople — legalised Christianity throughout the Roman Empire. There is a strain of academic belief that most ordinary people, those not within the social 'elite' of Romano-British society, would have been little affected by such events. Yet, fortunately, there is now a body of physical evidence showing at the very least that early Christianity had a presence in Nottinghamshire. Some idea of the texture and colour of local life can also be gained from what is known about people's diets, their industries and the art and craft that was produced in Nottinghamshire in the period. What's more, the names of around 40 individuals are known from the region including those of soldiers, town councillors, freed slaves — and even a gladiator.

Notes

1. *The Conquest of Gaul* — Julius Caesar. Penguin Classics, 1974.
2. *Agricola* — Tacitus. In: *On Britain and Germany* Penguin Classics, 1964.
3. Roman Leicester, a corrigendum: for 'Coritani' should we now read 'Corieltauvi'? — R.S.O. Tomlin. *Transactions of the Leicestershire Archaeological and Historical Society*, 58, 1982–83.
4. *The Name of Margidunum, Roman Settlement, Nottinghamshire* — Andrew Breeze. *Transactions of the Thoroton Society of Nottinghamshire* 109, 2005.
5. *An Imperial Possession: Britain in the Roman Empire* — David Mattingly. Penguin Books, 2007.
6. Ibid.
7. *Trent Valley Landscapes: the Archaeology of 500,000 Years of Change* — David Knight and Andy J. Howard. Heritage Marketing and Publications, 2004.
8. *The Population of Nottinghamshire in 1086 and the Roman Period* — Mike Bishop. *Pers comm.*

Chapter 3

Margidunum II: the excavations of Oswald and Todd

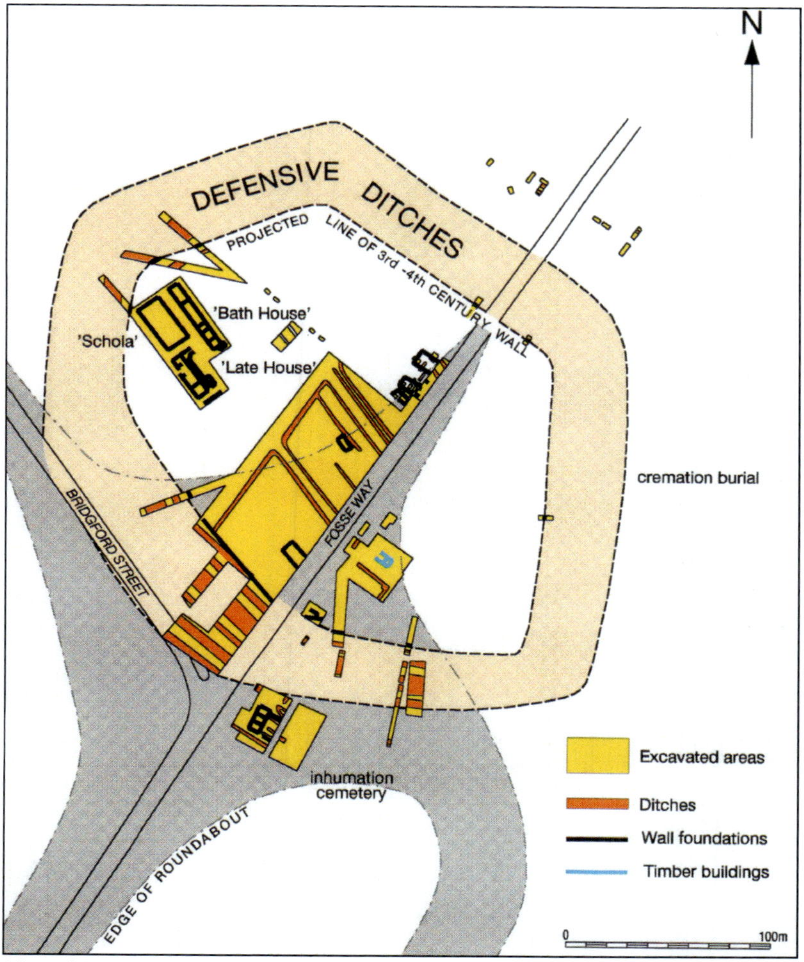

Map of *Margidunum* and the modern roundabout on the A46 Fosse Way that takes it name. Building names such as 'Schola' were the ones given by Felix Oswald.

Margidunum has been the subject of two main series of digs, the first being conducted by Felix Oswald, who excavated it almost single-handedly on and off between 1910 and 1936. In the early stages he was helped by a medical doctor called T. Davies Pryce, of University College, Nottingham, and Oswald's son, Adrian. Work was brought to a halt by the First World War, but was resumed afterwards by Oswald himself, 'working single-handed in my spare time down to the year 1936', as he wrote in a paper signed by him which is now in the possession of the University of Nottingham's Department of Manuscripts and Special Collections. Oswald's dedication to the site was impressive by any standard; he excavated a quarter of the interior, mainly on the western side of the Fosse, recovering scores of intact artefacts and thousands of broken fragments, including a mass of pottery which he reassembled into complete vessels whenever possible as he went along. He also provided many drawings for his excavation reports, the first of which was delivered in 1911.

Although the main report was published in 1927, Oswald described his interpretations and many finds in several shorter reports. In one he described how he literally groped through the mud at the bottom of a well and plucked out a flagon. Oswald's drive to investigate *Margidunum* even conquered hostile farmers. When a farmer refused to give permission for excavations to

Felix Oswald.

continue on land adjacent to the Fosse, a generous supporter of Oswald simply bought one of the farmer's fields and allowed the dig to continue. While Oswald's overall conclusions about *Margidunum* were substantially reassessed in the 1960s, it was his painstaking effort that produced most of the Roman artefacts for which *Margidunum* is known today.

The larger items included cooking pots, urns, storage jars and metalware such as iron weapons, a fire gridiron, large keys and door hinges. One large piece of tile still bore the clear imprint of a hobnailed Roman shoe; a complete flue brick was evidence that at least some of *Margidunum*'s residents had enjoyed central heating. Oswald also found many items of jewellery and coins from throughout the Romano-British period. And he seems to have found these and other artefacts almost everywhere he looked, including wood- and stone-lined wells, cellars and ditches. The wells proved to be particularly fruitful. In one he found a wooden comb, and a collection of earthenware roundels which he thought had probably been used for the game of five-stones or 'Snobs' — 'as it usually called, for the children of East Bridgford still cut out roundels of pottery for this game, just as in Roman times', he said.

In a well lined with oak, the planks still bore the marks of the Roman workers' saw and adze. As well as the larger objects there were the thousands of fragments of pottery plus window glass and plaster, some of which was coloured and suggested how the Roman buildings had been decorated. Pagan religious

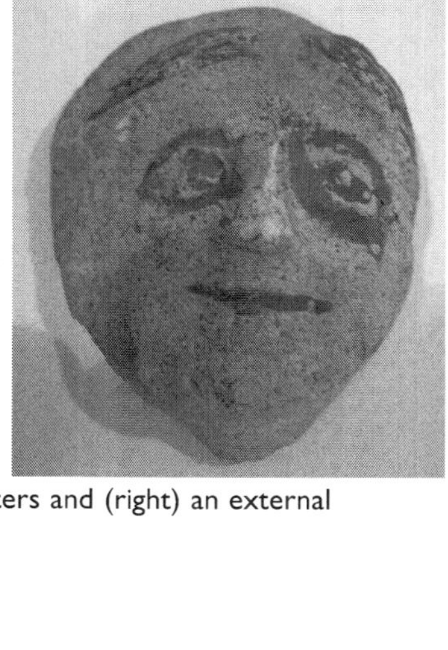

Finds from *Margidunum*: Roman gaming counters and (right) an external attachment from the neck of a jug.

items included the heavy carved figure of a 'Warrior God' and the smaller and now headless figure of a domestic 'Mother Goddess'. Both of these artefacts, and many other finds from *Margidunum*, are on display in the University of Nottingham Museum — the museum that was effectively founded by Oswald in 1933 when he donated his *Margidunum* collection to the university.

Yet thirty years after Oswald put down his spade at *Margidunum,* the site was substantially re-excavated. The year was 1966 and the archaeologist in charge was a professional, Malcolm Todd, then a newish lecturer at the University of Nottingham who later went on to be Professor of Archaeology at the University of Exeter. The reason for the new work was the imminent construction of the roundabout which was to be built over the southern half of the defences and interior. With destruction pending, Todd devoted much of his effort to this area before it was covered with the concrete and tarmac which makes up the *Margidunum* roundabout today. Todd's significantly more precise excavation report brought with it a complete reassessment of the site. And without being at all derogatory about Oswald's huge personal effort, he was forced to disagree with most of Oswald's major conclusions.

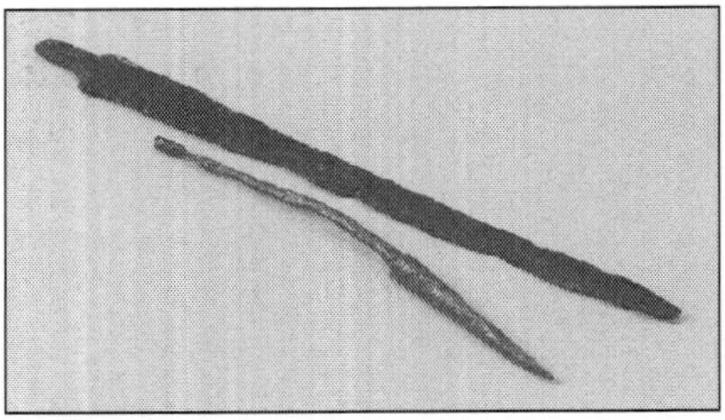

Roman sword blade and spear head found at *Margidunum.*

Oswald, for example, was confident that *Margidunum* had been established as 'one of the most important' military forts on the Fosse Way in around 47, its odd shape (described by Pryce as 'un-symmetrically rhomboidal') covering seven to eight acres and accommodating 1,000 men including cavalry. He based these assertions partly on the clear evidence of ditches and ramparts he found and a few items of recovered military equipment.

Working from this base, Oswald proceeded to fit the archaeology he found into a larger narrative of events in the history of Roman Britain, aided by colourful speculation of a kind that is seldom found in the rigorously scientific archaeology reports of today. For example, he suggested that discarded blackened archway stones were evidence that the fort had been burned by native Britons pursuing Legion IX as it retreated up the Fosse Way in the Boudican revolt. He asserted that the fort was rebuilt in stone, but subsequently levelled 'with Roman thoroughness' in the early 2nd century because the military front had moved north and *Margidunum* was no longer militarily important. The evidence for this was his uncovering of cellars, wells and ditches filled up with all sorts of pottery and camp rubble. The Roman garrison, said Oswald, was probably sent up to Hadrian's Wall.

Another vignette concerned his finding of a collection of unopened oysters on a layer of charcoal. Oswald extrapolated that just as the oysters were about to be cooked, on a day between the years 60 and 70, the chef's hut caught fire, 'causing the abandonment of this keg of oysters that had just arrived from the Lincolnshire coast'. After the fort's abandonment, Oswald reasoned that *Margidunum* continued as a civilian 'posting station', mostly given over to pasture for horses serving the station ('about 50 in number'). Then, based on coins he found, Oswald said the town was at least active during the reign of the Emperor Constantine in the first half of the 4th century. But finally disaster threatened *Margidunum* again when Picts and Scots overran Hadrian's Wall in 376. This led to the construction of a 'massive stone rampart' which would, said Oswald, have been 5.5–6 metres (18–20ft) high. After all that, *Margidunum* was abandoned and fell into decay.

Wrong, said Todd. Firstly, both in the unusual outline of its defences and supposed organisation of streets and buildings, *Margidunum* failed to resemble most known Roman forts. However, the site probably had a Roman military presence from 50–55. Todd's slightly later dating meant that *Margidunum* was established when, he said, 'the Vale of Trent will have long been under Roman control'. Like Oswald, Todd thought the site was abandoned by the army, but in around 75, far earlier than Oswald thought. Todd's diagnosis of Oswald's military misidentification also extended to buildings found inside the defences. Oswald, for example, found the remains of a stone building on the west side of the Fosse which he interpreted as having a central paved courtyard or verandah, surrounded by a corridor with a slanting roof, supported by pillars, as well as a latrine, well and adjacent stables. Oswald was confident that he had found the home of the fort's commandant and duly labelled this structure the Commandant's House. Todd, having already rejected the site as a fort, said that all that could be safely identified in this building were a single wall and some fragments of paving. The structure was probably a simple strip building facing on to the road.

Oswald's identification of the fort's main thoroughfares was also wrong, said Todd. 'In some cases, roughly metalled areas have been raised to the dignity of streets,' he wrote. The absence of evidence for barracks in the fort was recognised by Oswald, but he reasoned that the troops had probably lived in tents. In summary, the irregularly shaped settlement excavated by Oswald over 26 years had not been a Roman fort. Or at least it had not been *the* Roman fort. Although no 'certain trace' of a fort at the site was found by Todd, he reasoned that there was probably a fort somewhere very near *Margidunum*, perhaps on the northern side, where he found vague evidence of a defensive ditch. The fort, if one ever existed, remains unknown. Despite this, *Margidunum's* original *raison d'être* as a military site remains a distinct possibility. As well as Todd's ditch, both he and Oswald recovered metal weapons and pottery of a quality associated with a Roman military presence. The very suffix — *dunum* is also usually interpreted as meaning 'fort'. This all suggests that an original fort site lies very close to the known town and that what Oswald and Todd dug up was the civilian settlement that grew up next to the fort, and went on to have a separate existence for the duration of the Roman occupation. Incidentally, in questioning Oswald's assumption that *Margidunum* had been a fort, Todd queried the rationale for building a fort at this site at all since it was some distance from the Trent, which a fort might be expected to have guarded. Yet, clearly the site — fort or not — had strategic importance astride one of the Romans' main roads, the Fosse Way. It was also close to a natural source of fresh water from local springs. As one local man who has lived close to the site for many years told this writer in the summer of 2010: "Those Romans weren't stupid. They built this place halfway between Leicester and Lincoln, they had natural spring water from that field over there and took clay from the river banks to make their pottery."

Nonetheless, this all left the known *Margidunum* settlement as a defended civilian town. So what kind of town was it? The buildings were, we can suppose, built of timber (later stone) with thatch roofs, and the town was much larger than Oswald had thought. Finds by Todd and others since have established that there was building development up to 700–800 metres (half a mile) from the town centre and 200 metres (650ft) from the Fosse, with a concentration at the corner of the Fosse and the A6097 Lowdham road. This suggested a 'vast extent of occupation' in *Margidunum*'s first 25–30 years. Yet inside the defences, there was ample breathing space between buildings. 'The overall picture is of a scattered, discontinuous settlement, a layout well known from the other excavated roadside villages,' said Todd. 'Within the defences, large areas were never built over.' There were suggestions of a baking oven, smithy and outhouses. The industry here may have been the manufacturing of iron, perhaps making weapons for the army before it began its push into northern England. Oswald had found abundant evidence of iron smelting.

Oswald identified three principal buildings among the structures inside the defences: a 25 metre by 11.5 metre (84ft by 38ft) rectangular building of unknown purpose he labelled the Schola; another titled the Late House, or 4th Century House, which had a pool nearby; and a 40 metre (130ft) long Bath House, in which he found the remains of a cold room, an adjacent room retaining the pillar bases of a *hypocaust* central heating system and fragments of wall plaster decorated with bands of red, orange and green. A flue brick and fragments of waterproof floor concrete called *opus signinum* were further evidence that the building's users had regularly enjoyed hot water bathing. Diamond-shaped roof tiles made of Charnwood Forest slate were also recovered.

Todd's assessment of these was that the Late House had been 'relatively well-appointed' and may have been related to the bath house, but that Oswald had got the dating of all three wrong. Todd's overall dating of the site was that the earliest stone buildings didn't go up until around 150, 75 years after the army abandoned the site. Despite these disagreements, the finds suggest that the larger properties were relatively elaborate, with stone pilasters and glass windows, and were in contrast to the functional small rectangular buildings which stood end-on to the roads. With hearths and pits, these appear to have been used for industry. Separate surveys suggest there were streets and roads within this straggling town, running at right angles to the Lowdham road. Indeed, in an assessment of the archaeology written in 2004, Ruth Leary and Steve Baker wrote: '*Margidunum* can be re-classified as a road junction development with the possibility that a developed and regular street network remains to be discovered.'[1]

Coins and pottery suggested *Margidunum* had enjoyed 'widespread occupation' in the 3rd and 4th centuries, even though evidence of use of buildings in this later period was scrappy. In the early 5th century, as the Roman way of life broke down, the area may have been settled by migrating Saxons. How was this long history reflected in the town defences, the only part of *Margidunum* still slightly visible today? Oswald, interpreting what he found as military in origin, said the original defences consisted of earth-backed timber ramparts and six V-shaped ditches, separated by 'entanglements of stakes'. On the south side was a well-gravelled road between the two outermost ditches, 'perhaps a patrol-path for sentries, a very necessary precaution against a surprise on foggy nights'. Then, in the 4th century, a large stone wall built on a 2.7 metre (9ft) wide concrete foundation was added to the town defences. Todd, excavating the southern part of the defences which were soon to be covered by the roundabout, and defences to the north that Oswald hadn't touched, certainly couldn't substantiate speculation about foggy nights. Nevertheless, the 'unequivocal evidence for two main successive phases of fortification' he found was still impressive.

The first phase of the civilian town's defences had a 7.7 metre (25ft 6in) wide rampart and perhaps two ditches measuring 3 metres (9ft 6in) wide by 1.8 metres (6ft) deep and 5.4 metres (18ft) wide by 1.8 metres (6ft) deep. Sections of the earth rampart were still standing around a metre above the ground surface in Todd's day. This surviving section of the defences was among the parts of *Margidunum* flattened by the roundabout.

The second, later, defences had consisted of a 9 metre (30ft) wide earth rampart and a wall 2.7 metre (9ft) wide at its base made of limestone blocks. Todd couldn't date the wall to any later than 200 (against Oswald's 376). There were also two outer ditches, the inner one 8–9 metres (27–30ft) wide and 3 metres (10ft) deep, the outer 4 metres (13.5ft) wide by 1.5 metres (5ft) deep. The inner one had been used as a rubbish dump in the middle to late 4th century. Or as Todd put it: '...there had accumulated... such a large and noisome dump of vegetable refuse, dung and animal bone that, by the end of that century, the larger of the two late-Roman ditches must have been less of a work of defence than a public nuisance'.[2] The outermost feature of the defences was a 16 metre (52ft) wide pile of spoil from the ditches, still visible when Todd saw it. In summary, what Oswald had seen as a key military strongpoint on the Fosse Way was, under Todd's assessment, a somewhat untidy civilian village or small town encompassing 2.2 hectares (5½ acres) within its defences which may have had 'rural significance' as a settlement on a major road and played a minor administrative role in the province. Being located half way between Leicester and Lincoln, Todd speculated that *Margidunum* could have stationed servants of the Imperial postal service or an official such as a regional Roman police officer.

What about the large villa? After Todd finished his work in the late 1960s professional archaeological activity at *Margidunum* resumed in the early 1990s. Even then, the villa's discovery had to wait until 2003 and followed extensive surveys conducted in preparation for the dualling of the A46. The evidence for the villa, on Crown Estate land near the entrance to RAF Newton, was a combination of cropmarks, geophysical indications and rubble including brick, window glass, roof and flue tiles and possible roof tiles and mosaic *tesserae*. A plan of the villa, with a large gap in the middle, suggests that the building had a large walled courtyard, with a set of rooms, *hypocaust* and possible bath house. The full extent of the villa remains unknown, but Leary and Baker estimated the dimensions of the core group of rooms as 100 metres by 60 metres (328ft by 196ft). Their report continued: 'The complex compares in size with some of the large courtyard villas of Roman Britain... . In size the prominent compound can be compared with sumptuous villas in Britain and Europe, suggesting that in its final form at least it may be of remarkable dimensions. If the traces to the north are contemporary and of the same character, then the extent of the complex seems remarkable.'

Although the quantity of surface finds did not match projections of such grandiose luxury, the discovery of the villa and its proximity to the town have inevitably upgraded the perception of *Margidunum* and given it an enhanced relationship with the immediate countryside. Increasingly, it looks as if *Margidunum* was connected to several productive villa estates and had some wealthy neighbours living in the vicinity. As well as the Newton villa, at least two more villas were located close to the town. Just 2.5km (1.5 miles) east at Bingham, a skeleton and Roman pottery from the 1st to 4th centuries were found underneath a roadway by contractors when they were laying pipes for Carnarvon Primary School in the late 1960s. An accumulation of other finds including fragments of walls, roof tiles and a central heating flue tile has been interpreted as evidence that the school site supported a high status villa-type house from the late 1st century. The pottery found was similar to that found at *Margidunum*, suggesting the inhabitants here had trade connections with that settlement. Another villa close to *Margidunum* is also known about at Car Colston, on the eastern side of the Fosse Way. This second building is discussed further in Chapter Eight. Meanwhile, the sum of knowledge about the Roman town continued to grow thanks to the efforts of the Bingham Heritage Trails Assocation, whose extensive fieldwalking programme has covered 2,000 acres of land. The results have been published in a book titled *Bingham, Back in Time*.

Most recently, further extensive excavations conducted ahead of the building of the A46 dual carriageway have discovered new features, including another large building. Early results of these excavations at *Margidunum* were revealed in a public meeting held by the local history group at Colston Bassett, a village on the eastern side of the Fosse Way, in early March 2010. Archaeologist Peter Aspden, from A46 scheme designers Scott Wilson, said part of a previously unknown "substantial" Roman building had been found just outside *Margidunum's* defences close to the route of the new A46 . "We found the foundations were one metre deep, and some blocks were quite substantial, up to one metre across," he said. "It looks like it's got two wings. Is it a villa? It's difficult to say. It's certainly well made. We also recovered some [roof] slate, which you would associate with a building like this. We believe they originated in the Lake District, which suggests quite a wealthy building if they were transporting material from so far away."

The latest excavations also uncovered 12 Roman burials to the south of the town, plus a coin dated to the 330s. This wasn't the first time human remains were found at *Margidunum*. Oswald's human finds had included skeletons and the lower jaw of 'a young man with a very pronounced chin who had just cut his

Excavated foundations of the 'substantial' building found just outside *Margidunum*'s defences.

wisdom teeth' and, to the east of the town, cremated remains in a pot. In 1966, four graves were also found to the south. Todd accordingly investigated and, in 1968, six further human skeletons were found in shallow graves. Todd dated the graves to the mid to late 4th century or early 5th century and believed that there were more in the area.

In the years after the Roman abandonment of Britain *Margidunum* disappeared stone by stone. The earliest evidence of stone removal from the town was dated to the medieval period by Todd, who found that sections of the foundation and the stone blocks of the late stone defensive wall were removed almost entirely in the 14th century (he found two pots from the period). The stone-robbers had dug a trench 3 metres (9–10ft) wide and removed stone from the outer part of the wall. In the 16th century, the Elizabethan

One of the 12 human skeletons unearthed at *Margidunum* during excavations ahead of the A46 dualling.

scholar and traveller William Camden noted that 'plaster stone' was dug up in the area. But the clearest graphic evidence for how *Margidunum* was dismantled was given by the 18th century antiquary William Stukeley, who travelled south down the Fosse Way in 1722. Although Stukeley mistakenly thought he had arrived at *Ad Pontem* when he arrived at *Margidunum* there was plenty to see of the old Roman 'castle'. And also much that had been taken away:

> *Hereabouts I saw the Roman foundations of walls and floors of houses, composed of the manner before spoken, of stones set edgewise in clay, and liquid mortar run upon them. There are likewise short oaken posts or piles at proper intervals, some whereof I pulled up with my own hands... . houses stood all along the Foss, whole foundations have been dug up, and carried to the neighbouring villages. They told us too of a most famous pavement near the Foss Way. Close by in a pasture called Castle Hill Close has been a great building, which they say was carried all to Newark. John Green of Bridgford, aged 80, told me he had taken up large foundations there, much ancient coin and small earthen pipes for water. His father, aged near 100, took up many pipes four score yards off the castle, and much fine free stone, some well cut and carved. There have been found many urns, pots and Roman bricks, but the people preserved none of them. And some that had coins would by no means let us see them, for fear we were come from the lord of the manor.*[4]

No wonder Stukeley said he felt regret for 'the oblivion of so many famous antiquities'.

Despite such large-scale stone removal, there was still something to see in the 19th century. According to the *Victoria County History*, the outline of the defences was still 'clearly marked' on the ground in 1857 and these were investigated by the wife of the Rector of Bingham, a Mrs Miles. Mrs Miles' curiosity was well rewarded, for she reported finding a mass of material on the surface of fields including lead, flue tiles, stone tiles, deer horns, a knife handle, Roman coins and 'thousands of pieces of pottery of different colours, quantities, and materials'. The narrative went on: 'Several fields on each side of the Fosse were full of remains, especially a ploughed field on the west side through which runs the bridlepath known as "Newton Street". Stukeley's story of buildings here was corroborated to some extent by an old inhabitant who had seen a considerable portion of a wall, and it was a common practice with the residents to dig up the stones of Roman dwellings for building purposes.'

Oswald, in the 1920s, said that the late stone wall had been visible several decades before. 'But it gradually disappeared, for it furnished a convenient quarry in the Middle Ages for churches, as at Bingham and East Bridgford, and in more recent times for country houses such as Flintham Hall,' he said. 'Evidence of this 4th century refortification was still standing 60 or 70 years ago [i.e. the 1860s?] and gave rise to the modern name Castle Hill.' Pryce, in his own account of the 1910–11 excavations, published in 1912, said there had been a 'local tradition of the site having been used as a quarry for neighbouring buildings. An arch and other masonry were laid bare in the south west corner of the site some sixty years ago.' In a note in the *Victoria County History,* the author of the Roman section said he explored the defences of the settlement in 1905 with the help of an old parish map.

The remains of the defences seen by Todd in 1968 seem to have been *Margidunum*'s last hurrah. Before the roundabout, Todd said that the best preserved section was on the east and south east sides, where the original ditches were marked by a hollow nine metres (30ft) wide and three metres (10ft) deep. Angles of the defences at the north and north east were also 'fairly well defined'. The remains of the ramparts stood at a height of 46cm (18ins) on the south and south east, so perhaps this was part of the 'low mound' mentioned by Roger Wilson in *A Guide to the Roman Remains of Britain.* The only other reminder of the town's existence is the purported line of an early Roman road on the northern side of the site running parallel to the Fosse Way. This is believed to mark an early course of the Fosse Way and was first noted by Felix Oswald. It is discussed more fully in the section about the modern remains of the Fosse Way.

Felix Oswald died in 1958, having written a string of successful reports on geological and archaeological matters. Born in 1866, his early successes were in mapping and geological surveying in places such as Armenia, the Caucasus and Lake Victoria in equatorial Africa. In archaeology, he may not have regarded his long labours at *Margidunum* as his greatest success since his abiding passion was for collecting and analysing Roman high quality glossy red *samian* tableware, sometimes called *Terra Sigillata.*

Oswald established his collection from pieces collected at *Margidunum* and subsequently enlarged it with the purchase of a large collection from a French antiquarian called Albert-Edward Plicque. Oswald spent many years analysing the potters' stamps and decorative forms on the pottery, leading to the publication of three major works on the subject between 1920 and 1937. Oswald's guide to *samian*, written with Pryce, is only now being superseded by a ten-volume guide identifying more than 300,000 stamp marks belonging to around 4,500 potters. As much as anything, this is a reminder of the diagnostic importance that archaeologists attach to pottery. A brief memoir of Oswald by another *samian* expert, Grace Simpson, said this:

> *At the bungalow he designed and partly built with his own hands in Solva, Pembrokeshire, he played the piano until he was 84 years old, and he enjoyed gardening. He corresponded with scholars in many countries and he continued to write archaeology reports. He was small, and strongly built. He kept a cheerful, alert and energetic manner all his life. He was kind to young colleagues, and humorous in conversation. He died on his 92nd birthday in 1958 and his memory is honoured in many countries beside his own country.*[5]

Oswald donated much of his *samian* collection to the University of Nottingham; the rest was given to Prof. Eric Birley of Durham University, whose grandson now runs the on-going excavations at *Vindolanda*, near Hadrian's Wall.

A final note on the name *Margidunum*: some scholarly energy has gone into the meaning of the name, which has usually been translated as 'fort in the marly place', referring to the site's underlying marl bedrock. Camden had a shot at the etymology of the place, suggesting that *Margidunum* 'was borowed from *marga* and the situation of it. For *marga* among the Britans is a kinde of earth named Marle wherewith they nourished and kept their grounds in heart, and *dunum*, which signifieth an hill, agreeth onelie to places higher mounted than others.' However, with the overlying soil being rocky, a newer translation is 'fort at the stony place'. Lecturer Andrew Breeze, who offered this interpretation in 2005, wrote: 'In digging its defences, Roman soldiers would become very familiar with the "abundant pebbles and rock fragments" mentioned by modern geologists and were more likely to remember the tons of rubble they had to remove in baskets, than marl in bedrock beneath.'

Trackway running east (seen left of the modern road) from *Margidunum* and the Fosse Way... towards Bingham? Another feature revealed during excavations ahead of the dualling work on the A46.

Notes

1. *Margidunum Roman Villa and Small Town* — Ruth Leary and Steve Baker. Trent and Peak Archaeological Unit Report, 2004.
2. *The Roman Settlement at Margidunum: the Excavations of 1966–68* — Malcolm Todd. *Transactions of the Thoroton Society of Nottinghamshire* 73, 1969.
3. *Margidunum Roman Villa and Small Town* — Ruth Leary and Steve Baker. Trent and Peak Archaeological Unit Report, 2004.
4. *Itinerarium Curiosum, Or an Account of the Antiquitys and Remarkable Curiositys in Nature or Art, Observ'd in Travels thro' Great Britain* — William Stukeley. Printed for the Author, 1724.
5. *Felix Oswald 1866–1958: a Memoir and a List of his Works* — Grace Simpson and Adrian Oswald. Pamphlet, publisher unknown.

Chapter 4

Life's essentials in Roman Nottinghamshire: food, work, art and belief

Quintus Cornelius, Flavius Helius, Marcus Aurelius Lunaris... many of the names of the soldiers and civilians who lived in the eastern Midlands region of England during the Roman period are known from formal inscriptions written in enduring stone on heavy tombstones, altars and civic dedications. But a few others are recorded informally on small, stray items that have also survived the ages. A central heating flue tile maker called Primus, for example, scratched his name into one of 60 tiles he made in Leicester. A piece of pottery from the city also records Verucunda the actress and Lucius the gladiator, the implication being that Verucunda had *a thing* going with Lucius. In Lincolnshire, in the Fosse Dyke at its junction with the Trent, a statuette of Mars was found that carried the name of its creator, Celatus the coppersmith. Yet the single largest addition to the number of named individuals in the region only came to light in 2005 when two lead pagan curse tablets, *defixiones*, were found in excavations of a Roman house in Leicester. These tablets, on which the deities were asked to punish miscreants for various crimes, listed 24 previously unknown individuals and, with their intriguing mix of Roman and native names, offered a glimpse into the rich ethnic backgrounds of people who lived in the regional capital in the 2nd or 3rd century.

Nottinghamshire also has its curse tablets. Since the early 1960s four tablets have been found at Redhill, near Long Eaton, but these have recorded the name of only one person, Canius Dignus. In contrast, one of the Leicester tablets records four people while the other records 20. In the longer tablet, Servandus asked the god *Maglus* to 'take away' within nine days the person who stole his cloak from the slave quarters. It begins, 'I give to the god *Maglus* him who did wrong from the slave-quarters' and proceeds to list the suspects, all presumably slaves from a single household: Silvester, Ri(g)omandus, Senilis, Venustinus, Vorvena, Calaminus, Felicianus, Ruf(a)edo, Vendicina, Ingenuinus, Iuventius, Alocus, Cennosus, Germanus, Senedo, Cunovendus, Regalis, Ni(g)ella and Senicianus (this last name was scratched out). The other Leicester tablet recorded the wrath of Sabinianus, who asked 'a god' to strike down within seven days Similis, Cupitus and Lochita for the theft of his silver coins. This curse specified that the killing would occur in 'this *septisonium*', thought to be a monumental façade which included statues of the seven planetary gods who gave their names to the days of the week. Similar façades elsewhere had public fountains, suggesting that the curse tablet may have been intended to be thrown into water.

Another notable aspect of the Leicester *defixiones* is the Servandus tablet's mention of the 'slave quarters', which is one of very few written reference in the region to this ubiquitious aspect of Roman society. There are no figures for how many slaves lived in Britain during the Roman period, but one estimate has put the proportion of slaves among the population of late Republican Italy as high as 30 per cent. As already noted, slaves had long been one of Britain's exports to Rome and while Roman literature does contain occasional sympathetic references to slaves, the existence of slavery as an integral aspect of Roman social hierarchy appears to have been unquestioned (except perhaps by the slaves). Slaves could be freed through a legal process of manumission and one possible freedman in the region was a religious functionary called Marcus Aurelius Lunaris (see below) who served in a municipal organisation that was mostly made up of freedmen. The same man is also believed to have been a wine merchant. The Servandus tablet's listing of 24 names further suggests that some households in the region were wealthy enough to have a long roll call of slaves at their disposal.

At the other end of the region from Leicester, tombstones in Lincoln recorded the names and careers of several Roman soldiers who were stationed in the city. Legion IX *Hispana*'s men included Gaius Saufeius, Quintus Cornelius, a Spaniard called Lucius Sempronius Flavinus and Gaius Valerius, standard bearer of the *Hospes* century of 80 soldiers. The next legion in the city was II *Adiutrix*, which left behind Lucius Licinius Saliga, dead at 20, and Titus Valerius Pudens, from Saveria in *Pannonia Superior*, now modern Hungary. Tombstones also record the deaths of a Legion VI veteran called Gaius Julius Calenus and a freedman called Marcus Aurelius, son of a Legion XIV veteran called Marcus Aurelius Maximus.

The names of several civilians are also recorded in Lincoln. One tombstone preserves the name of a Greek-born citizen, Flavius Helius, who died when he was 40 and whose dedication was set up by his wife, Flavia Ingenua. An altar dedicated to 'the goddesses, the Fates and the divine power of the Emperors' was set up by a guild-treasurer called Gaius Antistius Frontinus. And a *decurion* (basically a town councillor) called Aurelius Senecio set up an altar to his dead wife, Volusia Faustina. In 1921 an altar dedication was also found in Bordeaux on which Marcus Aurelius Lunaris, a religious official at both Lincoln and York in *Britannia Inferior*, recorded his vows to the gods. Although the number of named individuals in Nottinghamshire itself amounts to one, the information gleaned from tombstones, altars and the Leicester curse tablets about the lives of people across the region raises some burning questions about the identity of native people in the Roman period. Did they come to view themselves as Roman? Was there a lingering sense of *Corieltauvi* identity that was passed down from generation to generation among the native-born? Dr Will Bowden, Associate Professor in Archaeology at the University of Nottingham, believes such identity issues would have become meaningless over time. "By the 3rd century Britain had been Roman for 200 years," he says. "That's a long time and the Roman invasion of Britain would have had no more relevance to people then than the Bloodless Revolution of 1688 has to us now. Who was Roman? Who was British? It was a non-question by that time."

Historian Peter Salway dealt with similar questions in a book about the English Fenland in the Roman period and his response could apply just as well to Nottinghamshire and the East Midlands. 'Because of the extraordinary mixing of cultures and populations that took place in the Empire it is extremely difficult to differentiate between "Roman" and "native"... [but] after the granting of citizenship to most of the inhabitants of the Empire in AD 212 or 214 it would be logically correct to apply the term 'Roman' everywhere.' Salway argued, in fact, that the biggest cause of differentiation between people in rural areas would have been economic (or class, if you prefer) — between the peasants on the one hand and landowners and government officials on the other. Apart from the Romanised immigrants (perhaps including the Greek-born Flavius Helius), the stew of identities in the East Midlands would have been further spiced by the Roman army veterans who were given land around Lincoln, and foreign auxiliary troops, who were granted the right to marry at the end of 25 years' service.

Religion

A second important issue that the epigraphic record underlines is the saturation of everyday life by religion and supernatural belief. This was a time, after all, when faith was put in omens and divination via inspection of animal entrails by Romans from the Emperor down. 'The main omens of Claudius' death included the rise of a long-haired star, known as a comet, lightning that struck his father's tomb, and an unusual mortality among magistrates of all ranks,' wrote the biographer Suetonius. In Nottinghamshire there is much fascinating evidence of pagan belief and then early Christian worship, with the spread of Christianity perhaps being greatly influenced from the early 4th century onwards by the probable creation of Lincoln as a bishopric following Constantine's recognition of Christianity in 313. Long before this, though, and almost certainly after it too, the people of Roman Nottinghamshire and the region worshipped and attempted to gain the favours of an array of native and sometimes local 'Celtic' pagan gods and the imported Roman equivalents with which they often became associated. These practices continued despite the importation into Britain of the official Roman state religion which had Jupiter Optimus Maximus at the apex of a Capitoline Triad comprising Juno and Minerva, followed by the Graeco-Roman pantheon including Diana, Apollo, Vulcan and so on.

In Nottinghamshire Roman shrines or temples are suspected at two settlements: on the Fosse Way at *Vernemetum*, near Willoughby-on-the-Wolds, and at Redhill, near Long Eaton. The evidence for the first comes from the name *Vernemetum*, which translates as 'great sacred grove' and perhaps suggests an earlier British shrine, and the finding of a fragment of base from a building column which may have been part of a classical temple. At Redhill, there has been stronger evidence for the existence of a cliffside temple overlooking the confluence of the Trent and

Soar. Despite the apparent loss of the building remains through a mixture of clearance, vandalism and cliff erosion, the case for a temple there has been strengthened by the discovery of four *defixiones*. The first and best known of these curse tablets was found by former University of Nottingham archaeology lecturer Roger Wilson, who then lived in Thrumpton, when he was walking near Red Hill Farm in December 1960. Wilson's lead artefact was initially described as a 'dirty little piece of brownish red metal bearing faint and vague lines of inscriptions on either side'. The object was subsequently sent to the British Museum, then Durham University, before a translation was made by Professor E.G. Turner, Director of Classical Studies at the University of London, who dated it to the late 2nd century or early 3rd. Some 300 curse tablets have now been found in Britain, their common purpose being to invoke the corrective influence of a god or gods on a person or persons for some specified crime or misdemeanour — usually theft. For example, in a tablet found in Hampshire, the writer asked Neptune to consume the blood of the person or persons who stole money from him. In another tablet found at Lydney, in the Forest of Dean, one Silvanius asked the god *Nodens* to damage the health of Senicianus until he brought a 'lost' ring to a temple. The pleas to gods expressed on such tablets, and their possible use in temples or some other religious context, encourage the belief that Redhill had a Roman temple or shrine.

So who was cursed at Redhill, and why? The text of the best-known tablet — the so-called 'Jupiter Curse' — has been translated thus:

> *To the god Jupiter best and greatest there is given that he may hound through his mind, through his memory, his inner parts(?), his intestines, his heart, his marrow, his veins... whoever it was, whether man or woman, who stole away the denarii of Canius(?) Dignus, that in his own person in a short time he may balance the account. There is given to the god above named a tenth part of the money when he has repaid it.*[1]

In other words, 'I hope whoever stole my cash suffers, and if you get the money back for me you get a reward'. It's the same old story. Three more lead tablets have been found at Redhill. One was found in 1963 and contained five lines of text that reportedly did not make any sense; a third was found in 1992 and seemed to have no writing on it; but a fourth tablet, found in

1990, contains a curse concerning the possible loss of a mule. The text was written right to left in mirror-image capital letters:

> *In the name of Camulorix and Titocuna I have dedicated in the temple of the god the mule(?) which they have lost. Whoever stole that mule(?), whatever his name, may he let his blood until the day he die. Whoever stole the objects of theft, may he die; and the [unintelligible], whoever stole it, may he die also. Whoever stole it and the [unintelligible] from the house or the pair of bags(?), whoever stole it, may he die by the god.*

The Redhill *defixiones* are now in the possession of various individuals and organisations including Nottingham City Museums & Galleries.

Elsewhere in Nottinghamshire, a handful of votive objects and solid stone carvings portraying pagan deities have also been found during excavations. From *Ad Pontem* (Thorpe) came the heavy carving of a pair of deities which have variously been identified as *Herecura* and *Dispater*, and *Pluto* and *Prosperine*. But the consensus now is that the figures are those of the hammer-wielding *Sucellos* ('the Good Striker') and the household god *Nantosuelta* ('Winding River'), an identification which originated with one of the 20th century's leading Roman art historians, Jocelyn Toynbee, who selected the carving for inclusion in her 1960s book *Art in Roman Britain*. Perhaps one reason for her selection is that *Sucellos* was a Gallic deity rarely found in Britain. Toynbee described the two deities thus: 'On the left is an unprepossessing, broad-faced, curly-haired goddess, naked to the waist... on her right is an elderly, but apparently beardless god, curly haired...' It was the only example of Roman art and design recovered from Nottinghamshire to be mentioned in her book. *Sucellos*' hammer has been interpreted as symbolising thunder, rain and fertility. The carving, which was in Elston Hall, near Newark, for many years (the hall was owned by the Darwin family until the Second World War), was discovered in 1789 standing upright around 70cm (2ft 6in) under the surface of a field called Dead Man's Grave at Thorpe. The surrounding material, including bone, decayed brick and 'mouldered wood', has led commentators to assert that the site had been a shrine. It may be important in this respect that Dead Man's Grave faces directly on to the Fosse Way and so would have been seen by countless travellers. Similar carvings of paired deities have been found in the region at Lenton and Wilsford in Lincolnshire.

Another crude but impressive carving showing a horsed 'Warrior God' is believed to have been found at *Margidunum* by Felix Oswald, although there is apparently no record of its finding at the University of Nottingham Museum where it and the *Ad Pontem* carving are both on show. Malcolm Todd said the warrior god looked as if it had once been 'built into the wall of some unknown Coritanian rural shrine'.

Carving of Sucellos and Nantosuelta found at the Roman town of *Ad Pontem*, or modern-day Thorpe.

Both the *Ad Pontem* and the *Margidunum* carvings are usually described as portraying 'Romano-Celtic' deities, which denotes how the Romans sought to absorb native beliefs and deities by pairing them with classical Roman gods. The pairing process, called *interpretatio*, was encouraged by the colonisers and occurred throughout Romanised Britain. One regional example came to light in 1961 in a drainage ditch at Nettleham, near Lincoln, when a stone tablet was found that recorded the dedication by one Quintus Neratius Proxsimus to DEO MARTI RIGONEMETI, or *Mars Rigonemetos*, thus matching the Roman god of war with a native deity whose name translates as King of the Sacred Grove. Although this was the first known appearance of *Mars Rigonemetos* in Britain, Mars was evidently a promiscuous partner since he has been matched with around 70 Celtic deities, perhaps suggesting the importance of the warrior spirit to the Iron Age tribes.

Quintus' archstone appears to have been originally placed over the entrance to a temple dedicated to Mars. Yet the native deity's name is also a reminder of the importance of rural shrines and woodland groves as sites for veneration among the native Britons. The name *Vernemetum*, associated with the Roman town near Willoughby-on-the Wolds, reflects this sacred importance of woodland groves. Tacitus described such a place in his book about *Germania*: 'In the territory of the Naharvali one is shown a grove, hallowed from ancient times. The presiding priest dresses like a woman; the gods, translated into Latin, are Castor and Pollux. That expresses the character of the gods, but their name is Alci... .'

Roman encouragement of continuing native beliefs shows a canny sense of toleration by the invaders; canny because they probably realised that outright banning of the old religions would cause deep resentment among the Britons. This toleration also seems to have accepted the existence of local cults, including a cult evidently based around a Gallic god which has only recently become associated with the East Midlands. This association is based on the finding of nearly 70 finger rings bearing the three letters 'ToT'. The majority of the rings, mostly made of silver, have come from Lincolnshire but a handful have also been found in Nottinghamshire. All have been dated to the 2nd or 3rd century.

The letters 'ToT' were long believed to have been an abbreviation for *Toutates* (or Teutates, or Toutatis, or variations thereof), a Gallic deity paired with both Mars and Mercury, the latter described by Julius Caesar as the most revered deity of the Gauls. 'They have very many images of him, and regard him as the inventor of all arts, the god who directs men upon their journeys, and their most powerful helper in trading and getting money,' he wrote.[2] But proof that the letters were indeed a short form of *Toutates* came when a ring was found in Bedfordshire bearing the words DEO TOTA. Another ring appears to have read VTERE FELIX, or 'use (this and) be happy'. Although the deity's name has been found in places well beyond the region — including the neck of a jar found in a gas mains trench in Essex — 47 of the 68 ToT rings found so far have come from Lincolnshire. Eight have been found in Nottinghamshire at *Vernemetum*, East Stoke, Mansfield, Linby, Gringley-on-the-Hill, Redhill, Stanton-on-Soar and Caunton. With the name *Toutates* translating as 'tribal protector', the deity appears to have been venerated for its protective powers over the old *Corieltauvi* territory well into the period of Roman occupation, providing a rare insight into a deity's connection with a specific tribal area. 'The series of ToT rings provides a fascinating insight into the religious and territorial characteristics of the *Corieltauvi* in the 2nd and 3rd centuries AD,' writes Adam Daubney, who has collected data and analysed the rings.[3] Daubney, who is finds liaison officer of the Portable Antiquities Scheme in Lincolnshire, adds: 'With every new discovery of ring and inscription the deity who was once just an enigmatic abbreviation becomes more established as a key tribal deity in Roman Britain.'

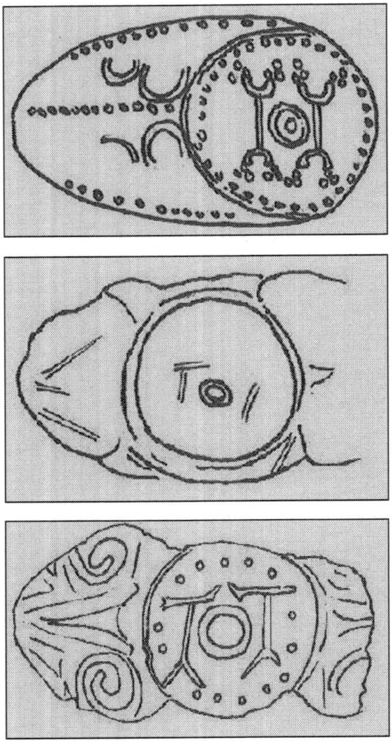

ToT rings including examples from Mansfield (top), Stanford-on-Soar (middle) and Linby.

Despite the Roman encouragement to match native gods with their own pantheon, unpaired and perhaps highly local deities also appear to have been worshipped. The god *Maglus*, invoked on the Leicester curse tablet, is otherwise unknown as is the deity *Viridios*, whose name was found inscribed on a limestone grave cover in Ancaster in 1961. The stone had originally been used as an archway in a Roman building and had been paid for by the dedicator, Trenico. *Time Team* fans will remember the excitement when the team discovered a second inscription to the same deity in the Lincolnshire town.

However, in the cities and larger Roman towns, the worshipped deities appear to have usually come from the state-approved pantheon. And alongside the highly regulated rites and customs associated with the worship of Jupiter there was also a relatively new Imperial cult which encouraged the worship of deified Emperors. The first instance of this in *Britannia* seems to have been the large temple dedicated to Claudius that was built in *Camulodunum* and which so enraged the Britons. But an Imperial cult also existed in Lincoln, as was shown in 1921 when the inscription by Marcus Aurelius Lunaris was found at Bordeaux which recorded that he was *sevir Augustalis* at Lincoln and York, meaning that he was a member of the municipal organisation responsible for the maintenance of the Imperial cult. The inscription dates from 237 and on it the official also honoured the 'Goddess Tutela Boudiga'. *Tutela* was a Celtic deity; *Boudiga* an epithet meaning victorious. Other dedications to the Emperors are known from the region, including the one at Nettleham where Quintus Neratius Proxsimus dedicated himself to the Divine Emperors as well as *Mars Rigonemetos*. In Lincoln itself, guild-treasurer Gaius Antistius Frontinus hedged his bets three ways by dedicating his altar to the goddesses, the Fates and the divine powers of the Emperors.

A further religious influence in the region may have been the presence of two mystery cults originating in the Middle East: the cult of Mithras and the cult of Attis. Attis was the mythic associate of the Anatolian Mother Goddess, Cybele, who drove him to frenzied self-castration when she suspected his love for her. Worship of Attis involved dancing and bull sacrifice and, at its most extreme, led priests of the cult to castrate themselves.

The figurine purporting to be Attis.

Attic cults in Britain are known mostly from Roman towns but evidence for their possible existence in Nottinghamshire comes from a small (6cm × 4cm) cast bronze figurine found at North Leverton during metal detecting in 1998. Its identification by Bassetlaw Museum could have involved some guesswork since the main feature identifying it as Attis appears to be the figurine's headwear, which resembles a characteristic soft, conical Phrygian cap. But are those breasts on the male consort's chest? And if so, why is the face so masculine? Bassetlaw Museum reports that the identification of Attis was probably made by a former member of staff and there are no records to shed light on the deduction process.

The evidence for a Mithraic cult may also be slight but its existence in Leicester, as the capital of the *civitas*, is certainly plausible. Mithraism, based around a complex mythology involving the death of a cosmic bull and the promise of rebirth, had spread west to Britain by the 2nd or 3rd century, mainly via the movements of legionary soldiers. Mithraic temples are known from Hadrian's Wall, London and York, and a Roman building now under the Holiday Inn, adjacent to the Jewry Wall in Leicester, has also been posited as a temple. The 'mystery' of the cult refers to the passage of worshippers through several stages of initiation leading to an epiphany, this being a disciplined and exclusive process which seems to have had particular appeal to soldiers up to the rank of Centurion, but also slaves and ex-slaves. The fact that all but one of the other Mithraic temples known in Britain are at military sites (three alone are near Hadrian's Wall) may be a problem for Leicester's claim, since the city is not known for having had a large military garrison. Nor does the shape of the building in Leicester follow that of other known *Mithraea*, although there is little doubt that it was used as a temple since incense burners, carvings and stone columns were found there. Indeed, a more suitable location for a Mithraic cult in the region would have been Lincoln which, like York, was a *colonia* with a population of army veterans. And as altar stones and relief inscriptions found in the city attest, Roman York did have a Mithraic temple. Today, remnants of the Mithraic belief system survive among the minority Yazidi people of Iraqi Kurdistan. Meanwhile, in Britain, the altar at the Mithraic temple near *Brocolitia* at Hadrian's Wall attracts gifts such as flowers and money from visitors every year.

The hint of the existence of other eastern influences in the region only came to light a few years ago, when a small rectangular ivory panel from a box was found during excavations in Vine Street, Leicester, ahead of the building of the High Cross shopping centre. The panel, which appears to show the Egyptian deity Anubis clasping lances above a motif of lotus flowers, has been described as extremely rare and 'an extraordinary find, not just from Roman Britain but also from many other western provinces'.[4] Ivory items of this type were so rare that the box from which the lid came would have been considered a luxury item in Egypt. A report on the ivory piece added: 'It may also be noted that in Egypt soldiers in the Roman army favoured Anubis, and the fact that the figure is shown holding lances here might hint at a link to military personnel. Given the presence of the seal of an eastern legion on the site this piece might thus be additional evidence for an unusual military presence at Vine Street.' Anubis was an associate of Isis, who was the subject of a popular cult. In Britain, the only evidence for a temple dedicated to the cult of Isis so far comes from London. Yet describing the worship of such non-Roman deities as cults is not to infer that they were furtive or illegal. Far from it. A sanctuary of Isis and Sarapis on the Campus Martius in Rome was a highly visible building, featuring an arched entranceway, colossal statues, a courtyard 140 metres long and images of crocodiles and baboons, all administered by priests with shaved heads and white cloaks.

Gifts left at the Mithraic temple near *Brocolitia* fort, Hadrian's Wall, photographed in the summer of 2010.

One more minor suggestion of the survival of native beliefs came when the small bronze head of a three-horned bull was found at Thorpe in the 1970s. This fine and 'carefully cast' piece measured just 3cm wide and 3.25cm long but brought with it a weight of cultural associations with a widespread 'Celtic' bull cult which had links with finds in Leicester, Dorset and the former Yugoslavia. The bull deity was identified as *Tauros Trigaranus*, associated with springs, streams, pools and the fertility of land.

Although the evidence from Nottinghamshire and the region underlines the scope of Roman religious tolerance and inclusivity in the provinces of the Empire, that tolerance did not extend to the powerful priestly Druids in Britain. Caesar, in the 1st century BC, had described the Druids of Gaul with horrified fascination but remarked that 'even today, those who want to make a profound study of it generally go to Britain for the purpose'.[5] However, active suppression of the priesthood seems to have arrived in 43 with Claudius' army. Roman intolerance was based partly on the Druids' practice of human sacrifice and general promotion of perverted 'magic'. As the 1st century Roman naturalist Pliny the Elder wrote: 'Today even Britain, in awe, practises magic with such impressive rites that one might think that she had given the Persians the art of magic... . An incalculable debt is owed to the Romans who destroyed these monstrous practices, in which human sacrifice was considered an act pleasing to the gods and eating the victim was thought to be beneficial to one's health.'[6] Yet the removal of the priesthood (by military means where necessary, as happened at Anglesey) also rid the invaders of a powerful and influential caste which might have inspired resistance to Roman rule.

But intolerance worked both ways and the eventual destruction of Mithraic temples in Britain has been put down to the vandalism of Christians as the new monotheistic religion spread in the provinces following Emperor Constantine's legal recognition in 313. This was eventually followed by the Emperor Theodosius' declaration of Christianity as Rome's official religion in 380. Yet Christian worshippers did not have an open field between these two dates, as might be thought from this two-line summary of nearly 70 years of history. The main initial period of Christian expansion in Britain has been placed between 340 and 360, this being followed by a brief pagan revival under the philosopher-Emperor Julian, known as the Apostate, because of his fervent commitment to the old polytheistic beliefs. Upon Julian's death in battle with the Persians in 363, when he refused to wear armour because of the desert heat, Christian believers looked forward once more to an end to Imperial policies against their religion. As Edward Gibbon wrote in *The Decline and Fall of the Roman Empire*: 'One party

Coin of Constantine, the first Christian Emperor, found at Warsop. Minted in *Lugdunum*, now Lyons in France. *Lugdunum* was a very productive Roman mint, most active in the 4th century. The reverse of this coin reads 'Beata Tranquillitas', meaning 'Blessed Peace... of the state.'

lamented the approaching ruin of their altars, the other celebrated the marvellous deliverance of the church.'

All this makes it more difficult to interpret the physical evidence which has been found in Nottinghamshire for the early spread of Christianity in the Roman period. Since the 1950s a crushed baptismal font and two fragments of lead believed to have been part of other fonts or coffins have been found, all of them bearing Christian motifs such as the Chi-Rho symbol, Chi and Rho being the first letters in the Greek spelling of the word Christ. The two fragments have been unearthed at Thorpe and Brough while the complete font, or water tank, was found, crushed, at Flawborough in 1998 during metal-detecting. This lead tank, also decorated with human figures, had been placed in a pit in two halves which were both crushed inwards as if to fit the hole which had been dug for it. The tank, dated to the late 4th century, had at least one striking similarity with the piece of decorated lead found at Thorpe: both bore the words VTERE EELIX, a mis-spelled form of the commonly used phrase VTERE FELIX. The similarity of the decoration, and the fact that the 'F' in FELIX on both pieces was written like an 'E', suggested they were the products of the same artist or workshop — and were perhaps also made by a partly illiterate artist. But an additional feature on the Flawborough tank was a line of four human figures, all with their arms raised in a position known as the *orans* posture which is known from other Romano-Christian sites such as a villa at Lullingstone in Kent. The tank's decoration and scarcity (only 22 partial or complete lead tanks are known in Britain) makes it an item of national significance. It can be seen in the University of Nottingham Museum. The lead fragment at Thorpe was found in 1954 and at the time was described by the Thoroton Society as 'the oldest evidence for Christianity in Nottinghamshire, and certainly one of the most important finds to have been made in the country'.[7]

Further up the Fosse Way, another piece of lead decorated with Christian motifs was found at Brough in the late 1970s. Initially thought to be part of a coffin, it was later regarded as part of another circular lead tank. These lead pieces are open to interpretation. Was the Flawborough tank hidden by Christian worshippers at a time of pagan revival? Were the lead fragments hidden to protect them or were they cast aside after their owners were attacked? Nobody knows, but the three pieces certainly

Detail of the lead fragment found at Thorpe showing the Chi-Rho Christian symbol.

provide firm evidence for the spread of Christianity into southern Nottinghamshire. Small Christian cemeteries appear to have been located at *Margidunum* and Brough, where lead coffins have been found. Two datable Christian cemeteries have also been located in the region at Ancaster and Lincoln, founded in around 340 and 390 respectively.

Art and design

These intriguing decorated metal pieces also allow us to segue seamlessly into a brief discussion of the evidence for Roman art in Nottinghamshire. But, straight away, we strike a problem in defining what we mean when we use the word art. The major hindrance to clean debate is that so much *contemporary* western art has become divorced from any kind of material usefulness apart from its investment value. While all great art does encourage you to think differently, and the great paintings of the past often imparted a useful moral lesson about vanity or mortality, it's rare that you can use it for anything else — which is in complete contrast to much of what we think of Roman art such as decorated tableware and complex floor mosaics. There were 'art' collectors in Rome and writers such as Pliny the Elder devoted short essays to subjects such as portraiture, Greek painters and changing tastes in painting. But an argument concerning pure design vs art-for-art's sake may have been meaningless to many

Romano-British people, for whom design was largely an embellishment upon the functionality of items they used in their day-to-day lives. Exceptional items would have been busts and statuary in the classical mould such as the naked and helmeted statuette of Mars that was recovered from the Fosse Dyke in Lincolnshire in the 18th century. The inscription on it tells us that it was made by Celatus the coppersmith for Brucius and Caratius at a cost of 100 *sesterces*. Yet even this figure, regarded by some as the most vibrant portrayal of Mars in Roman Britain, had a religious function.

Whatever its religious or aesthetic value, in the modern era it is only in the past half century or so that Romano-British art has been recognised as possessing any merit at all. R.G. Collingwood, an influential archaeologist of the early 20th century, thought that Roman art was bad enough but, in the hands of the Britons, attempts at imitation produced something even worse.[8] 'Before the Roman conquest the Britons were a race of gifted and brilliant artists,' he wrote in 1936. 'The conquest, forcing them into the mould of Roman life with its vulgar efficiency and lack of taste, destroyed that gift and reduced their arts to the level of manufacture.' Collingwood added that as well as having 'bad taste', the Roman Empire had a 'common vulgar ugliness' which inspired in the Britons 'a blundering, stupid ugliness that cannot even rise to the level of that vulgarity'.

In the early 1960s the art historian Jocelyn Toynbee, who included the carving of *Sucellos* and *Nantosuelta* from Thorpe in her catalogue *Art in Roman Britain*, was among those who began to correct this view. And as the inclusion of the crude Thorpe carving suggests, the definition of Roman art has come to embrace any item with some kind of decorative or design element: votive objects, tombstones, jewellery, gardens, coins, spoons, pan handles (some of which could be highly ornate), as well as the marble busts and statues you are never allowed to touch in museums. Meanwhile, contemporary historians of the subject have grappled with the issue of whether there was such a thing as a uniquely British provincial form of Roman art. As the archaeology writer and former Nottinghamshire resident Jennifer Laing has pointed out, native British art and Roman art had nothing in common. But, brought together in the Romanised province, the two cultural influences became fused and produced art that, she says, ranged from the inept to the exquisite. 'It is possible to view Romano-British art as a seminal lesson in the ability of two totally different and opposing cultures to find a harmony of purpose,' she wrote in *Art & Society in Roman Britain*. 'As sociological phenomena, even the aesthetically unsatisfactory items have exceptional value.'[9] The eminent Roman coin expert Harold Mattingly was thinking on the same lines when he analysed the contents of two Roman coin hoards found in Calverton in 1959 and '60. Many of the coins were locally produced imitations of Roman coinage, and examining the rough copies of Imperial imagery on them he commented that they offered 'casual glimpses of the half-submerged Celtic culture'.[10]

Although not all art historians agree with Laing's view about cultural fusion, this is a good place to start talking about the examples of aesthetically pleasing Roman art found in Nottinghamshire such as the ornate villa floor mosaics at Mansfield Woodhouse, Southwell, Barton-in-Fabis, Flawford and Oldcotes — all presumably produced, in their thousands of small *tesserae*, by Britons who had been taught Roman techniques. Collingwood described Romano-British mosaics as examples of 'third rate artistic achievement', but this helps explain why his views on art are largely unread these days. The Nottinghamshire mosaics are discussed in detail in Chapter Eight. But suffice to say here that while three of them have been irretrievably lost through a combination of theft, vandalism and seeming natural decay, detailed colour drawings of the remains of two mosaics when they were found at Mansfield Woodhouse and Barton-in-Fabis give us a sense of what they must have looked like in the glory days. And the mosaic at Mansfield Woodhouse, with its repetitive and hypnotic patterns of interlocking knots, diamonds and flower motifs, bears comparison with some of the finest in the region.

At Southwell, remnants of the large villa's mosaic are still *in situ* underground, but enough fallen painted plaster from a bath suite in the building was recovered to recreate an image of a Cupid figure that is on display in Southwell Minster today.

A few examples of recovered painted wall plaster from sites such as *Margidunum*, Redhill and a villa near Epperstone also offer a tantalising glimpse into how some of the county's grandest Roman buildings were decorated. Leicester has the best remnants of décor from Roman town houses and villas in the

CONSERVATION OF ROMANO-BRITISH PAINTED PLASTER 267

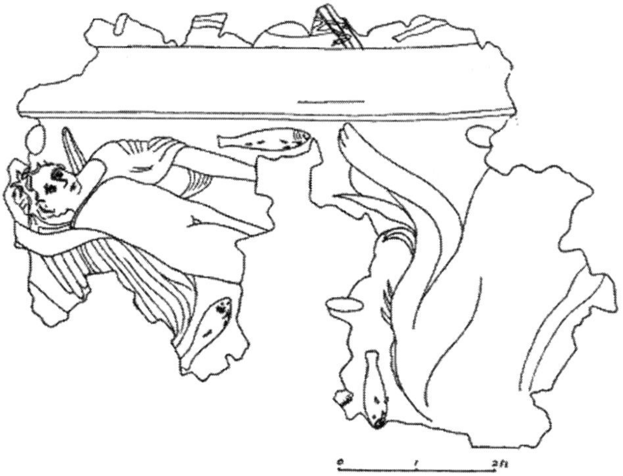

FIG. 14

Southwell: decorated plaster from the wall of a cold bath (cf. PL. XXII *b* ($\frac{1}{25}$).

FIG. 15

well: another fragment of plaster from the same cold bath as that from which the plaster shown in FIG. 14 came ($\frac{1}{25}$).

Drawings of two scenes that were painted on the walls of the bath suite in the Southwell villa. Cupid is the figure at the top. This image is shown in colour in the chapter on villas.

region, which suggest how some of the wealthiest homes in Nottinghamshire may have looked inside (this is assuming, of course, that interior décor is accepted as art...). For example, remnants of the 2nd century Norfolk Street villa, which was a little way out of Roman Leicester, had vibrant wall frescoes of bright greens, reds and yellows and panels that imitated the look of marble; the mid-2nd century town house in Blue Boar Lane, with its colonnaded walkway surrounding a courtyard, had decorated wall panels incorporating architectural designs and human figures. Near the ceiling there was also a painting of a theatrical mask which, put together with the mention of Verucunda, has suggested the existence of a theatre in Leicester. No trace of a theatre has been found in the old regional capital; in fact the archaeological evidence suggests that the nearest theatre was in Humberside, where, at *Petuaria* (Brough-on-Humber), a new stage building was presented as a gift by a magistrate in the 140s. Apart from the Cupid image at Southwell, no large chunks of décor from a house or villa have been recovered in Nottinghamshire. Nonetheless, published reports and various small pieces of recovered painted wall plaster indicate that there were villas and other buildings in Nottinghamshire that may have been as richly decorated as those found in the *civitas* capital. This décor is described in the chapter on villas.

The county has also produced some striking and contrasting examples of designed objects that were intended for domestic use. These include a drinking vessel of a type known as hunt cups and some larger vessels with slightly unnerving faces carved into them called head pots. Felix Oswald recovered two complete head pots from *Margidunum* while the fragment of another, with a trident carved in its forehead, was found at Brough.

Although possibly descended from earlier facial vase designs in the Mediterranean world, vessels of this type seem to be unique to Britain and have been found mostly down the civilianised eastern side of the province. Indeed a distinctive East Midlands style of head pot, featuring 'rather heavy applied eyebrows', has been suggested. There may well have been some religious or superstitious meaning to these vessels (a pot found in Lincoln had MERCURIO written on its base), but their precise use and the significance of the faces remain unknown. The

Fragment of a 'head pot' found at Brough. Two complete head pots were found at *Margidunum* while fragments of others have been recovered from Lincoln and Old Sleaford.

Detail from the 'hunt cup' showing a hound in pursuit.

'hunt cup', so called because it shows two hounds pursuing a deer, was found in fragments at Thorpe in 1953 and has been restored to its present complete form. Such vessels are usually associated with the productive pottery kilns of the Nene Valley area. Another hunt cup was found at Littleborough during excavations in the late 1960s.

A more poignant vessel was found at Redhill in 1995. This was a cup, or beaker, also made in the Nene Valley, but containing burned bones. Analysis of the bones suggested they were those of a four- or five-year-old child. The beaker was decorated with four bird motifs resembling modern children's bath ducks. The vessel's decoration and contents together suggested the early death and cremation of a child, and the disposal of the ashes in a cup that was significant to the child and the parents.

Other large finds recovered from Nottinghamshire include an altar stone from Littleborough and a marble portrait bust from nearby Clarborough. The digging up of two 'handsomely moulded' altar stones from Littleborough was mentioned by the antiquarian William Stukeley in the 1720s. By 1909, the amateur archaeologist T. Cecil Smith Woolley, from Collingham, reported that one of altars, inscribed with the words LIS ARAM DD, had disappeared but that another had been found and was in the possession of the local landowners, the Foljambes of

Osberton Hall. The Osberton Hall altar was then examined by the eminent Roman archaeologist Francis Haverfield who thought it was the one which had supposedly gone missing. It was described as sandstone, just under a metre high and with a 38cm (15in) square panel.

The Clarborough bust of a man, apparently in military uniform, was reportedly found by a labourer in around 1860 and was acquired by one Henry Hill at the sale of the effects of Canon Brookes, of Nottingham, formerly of Clarborough. The bust was shown to the public in January 1899 in the Exchange Hall, Nottingham, as part of an exhibition and *conversazione* held by the Thoroton Society. This event certainly gave a rounded view of Nottinghamshire culture. The bust, exhibit no. 354, described as 'bust, in marble. Roman', preceded 'Lord Byron, bust of' and came after 'Sword, taken from Blackburn the Luddite'. Photographs of both the Littleborough altar and the bust were published in 1910 in the *Victoria County History*. Both items are among the largest complete finds of Roman art in Nottinghamshire and one can only speculate as to where they are today. However, Todd, in *The Coritani*, said that the bust was 'now sadly lost'. Another altar stone was excavated in Granby churchyard in 1812 but has also long since disappeared. The item reportedly bore the image of a Roman figure with helmet and toga and with sword in the left hand. On the side was a creature with the head of a lamb and the wings of a dragon, while the back had a 'finely-cut vegetable figure'.

However, arguably the most celebrated example of Roman art found in Nottinghamshire remains the right-hand copper cheekpiece from an auxiliary cavalry parade helmet, found at Brough, in the early years of the 20th century by T. Cecil Smith Woolley. Measuring 18.5cm by 12cm (7in by 5in), this gorgeous and delicate item is decorated *repoussé* style, and was exhibited at the Society of Antiquaries in London in 1903. It appears not to have attracted serious scholarly attention until the art historian Jocelyn Toynbee heard about it in 1949. Documents accompanying the piece at Newark and Sherwood District Council include correspondence between Newark Museum and Toynbee, who, in hand written letters, described the item's decoration as 'truly remarkable'.

Toynbee's interest had been spurred on by the finding of a decorative Roman bronze helmet in a river near Norwich and she was compiling information on other ceremonial helmets for an article that was eventually published in *The Journal of Roman Studies*. She knew of 70 such surviving helmets or fragments of helmets, 13 of which had been found in Britain, including the two best known examples found at Ribchester and Newstead in Scotland. Toynbee's interest appears to have made Newark's curators aware that they had something quite special on their hands. In one of several typed responses to Toynbee, a museum curator (probably Arthur Smith, whose name crops up elsewhere in this book) told her that 'the information you have given to me makes it possible to give an additional local press boost to the Museum and we shall make the most of the opportunity'.

As for the item itself: the cheek-piece's fragility and decoration suggests it was never intended for combat operations but was designed for ceremony and cavalry sports. The figure on it was first thought to be male, then female, and as such has been interpreted as *Epona*, a Celtic horse-goddess. Latterly, though, it has been regarded as representing one of the mythological twins Castor and Pollux. A similar cheek-piece in much worse condition, found in Leicester in the 1980s, was decorated with a figure of Cupid while a piece found in a river near Nijmegen in Holland bore a *repoussé* image of Mars. The three cheek-pieces share stylistic similarities. Despite the non-combat use of the helmet to which the Brough cheek-piece belonged, the item has been 'stabbed' with sharp objects twice at some point in its long history. It has recently benefited from conservation work at the University of Lincoln.

One other large find worth mentioning is a striking piece of decorated lead that was discovered by a metal-detectorist at Gateford, Worksop. The item was acquired in 1999 by Bassetlaw Museum, which describes it as part of a 3rd century coffin.

Finds of small Romano-British decorative objects in Nottinghamshire are so numerous that it is impossible here to do the subject justice. Jewellery, including brooches, bracelets and engraved gemstones or glass (intaglios), have been found on excavated sites across Nottinghamshire (as elsewhere in Britain), reflecting their wide use and probable low manufacturing and purchase cost.

Piece of decorated lead found at Worksop.

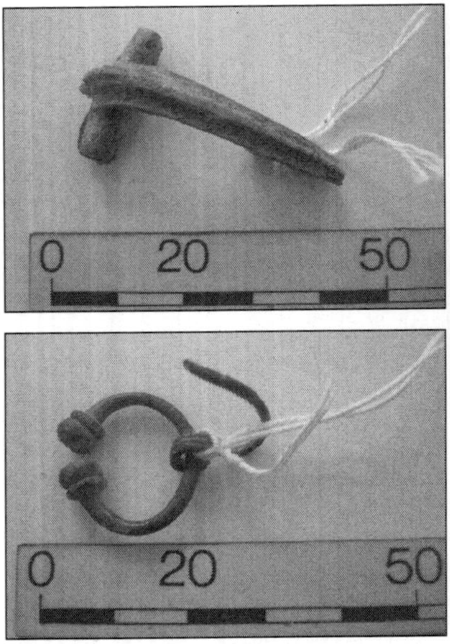

Two typical items of mass-produced Romano-British jewellery found at Broxtowe fort, north Nottingham.

This 'seal box lid' was found by Felix Oswald at *Margidunum* and described by him in his 1927 excavation report.

At *Margidunum*, Felix Oswald listed 19 small finds including many brooches, one of which was wrapped around the left little finger of the skeleton of a man whom Oswald reasoned had been partly devoured by wolves. A fairly representative list of 'small finds' from Redhill included a broken brooch of simple 'Aucissa' type (meaning D-shaped), an intaglio and part of a bracelet made of a fine chain linking three opaque blue glass beads.

In 1985, archaeologists were given just a week and a weekend to excavate a small D-shaped Romano-British farmstead in the brickwork field system on Chainbridge Lane, Lound, north of Retford, before the site was due to be destroyed by quarrying. In this short time the metal items found here included a Corieltauvian coin and three bronze brooches, one of which was in the shape of a sitting hen still bearing traces of red and green enamel.

The small finds from Lound and Redhill are mentioned here not to make a point about their rarity, but rather to emphasise how often items of jewellery like these have been found at Romano-British sites in the county. Unfortunately, despite the quantity of finds, no single piece of Romano-British jewellery or other small decorative item found in Nottinghamshire has matched the exceptional nature of the gold Iron Age torc found in Newark in 2005, which was purchased with financial assistance by Newark and Sherwood District Council for £350,000. That said, some more notable Romano-British items have turned up, such as a finely crafted bronze bracelet, with a delicate loop and hoop lock, which was found when a subway was being dug near Warwicks Brewery in Northgate, Newark, in 1898.

Bronze bracelet, approximately 3mm diameter, found in Newark in 1898.

Two beaded torcs of the 1st or 2nd century, made of cast bronze, have also been found at *Margidunum* and Brough while a large bronze Roman brooch, measuring 6.5cm (2.5in) tall, was unearthed in the Harlow Wood area near Mansfield in the late 1970s.

Industry

Although production of jewellery may have been the basis of many small cottage industries in the county, the region's major productive industries after agriculture were probably pottery production, stone quarrying and the mining of lead and ironstone for iron. These goods then required sale and transport in and beyond the region via rivers, roads and possibly canals. The potential of the region as a source of mineral wealth inevitably leads on to the question of what it was that — financially — attracted the Roman invaders to Britain in the first place and then persuaded successive dynasties to maintain an expensive troop presence in the province.

In the late Republican era, Julius Caesar had noted the presence of gold, iron, tin and timber in the country, and under the Empire the island's resources in precious metals as well as lead and iron must have been regarded as increasingly important sources of wealth to the Roman administration. That there was an expectation of treasure to be gained from Caesar's invasion appears confirmed by a letter written by the celebrated politician and lawyer Cicero to his brother Quintus, who was a general serving under Caesar in Britain. 'It has... been ascertained that there is not a scrap of silver in the island, nor any hope of booty except slaves; and I don't think you can expect any of those to have had a literary or musical education,' he wrote in 54 BC.[11] But after the Claudian invasion the East Midlands was to become exploited for its prize mineral resource, ironstone, which is concentrated in the Jurassic rocks of Lincolnshire and Leicestershire. Evidence of the iron smelting process has been found on several sites in Nottinghamshire such as *Margidunum*, where Oswald reported finding lumps of slag. There were also suggestions of smithery in the town, which was necessary to turn the iron into a variety of household objects, agricultural tools or weapons.

Lead, another useful metal to the Romans and widely used for everything from waterproofing and pipes to coffins and pewter, was also extracted from several regions of the province, including the Derbyshire Peak District. In 1848 a product of the Roman lead mining industry, a heavy inscribed ingot, was found in Nottinghamshire at Hexgrave Park, Farnsfield. Weighing 83kg (184lbs), the item was stamped C.IVL.PROTI.BRIT.LVT. EX.ARG. The 'C.IVL. PROTI' part has been interpreted as the name Gaius Julius Protus, the owner or manufacturer of the ingot; the 'LVT' has been read as an abbreviation for *Lutudarum*, believed to have been the location of lead mines at Wirksworth or Carsington in the Peaks; and the 'EX.ARG' is translated as *ex argentariis*, meaning 'from the silver works', suggesting that silver had been obtained from the lead. The ingot was reported to have been kept at Thurgarton Priory until it was purchased by the British Museum from one John Parkinson in 1879.

Coal was also used in the county area since coal deposits have been found on a handful of sites including the farmsteads at Menagerie Wood and Scratta Wood and the small Roman towns at Thorpe and Redhill. Little is known about Roman coal mining in the province except that coal was probably extracted from exposed seams. Coal, like lead and ironstone, may have been imported into Nottinghamshire but a possible extraction site in the county has been suggested at Sutton-in-Ashfield. Although wood was widely used for cooking, coal may have been useful in the *hypocaust* fires that were necessary for the central heating systems of wealthier households.

Another important regional industry was stone quarrying and one of the most widely used kinds of stone in Roman

Nottinghamshire was Swithland slate from Leicestershire. Shaped into roofing tiles, the slate was used on buildings at Thorpe, Brough, Epperstone and *Margidunum*, where diamond-shaped tiles with nail holes in them were recovered. Swithland roofing tiles were also used on the villa at Norton Disney, some 64km (40 miles) from the source of the slate in ancient Charnwood Forest. A study of distribution concluded that such heavy loads of slate must have been transported by cart on roads such as the Fosse Way, suggesting that towns that lay on or close to the road offered the most accessible markets. Swithland slate was also transported to the fort of *Derventio* in Derby, this route perhaps passing through the important communication hub at Redhill. Other kinds of stone used for building construction included local skerry sandstone, Derbyshire millstone grit and Lincolnshire limestone, all of which were used at *Margidunum*, showing that there was trade and transport of these materials within the region.

Despite the absence of any remains of Roman quays or loading docks along the Trent in Nottinghamshire, transport of heavy freight such as stone along the river has long been theorised. A problem in speculation about the Roman regional freight and transport network is the Fosse Dyke, the 17km (11 mile) canal that links the Trent at Torksey in Lincolnshire with the river Witham at Lincoln. Although long believed to have been a Roman feat of engineering, there is a more recent suspicion that the canal originated in the early medieval period. There is no consensus. But the Romans did build canals (the 140km-long Car Dyke that connects the Cambridgeshire and Lincolnshire Fens to the Witham at Lincoln is accepted as being wholly or partly Roman) and if the Fosse Dyke was Roman then it may have helped deliver freight to settlements in north east Nottinghamshire such as Littleborough.

Incidentally, there are no records from Nottinghamshire offering any insight into how any of these industries were owned and controlled. But evidence from elsewhere in the Roman Empire has suggested that the most valuable mineral extraction industries may have been controlled directly by the Roman state, while other industries were controlled by private concerns operating on a contractual or concession basis. Agriculture was, however, probably the area of production which employed most people in Roman Nottinghamshire. And farming in this naturally organic, pre-chemical era may have been more productive than most people believe. In trials of Iron Age farming techniques using ancient wheat types conducted in the 1970s and '80s at Butser Ancient Farm in Hampshire, yields were much higher than expected, averaging 1.65 tonnes per hectare for emmer wheat and 1.49 tonnes per hectare for spelt. One year saw a bumper emmer wheat yield of more than 4 tonnes per hectare. Although 4 tonnes per hectare is about half the yield that conventional UK farmers obtain today from more productive modern wheat strains, and using chemical fertiliser, the results at Butser suggested that Iron Age and Romano-British farmers may have obtained surprisingly high crop yields using manure and the best soils.

The other industry of importance to Nottinghamshire, and indeed the entire Romanised world, was pottery production. Professional archaeologists will now start gasping in disbelief at the brevity of the information on the issue given here since pottery sherds are by far the most commonly found artefacts in excavation, giving them an unparalleled diagnostic role in dating Romano-British settlements. The large quantities of pottery sherds that are so often recovered in excavations (and from the surfaces of fields) are easily explained by two factors: the Roman world's universal use of pottery vessels for food storage, mixing, cooking, drinking and eating and the very durability of the vessels' broken clay sherds for centuries after their disposal. No excavation report is complete without a comprehensive analysis of pottery detailing decorative styles and colour of all identifiable sherds and what these suggest about the date and place of production. And sometimes hauls of pottery can be huge. In 2008 a report was published into the results of a major fieldwalking exercise that took place across the brickwork field system of north Nottinghamshire between Ollerton and Bawtry. Led by archaeologist Daryl Garton, volunteers picked up 2,547 pieces of pottery plus items of Roman brick and tile, quernstones and firecracked pebbles. This is not, in fact, a large quantity at all compared with the tonnes of sherds which have come from some sites — but it does indicate just how much can still be picked up from the surface of Nottinghamshire fields some 1,600 or 1,700 years after the end of the Roman occupation. The commonly heard statement, 'oh, you can find bits of pottery lying all over the place at this site' turned out to be true when this author visited the excavations at Besthorpe; large fragments of pottery, Roman and Iron Age, were scattered over the sand. Such sights may be old hat to an archaeologist; but they are a little magical to everyone else.

But what can you learn from it? After the fieldwalking haul in north Nottinghamshire had been analysed few single items were picked out as being remarkable. But the dating of most of the potsherds to the 2nd and 3rd centuries suggested that the area had seen its highest occupation levels over this span of time. In the south of the area there was also a higher quantity of Roman pottery originating in the kilns of the Nene Valley, providing evidence for the direction and length of lines of trade and communication between this part of Nottinghamshire and the furthest south of the region. The sherds also suggested that some Romano-British farmers in this apparently impoverished area of Nottinghamshire at least had the means to purchase vessels produced outside their immediate locale. Meanwhile, in the north of the brickwork farming area, farmers bought some of their cooking pots from south Yorkshire, where there were concentrations of kilns around Doncaster and Rossington Bridge. Information like this may not offer revolutionary insights, but the accumulation of additional information these hundreds of little sherds present about life in Roman Nottinghamshire helps explain why archaeologists are generally fixated by bits of pot.

Nottinghamshire was surrounded by highly productive pottery industries in the Roman period. To the north were the kilns of south Yorkshire including 17 kilns at Rossington Bridge (one site is marked just north of Bawtry on OS Explorer 279) and more than 40 kilns just south of Doncaster. To the north east and east were the many pottery producers of Lincolnshire including kilns on the east bank of the Trent at Little London, Lea and Knaith, which supplied settlements in Nottinghamshire such as Littleborough. There was also a cluster of kilns in and around Lincoln such as North Hykeham on the Fosse Way. To the south were kilns around Leicester and, further south, the major pottery industry of the Nene Valley area and *Durobrivae*, Water Newton. And to the west there was another cluster of pottery producers around Belper in Derbyshire which produced a distinctive form of tall, coarse-grained pottery now called Derbyshire ware. Yet in Nottinghamshire there is no evidence of anything that might be called a comparable pottery industry. Indeed, surviving pottery kilns on Romano-British sites in the county are few and far between. One exception is the settlement at Raymoth Lane, Worksop, where a rare kiln, filled with pottery shapes, was found during the excavation there in 2004. The recent finding of another kiln at the generally impoverished settlement of Mons Pool, at Besthorpe, may suggest that more kilns are waiting to be discovered in Nottinghamshire. At Littleborough, the existence of kilns was suspected because the native pottery was so similar to that made across the Trent in Lincolnshire. A pottery kiln and its contents were also dug up in the late 19th century at Newark, according to Cornelius Brown's *A History of Newark-on-Trent*, published in 1904.

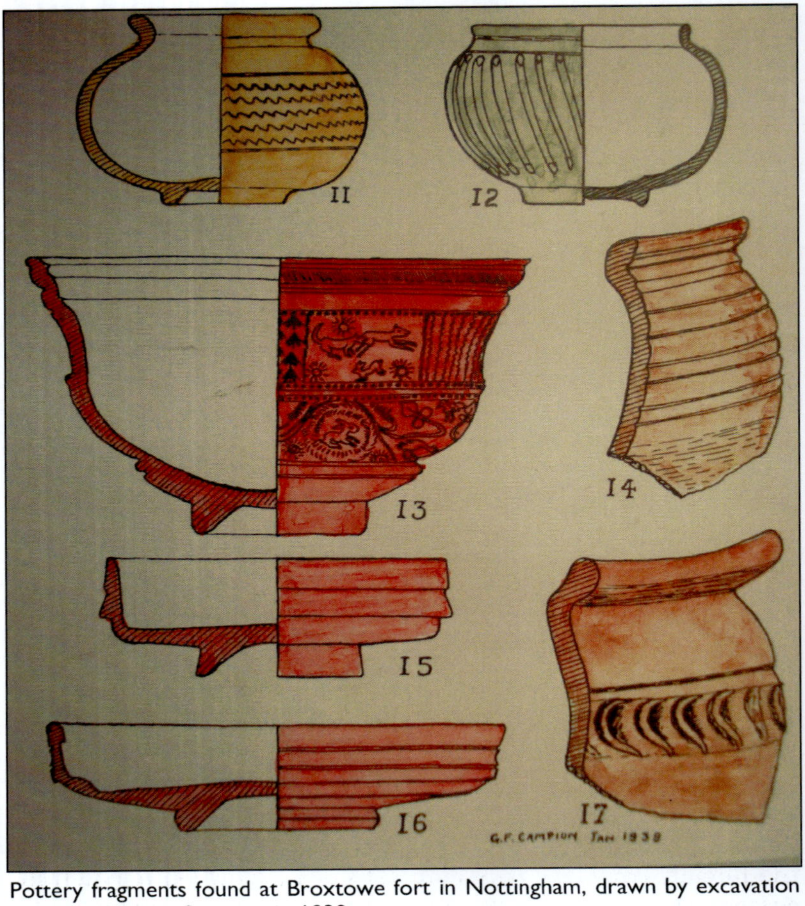

Pottery fragments found at Broxtowe fort in Nottingham, drawn by excavation director George Campion in 1938.

The result of this is that while there is lots of evidence showing where Nottinghamshire people got their pottery from, and how far that pottery had travelled, there is scant evidence to support the existence of an 'industry' in the county itself. However, the existence of a regional pottery style called Trent Valley ware has been identified. This range of rough, tall, dark grey storage jars and deep bowls has been found in large quantities at *Margidunum* and also at Epperstone villa, Littleborough, Shelford, Thorpe, Meering, Brough and sites in Lincolnshire such as Lincoln, Dragonby, Ancaster and Norton Disney. Malcolm Todd believed these wares were mainly, but not exclusively, used by the Roman military and were produced over a period of 50–100 years. This is a reminder that pottery-makers in the region and across the province were not active at the same time or serving the same markets. It is usually accepted, for example, that most pottery made in Britain was limited to local or regional markets, travelling no further than around 30–40km (20–25 miles) from its source. Pottery used by the farmers living at the enclosed farmstead at Dunston's Clump, Babworth, obtained most of their pottery from within a 25km radius which included kilns in south Yorkshire and the Trentside kilns of Lincolnshire. But there were many potters who sold their wares further afield. One prolific pottery-maker called Sarrivs, who had a manufacturing centre in Rossington Bridge, was an important supplier to the military in the 2nd century and his *mortarium* spice and herb mixing bowls (today called mortars, paired with pestles) reached the temporary Antonine Wall frontier in Scotland as well as the forts at Corbridge, Catterick and Aldborough in northern England. Other regional manufacturers such as the Derbyshire ware makers had markets in Nottinghamshire but also extended their range by supplying wares to the military in the north.

One of the largest manufacturing centres in Britain was located in the Nene Valley, where large volumes of fine pottery were produced from the 1st century onwards and were used by people across the province — including the farmers of north Nottinghamshire. The Nene Valley kilns also produced imitations of high quality, glossy red *samian* ware, which was imported into Britain in massive quantities with the arrival of the Roman army in 43. Despite the huge expansion in potential custom presented to British pottery-makers by the arrival of the military, the army was initially a major user of imported *samian* tablewares and today their remains on archaeological sites are a classic sign of the Roman military presence in the 1st and 2nd centuries.

Most of the *samian* that came into Britain was made in southern and eastern Gaul (which included the Rhine and Mosel valleys of modern Germany) where, helpfully for modern analysis, the manufacturers stamped their names onto their bowls and dishes. Such stamped vessels have been found across Roman and Romano-British sites in Nottinghamshire. Felix Oswald became a leading expert in *samian* and at *Margidunum* he found Gaulish *samian* stamped with the names Advocisi, Of Felicis, Probus F and Secvndini M as well as items he suspected were made by the fabulously named Mommo, Germanvs and Mercator. At Brough, T.C. Smith Woolley found *samian* bearing names such as Jvstvs, Qvintvs and Reginvs. The common finding of pottery sherds such as this at Roman sites, and the fact that there is now a huge corpus of literature devoted to their study, can sometimes make it seem as if inscriptions like these do not

Fine *samian* pottery from Brough marked with its maker's name, made in the Lezoux area of Gaul.

warrant special attention. However, for the interested lay person, seeing the prosaic name stamp of the potter first hand can telescope time, creating a tingling sense of coming just within reach of the silent people of antiquity.

Diet

What did people put in their cooking pots? What did the people of Roman Nottinghamshire eat? First of all, the diets of the local people and the Roman army need to be distinguished. A good deal of research has been conducted into the diet of Roman soldiers; far less into the diets of native Britons on a regional basis. The soldiers' basic peace-time rations consisted of corn, bacon, cheese, vegetables, salt, olive oil, and sour wine to drink. However, supplemented by personal food gifts and additional supplies gained from the local countryside, the meat intake of many ordinary soldiers was probably more varied than this basic list suggests since the bones of ox, sheep and red deer as well as pig have commonly been found at forts. Those two essentials in the diet of soldiers used to the Mediterranean sun, olive oil and wine, were imported, although wine was produced in Britain and native ale and mead, produced from barley and honey respectively, had been consumed since the Iron Age.

Valuable new evidence about the diet of the army in Britain came to light when letters listing or mentioning food supplies were found during excavations at *Vindolanda* fort at Hadrian's Wall. The letters were written around the end of the 1st century and seem to have mostly concerned food supplies destined for officers rather than common soldiers. Nevertheless they show that the army, even on the frontier, had access to a wide range of food and drink including pork crackling, pork cutlets, roe deer, goat meat, ham, chicken, wine, beer, butter, beans, lentils, pancakes, apples, honey, olives, eggs, radishes, mustard-seed, beetroot, twisted-loaf and pig's trotters. These were in addition to basics such as flour, barley, wheat, meal and sour wine and such herbs and spices as garlic, garlic paste, caraway, anise, cumin, lovage and thyme. A third element of the diet at *Vindolanda* was seafood including small fish and oysters, which were consumed in vast quantities in the Roman world. If such was consumed in the permanent military zone of the north, then the diet of soldiers garrisoned in the south of the province is likely to have been at least as varied.

Nevertheless, a diet heavy in cereals for breadmaking, porridge and soup, calculated as 1.4kg (3lbs) per soldier per day, must have had an impact on the population of pacified areas such as Nottinghamshire since one major source of grain supplies was native farmers. As well as growing enough grain for home consumption and the permanent Roman army, Britain also exported grain to the continent. Although supplies may have been organised via contracts with the farmers, compulsory purchase was within the army's remit. Forts also grew their own crops or grazed livestock on an area of surrounding land called the *territorium*.

At *Margidunum* it was difficult in the archaeological record to distinguish who ate what. Yet Felix Oswald found evidence of a diet not short on flesh, noting the remains of small Celtic Shorthorn cattle, sheep, pig, goat, wild boar, red deer, fighting cocks, ducks and edible snails. Saltwater and freshwater creatures were also consumed. Oswald reported finding whelks and 'a large number of oysters and also many freshwater mussels'. The remains of what appears to have been a bread oven were also found at *Margidunum*. But it wasn't only the army or the people who lived close to forts who had access to seafood. Several oyster shells have also been found at the site of the Barton-in-Fabis villa, posing the question of how seafood would have reached landlocked Nottinghamshire in a fresh condition. One suggestion is that it was transported from the coast in saltwater tanks on carts. As previously mentioned, Oswald believed that the burnt oysters he found at *Margidunum* had come from the Lincolnshire coast. Britain had a reputation for the quality of its oysters in the Roman period and the Roman historian Suetonius mentioned that Caesar actually invaded the country because he was so fond of the pearls.

Away from the military sites, there is good evidence for the Romanisation of diet among Nottinghamshire's civilian population. When the settlement at Chainbridge Lane, Lound, was excavated in the mid-1980s archaeologists found fragments of *amphorae*, the tall two-handled storage vessels that were used for the transport of, *inter alia*, olive oil and wine, suggesting that Mediterranean products from the heart of the Empire were reaching north Nottinghamshire. In south Nottinghamshire, too, 3.2kg of *amphorae* fragments were found at *Vernemetum*. The pottery styles here were connected to manufacturers in Spain, one along the Guadalquivir river, one to southern Spain between Cadiz and Malaga. *Amphorae* imported from these factories were used to transport olive oil and fish-based products respectively. Fish sauces were a staple in the Roman diet and in the only surviving complete cookbook from the Roman world, Apicius' *De Re Coquinaria*, an entire chapter was devoted to nearly 40 sauces for mullet, perch, dory, red snapper and even broiled conger eel.

Another small but intriguing indication of diet came from the farmstead at Menagerie Wood, Worksop, where two grape pips were found as well as bones of cow and sheep, still bearing the marks of the butcher's knife, and the skeleton of a lamb foetus. The pips may have arrived in raisins or grapes preserved in must. There is the possibility that there were vineyards in the region, if not in Nottinghamshire. Wine grapes were certainly grown in southern England and there is some evidence that there were vineyards as far north as North Thoresby in Lincolnshire. However, most wine was imported into Britain from warmer climates; Marcus Aurelius Lunaris, the *sevir Augustalis* from Lincoln and York who set the altar up in Bordeaux, is thought to have been a wine merchant.

Fragments of quernstone found at the Menagerie Wood settlement and many other sites also remind us that the way many Romano-British people got their daily (unleavened) bread was by grinding cereal seeds by hand to make flour. Although evidence for diet in the Roman period has sometimes come via the unlovely examination of antique human faeces, in Nottinghamshire knowledge of the population's cereal consumption has usually derived from the recovery of surviving seeds in the soil. Sometimes the seeds are burnt, suggesting that they had been in a corn drier or roaster or had been thrown into a fire as waste. At Dunston's Clump, Babworth, for example, the haul included seeds of rye, spelt, emmer, bread wheat, flax, six-row hulled barley and flax, which is a fairly representative spread of cereals and crops from the period. Local people probably supplemented their diets with the leaves and seeds of edible plants of a kind now regarded as mere weeds. In the 1940s a Roman well was discovered at Bunny, in Rushcliffe, which was in use between around 100 and 300. In the well were traces of several edible wild plants including chickweed, nettle and fat-hen. Archaeologists said that the overall seed mixture in the well suggested a surrounding landscape of mixed farming, lush pasture and rich arable land.

A handful of complete cooking utensils have also been found in the county. At *Margidunum* Oswald found a colander with 30 small square holes in it as well as several flat 'platters' and pans. An iron ladle and cooking gridiron from the same town are also on show in the University of Nottingham Museum, as is an impressive complete skillet from Broxtowe fort.

The number of modern books now offering recipes and tips on Roman cooking renders similar advice here redundant. But one problem with attempting to reproduce Roman dishes is that recipes such as those in Apicius' book do not detail ingredient quantities. And it must be remembered that tastes have changed. Those who dare to cook full Roman meals should bear in the mind the scene from Tobias Smollett's 18th century picaresque novel *The Adventures of Peregrine Pickle*, where the eponymous hero and friends are obliged to consume a banquet based on recipes straight from Apicius. The soup alone is so dreadful that when one character puts a spoonful in his mouth, '*...he seemed to be deprived of all sense and motion, and sat like a leaden statue of some river god, with the liquor flowing out at both sides of his mouth.*'

The End of Roman Nottinghamshire

Did the end come with a bang or a whimper? In 410, the Emperor of the western half of the Roman Empire, Honorius, wrote a letter to towns in his British province bidding them to 'take precautions on their own behalf'. In other words, you must now defend yourselves from attack by bandits and raiders since the Roman Empire can no longer do so. Although there is some doubt as to whether this famous 'rescript' really was aimed at *Britannia*, the year 410 or thereabouts is generally accepted as the time at which Britain left the Roman Empire. In August of the same year, an army of Visigoth barbarians led by Alaric also entered and sacked Rome for three days, an event which retrospectively marked the beginning of the collapse of the Roman Empire in the west. The eastern half of the Empire continued Roman traditions as Byzantium, based at Constantine's capital Constantinople.

For the English historian Edward Gibbon, whose mammoth *The Decline and Fall of the Roman Empire* was published between 1776 and 1788, the Empire's golden age had run from just 98 to 180 — and the causes of 'decay and corruption' from then on included declines in civic or public pride, failing military vigour and the rise of Christianity. Such forces served to introduce a 'slow and secret poison into the vitals of the Empire'. Gibbon's vast erudition, penetrating language and gift for vigorous narrative story-telling remain greatly respected today. And while he is only occasionally quoted as an authority in contemporary histories of the later Roman Empire, his ideas continue to have currency. As has been remarked by a modern historian, the end of the Roman Empire — in Britain — was a process, not an event,[12] involving the breakdown of urban life, raids and invasions by Saxons, Picts and other tribes and the Empire's removal of troops to repel barbarian incursions along its vast continental frontiers. Gibbon's theory that loss of military spirit among the Romans was a factor has some relevance considering that the Roman state became increasingly reliant on barbarian troops to do its fighting into the 4th century. There is some limited evidence for this in the East Midlands; in Leicester, the finding of a bronze belt-plate and leather belt strap-end, decorated in a characteristic 'chip-carved' German style, have suggested the possible presence of a garrison of troops of Germanic origin in the late 4th century. A handful of late Roman buckles of German design has also been found in Lincolnshire.

Yet connecting a small area such as Nottinghamshire in a meaningful way to the process by which Britain became finally divorced from the Roman Empire is a frustrating task given the scarcity of local archaeological evidence. However, some Romano-British settlements in the county appear to have continued Roman ways of life into the late 4th or early 5th centuries, even if more precise dating for their length of occupation is lacking. For example, a Roman coin dated to 402 was found at *Vernemetum* during the 1960s excavations there. This is an important date: since no Roman currency was imported into the province after this year, 402 appears to mark the end of formal economic relationships between Britain and the Empire. And although this was deep into the 'end game' period, it followed perhaps a period of 150 years of intermittent economic and military crises which affected the Empire and Britain's place in it. These included the so-called 'barbarian conspiracy' of the 360s when *Britannia* was subjected to co-ordinated attacks by Saxons from the continent and Picts, Attacotti and Scotti tribes from Scotland and Ireland. It is these invasions which Felix Oswald's son Adrian thought had led to the deaths of the occupants of the Norton Disney villa.

A graphic picture of the chaos of those times was given by the Venerable Bede in the 8th century. Hadrian's Wall, manned by 'a dispirited British garrison', was overrun. Then: 'At length the Britons abandoned their cities and wall and fled in disorder, pursued by their foes. The slaughter was more ghastly than ever before...They were driven from their homesteads and farms, and sought to save themselves from starvation by robbery and violence against one another, their own internal anarchy adding to the miseries caused by others, until there was no food left in the whole land except whatever could be obtained by hunting.'

In response to the massed attacks, the Emperor Valentinian despatched the general Count Theodosius with four legions to clear up the situation. According to one of the key sources on this period, the 4th century Greek historian Ammianus Marcellinus, Theodosius completed the task and then began a concerted programme to repair and strengthen the defences of Britain's forts, cities and frontiers. At *Margidunum*, Felix Oswald was convinced that the town's thick stone wall had been added as part of this Theodosian building programme. '*Margidunum* in these circumstances would have become a city of refuge for neighbouring farms after the restoration of order by Theodosius,' he wrote.[13] But as already mentioned, Malcolm Todd couldn't date the wall to any later than 200. Another possible addition to the Nottinghamshire landscape in this late period was the small fortlet at Scaftworth, which guarded the crossing of the river Idle at Bawtry. A coin of Emperor Julian (the Apostate), whose reign slightly pre-dated the barbarian outbursts, was found in the fortlet during excavations in the 1950s. To bolster the existing 'Saxon Shore' coastal defences in Yorkshire and Norfolk, it is believed that new fortifications may also have been constructed along the Lincolnshire coast that have since been lost to erosion.

The Theodosian 'restoration' of Britain shows that the Empire at this stage was prepared to hang on to the province by pouring resources of money and manpower into its security. Yet within 16 years, resources began going in the opposite direction when the army in Britain rebelled and declared as Emperor one of Count Theodosius' former lieutenants, a Spaniard called Magnus Maximus. Maximus promptly took an army to the continent to fight, possibly stripping the province of its best troops. In 407, another rebel Emperor elected in Britain, Constantine III, took an army to the continent to take control of the western Empire and repel barbarian invaders who had reached Gaul. With the benefit of an overview of the grand narrative arc of antiquity, one can see the end in sight. The Empire, having been split into western and eastern halves by the Emperor Diocletian in the 280s, was under constant pressure to repel or accommodate invasions of Visigoths, Vandals and other migrating peoples from the east; the key battle grounds were not in Britain or Spain, but along the Danubian frontier and in the Balkans and Persia; the armies attempting to defend the frontiers were themselves increasingly composed of barbarian troops in the pay of the Empire; and in 409 the people of Britain, stripped of an army and Imperial cash to keep the economy going, rebelled against all Roman rule and took independent action to liberate their cities from their own latest barbarian scourge. The following year, Honorious told Britain it was on its own.

One might expect to see lots of evidence for the gradual unravelling of Roman patterns of existence in this period. But the evidence from the main urban centres of the *Civitas Corieltavorum* suggests instead that life in the larger towns, at least, may have continued on Roman lines up to and after the withdrawal of Imperial support for the province. Some of the more recent excavations in Leicester, for example, have suggested that new hearths were being built in houses in the late 4th century. While one of Leicester's wealthier houses (in Vine Street) suffered "massive decline" from around 340, the town's forum — the symbol of Roman urban order — may have continued in use until the end of Roman rule. Rather than suffering a drastic decline there was more "a sense of continuity" about Leicester in the late Roman period, according to Richard Buckley, director of University of Leicester Archaeological Services. At Lincoln, the forum also seems to have been in use until the end of the 4th century, some buildings were occupied after 370 or 380 and late Roman coins have been found throughout the city. This is according to City of Lincoln archaeologist Mick Jones who, like Richard Buckley, spoke at a University of Nottingham conference titled The End of Roman Britain in the East, in October 2010.

In the countryside, though, the sense of breakdown, and the reality of insecurity from bandits and marauding barbarian invaders, probably arrived sooner. As noted, the villas in Nottinghamshire were abandoned by between 350 and 380 and normal life in small rural communities may have come to an abrupt end as the cash economy ground to a halt. In already marginal settlements such as Besthorpe it is possible to imagine that people simply wandered off in search of other opportunities as work dried up. At Newark, whatever settlement there was seems to have contracted so much that the land eventually reverted to woodland in the late 4th century. Life in defended towns such as *Margidunum* and *Segelocum* at Littleborough may have been more secure for a while; the latest coin found at *Margidunum* by Felix Oswald was dated to 392 while the dating of pottery at Littleborough also indicated occupation until the end of the 4th century. But, with no further troops from the Roman Empire to repel them, Saxon raiders from the continent must have soon found opportunities to settle and begin building new communities, even as some Britons tried to remain true to the patterns of Roman life they had known for 350 years.

The Saxons, initially pagan, then Christian, founders of the later kingdom of Mercia, sometimes lived on or adjacent to the crumbling relics of Roman civilisation in Nottinghamshire. At Southwell, 'a pagan Saxon urn' was found in the ruins of the once luxurious villa and a Saxon church believed to have preceded the Minster may have been deliberately founded on top of the villa; at Flawford, a Saxon church was built directly over the site of the villa there; near Willoughby-on-the Wolds, the Saxons buried the remains of their dead on the unused, faded line of the Fosse Way; and at Newark, old Roman urns were even borrowed to bury the cremated remains of the dead at a large Anglo-Saxon cemetery in Millgate. Within a few years, perhaps, the villas and defended towns were 'tumbled and weed-grown, the fields gone back to heath and scrub', as W.G. Hoskins put it. Over time, the cut Roman stone was taken away to build churches and other structures while roads fell into disrepair and became choked by weeds. But even the ruins of the once great villas, towns and roads of the Romans must still have had an imposing presence in the British landscape for many centuries. The Venerable Bede, writing in 731, said that the existence of 'cities, forts, bridges and paved roads' still bore witness to the presence of the Romans. Hadrian's Wall was described as 'this famous and still conspicuous wall...' Anglo-Saxon poetry, too, expressed awe at what one poet called 'the work of giants'. The following lines are thought to have been written about the remains of Roman Bath, but perhaps Roman Nottinghamshire's collapsed villas, crumbled town defences and ruined public buildings in *Margidunum* inspired similar feelings in the Anglo-Saxons who took time to think about the Romans and Romano-Britons who built them:

> *Wondrous is this wall stone; broken by fate, the castles have decayed; the work of giants is crumbling. Roofs are fallen, ruinous are the towers, despoiled are the towers with their gates; frost is on their cement, broken are the roofs, cut away, fallen, undermined by age. The grasp of the earth, stout grip of the ground, holds its mighty builders, who have perished and gone; till now a hundred generations of men have died.*[14]

Notes

1. A Curse Tablet from Nottinghamshire — Eric G. Turner. *The Journal of Roman Studies* 53, Parts 1 and 2, 1963.
2. *The Conquest of Gaul* — Julius Caesar. Penguin Classics, 1974.
3. The Cult of Totatis — Adam Daubney. In: *A Decade of Discovery: Proceedings of the Portable Antiquities Scheme Conference 2007*, edited by S. Worrell, K. Leahy, M. Lewis and J. Naylor. British Archaeological Reports. *Forthcoming.*
4. The Small Finds — H.E.M. Cool. In: *Life and Death in Leicester's North-east Quarter: Excavation of a Roman Town House and Medieval Parish Churchyard at Vine Street, Leicester (Highcross Leicester) 2004–2006* — T. Higgins, Mathew Morris and Dan Stone. University of Leicester Archaeology Services Report No. 2009–134. *Unpublished.*
5. *The Conquest of Gaul* — Julius Caesar. Penguin Classics, 1974.
6. *Natural History: a Selection* — Pliny the Elder. Penguin Classics, 2004.
7. Archaeology in Nottinghamshire: Achievements and Prospects — R.M. Butler. *Transactions of the Thoroton Society of Nottinghamshire* 58, 1954.
8. *Roman Britain and the English Settlements* — R.G. Collingwood and J.N.L. Myres. Oxford University Press, 1937, 2nd edition, reprinted 1975.
9. *Art and Society in Roman Britain* — Jennifer Laing. Sutton Publishing, 1997.
10. Two Hoards of Roman Coins from Calverton — H.B. Mattingly. *Transactions of the Thoroton Society of Nottinghamshire* 64, 1960.

11. *Letters of Cicero* — edited by L.P. Wilkinson. Hutchinson, 1966.
12. *The Decline and Fall of Roman Britain* — Neil Faulkner. Tempus, 2004.
13. Margidunum — Felix Oswald. *The Journal of Roman Studies* 31, 1941.
14. *Anglo-Saxon Poetry* — translated by R.K. Gordon. Everyman's Library, 1976.

Chapter 5

Following the Fosse Way: Ivan Margary's road 5f

'One of the four principal highways of England, made by the Romans, and so called on account of its being ditch'd in on both sides; or because it was never perfected but left as a great ditch. It leads from Cornwall, thro' Devonshire, by Coventry, Leicester, Newark, & c. and to Lincoln.'
NATHAN BAILEY, *AN UNIVERSAL ETYMOLOGICAL ENGLISH DICTIONARY*, 1721

'I refer the curious to make their observations upon that causeway, call'd the Fosse, which is now remaining...''
DANIEL DEFOE, *A TOUR THROUGH THE WHOLE ISLAND OF GREAT BRITAIN*, 1724

"I apprehend the Foss is the name transmitted thro' the British, which comes from digging, as being an artificial road, whence they are often call'd dikes, a word of contrary significations...'
WILLIAM STUKELEY, *ITINERARIUM CURIOSUM*, 1724

The study of Roman roads forms a substantial subcategory within the vast outpouring of books and articles on Roman issues. But in Britain at least, all routes of enquiry ultimately lead back to Ivan D. Margary, who produced the most comprehensive study of the estimated 13,000–21,000km (8,000–10,000 miles) of major and minor roads built by the invaders in their most northerly province. Margary, a veteran of the Great War who had been wounded at Gallipoli, wasn't the first to tackle this feat in the 20th century.' In 1903, half a century before Margary published his major study, a civil engineer called Thomas Codrington brought out *Roman Roads in Britain*, having travelled the network by horse gig. Codrington reflected the state of knowledge on the subject — and included a very useful fold-out map — until Margary came on the scene and published his own two-volume *Roman Roads in Britain* in 1955 and 1957.

Despite having driven and walked 30,000km (19,000 miles) in pursuit of his subject, Margary modestly said he saw his books as an update and extension to Codrington. But half a century later again, and despite another five decades of growth in traffic and road building, Margary still provides the most popular and *most recent complete* reference for academics and the passionate lay historian. Like Codrington, Margary's approach was comprehensive and detailed. He was also systematic and bestowed on the world a numbering system for Roman roads that is still used by archaeologists. The numbers he gave to the best-known Roman roads in Nottinghamshire were the 5f and the 28 — better known respectively as the Fosse Way between Leicester and Lincoln, and the link road between Lincoln and Doncaster via Littleborough and Bawtry in the north east corner of the county. Furthermore, the dividing line between the contents of his two volumes was the Fosse Way, signalling that this was not only a major highway marking both the northern and southern areas of Margary's own investigations, but a convenient line dividing the southern and northern parts of *Britannia.*

The Fosse Way proper stretches around 350km (220 miles) north east across England from Exeter in Devon to Lincoln. That the Fosse Way is almost straight between these two points, and is very straight for long individual stretches, has long been marvelled at. 'As strait as a line can mark it out,' said Daniel Defoe in *A Tour Through the Whole Island of Great Britain* in the 1720s. The eminent archaeologist R.G. Collingwood noted that no part of its entire length was more than 10km (six miles) from the line joining Lincoln and Exeter while Codrington said that no part of a 46km (29 miles) stretch between Lincoln and Cotgrave was more than three kilometres from the straight line. The modern countryside writer Oliver Rackham remarked simply: 'Whoever set out the Fosse Way evidently knew in what direction Lincoln lay from Exeter, to within a fraction of a degree, and also knew that the Somerset Levels and multiple river-crossings in Nottinghamshire were insuperable obstacles to going there direct.'[1] This straightness today makes the road photogenically useful when book publishers want to illustrate the Romans' famed surveying engineering skills. But the Fosse

Way's stretch from one side of the country to the other, from Exe to Humber (or Severn to Trent as it is more often described), also makes it look as if it could have acted as a temporary frontier line established by the Romans in the first few years after the invasion. In modern times this belief has been repeated by popular archaeology writers such as Victor W. Hagan who, in *The Roads That Led to Rome*, boomed that in 47 the Romans 'drew an imaginary line from South Devon to Lincoln and legions and prisoners alike dug a trench 220 miles in length: it was at once frontier and road. On this *limes* [frontier] the legions and native-trained auxiliaries were stationed to hold all else in check.'

The fortified frontier theory, still repeated in literature on the subject, is neat, comfortable and makes sense of the linear landscape feature that the Fosse Way created. In the early 20th century it was confidently articulated as fact by R.G. Collingwood in the influential book *Roman Britain and the English Settlements*. This was published in 1936 and many other archaeologists adhered to his thinking. Collingwood's argument was that the line of the Fosse marked the frontier of lowland Britain that had been conquered by the time Ostorius Scapula took over the governorship of the nascent province from Aulius Plautius in 47. To make the frontier meaningful, Scapula decided to immediately disarm the conquered tribes to the south and fortify the line of the Fosse against intruders. These forts would guard the occupied territory against hostility by the unconquered tribes to the north, including the *Brigantes* in northern England who were attacking the more compliant *Corieltauvi*. The frontier, Collingwood argued, would also give Scapula a firm temporary base from which he could move onwards to deal with the Welsh tribes and the *Brigantes*.

The written records supporting the frontier idea seem slight at first glance, consisting of a few sentences in the writings of Tacitus — but these sentences are the only ones to survive that were written by a historian who was actually alive at the time (although Tacitus was a young man at this date, and never actually visited Britain). In his biography of his father-in-law, the Roman general and governor Agricola, Tacitus remarked that under Britain's first two Roman governors, 'the southern part [or 'nearest part', depending on your translation] of Britain took the form of a province, and received a colony of veterans'. More to the point, in his *Annals*, Tacitus said that Scapula 'proceeded to disarm the suspected tribes, and establish forts to hold in check all the country between the Trent and the Severn'. There is some debate as to whether this sentence really did refer to the Trent; other rivers put forward as a pairing for *Sabrinam*, the Severn, have included the Avon and the Nene. The argument turns, in fact, on an accepted late 19th century 'emendation' of a garbled sentence from Tacitus so that it includes the word *Trisantonam* for the Trent.

But if the Fosse Way was an engineered frontier between Trent and Severn, where were the forts? Collingwood said the major bases or legionary concentrations had been at the mouth of the Axe in Devon, at Cirencester, High Cross, Leicester, *Margidunum* and Lincoln. He continued:

> *Thus both ends and the middle were already well defended by legionary fortresses. It was the gaps between these points that were exposed to Silurian and Brigantian raids respectively and it was to protect these gaps that Ostorius planned his frontier line.*[2]

The Fosse-as-frontier idea was also trotted out by many other archaeologists including Felix Oswald. Sheppard Frere, whose book *Britannia* has been one of the big drivers of the narrative of Roman Britain since its publication in 1967, also elaborated on the idea by stating that the required frontier forts were either on the line of the Fosse or in front of it and were either already known or *suspected*. He added that the spacing of forts such as Broxtowe and Gloucester 'at uniform distances apart and at a uniform distance beyond the Fosse Way is systematic and significant'.

Unsaid in all this was also the old idea that the Trent itself was and is an unofficial frontier, marking a cultural and geographical border between southern England and northern Britain. As the author of *Portrait of the River Trent* wrote in 1968: 'It is tempting to believe that differences between people and cultures north and south of the river today are an echo of the distinction between Romanized Coritani and independent Brigante.' Highland and lowland, north and south, untamed and tamed: a lingering question over the Fosse Way's streak across the middle of England is whether it reflected an ancient border between different kinds of mental and physical territory, or helped to create it. Daniel Defoe said that passing over the Trent was like crossing the *Rubicon*.

But since the 1960s the Fosse frontier idea has largely fallen out of favour and few archaeologists now accept Collingwood's theory. One idea is that the road at most marked the temporary border of newly won land, making it one of the Romans' 'territory-holding roads', as it has been called. Another suggestion is that the road was carefully built to serve a large pacified zone after all major military campaigning activity had moved to the north and west. There are several reasons for the change of interpretation but even old Thomas Codrington, back in 1903, pointed out that the line of forts you would expect to see along a frontier are absent on the Fosse.

Certainly, a quick glance at the latest Ordnance Survey map of Roman Britain shows that the spacing of known troop concentrations along the road seems to have left a lot of unguarded space for northern barbarians to run wild through. Neither have some of the *suspected* forts mentioned by Frere and others materialised. The long suspected fort at *Margidunum*, for example, has not been conclusively found and a fort at Leicester has also proved elusive. In fact, in the wider geographical area touched on in this book, there seem to have been no large forts at all between High Cross in Leicestershire and Lincoln. The evidence suggests, instead, that this section of the Fosse Way was in the hands of only small garrisons of troops who could keep the road clear and maintain a watch over the surrounding tribal area in the first three or four decades after the invasion. In fact, south from High Cross, the next permanent Roman troop concentration was the early fort at *Corinium*, Cirencester in Gloucestershire. This all seems to move the Fosse Way some distance from being the fortified frontier or boundary imagined by Collingwood. His theory has also been rubbished on the basis that the Roman leadership was still some way off the idea of partitioning the new province of *Britannia* by borders and frontiers. When the Fosse Way was built Claudius and his generals probably saw no reason why they would not conquer the entire island. A tacit admission of failure in achieving this was marked by the creation of the Antonine Wall in Scotland and the permanent frontier of Hadrian's Wall in the early 2nd century. Ivan Margary, by the way, said that the use of the Fosse Way as a dividing line between his two volumes was 'entirely artificial'.[3]

Nevertheless, the Fosse Way is a remarkable highway which linked two far separate legionary bases and Roman towns on either side of the new province, Lincoln in the north and *Isca Dumnoniorum*, Exeter, in the south. Despite this military usefulness, the road still stands out as a road apart. Writing in 1924, when some parts of the Fosse Way were completely derelict, Collingwood remarked that, unlike many other Roman roads, neither railways nor modern traffic followed the route of the Fosse Way. 'And railway-system and the modern road-system thus conspire to prove that the Fosse, except at its two ends, is a line which no modern traffic wants to follow,' he said. Yet after two millennia of almost continuous use, the road has became hardwired into the psychogeography of Nottinghamshire, and Britain, itself. Fosse Way Farm, Fosse Farm, Foss Farm, Fosse Fields Farm, Foss Lodge, Foss House, the Fosseway Flier bus service.... in Nottinghamshire these are among the places and services whose names derive from the established English name for this Roman highway, the Latin word *fossa* meaning ditch or trench. Local names for the road have included the Causeway, Causey, Rampart and the Ramper (the latter in Lincoln).

An archaeological report published in 1992 described the Fosse Way as 'a linear archaeological resource of national significance'.[4] While that is a commendably efficient description, this scientific approach misses the magical subterranean influence that lurks in the ancient cobbles beneath the tarmac. At one level all of the Foss and Fosse names can be seen as the surface indicators of an ancient culture from the Mediterranean that took root centuries before Nottinghamshire was thought of as Nottinghamshire. But from a deeper level, that early rooted Roman presence, reflected in the very names of existing places and buildings, reaches out to shape and influence the lives of people today. Whether by driving along the road the Roman engineers laid out, or living in towns and villages built on the foundations of the Roman settlements by its side, the people who live in modern Nottinghamshire continue to feel the influence of the ghosts of Rome.

This sense of being shaped by the decisions of mostly unnamed and unknowable invaders 2,000 years ago must rank as one of the more delicious but lesser expressed characteristics of daily modern life — the ancient not just lying under the modern, but spiritually invading it. Yet despite all this, and despite the long history of the Fosse Way as 'a linear archaeological resource', acknowledgements of the road as a Roman road are few and far between in public places in Nottinghamshire. There's a Highways Agency sign on a windy knoll opposite Brough; a restaurant called Roman Way in Newark; a road sign in Car Colston; and a bar called *Via Fossa* in central Nottingham, miles from the road and in no way related to it in any case (*Caffe Nero* doesn't count either). However, this absence of acknowledgement of the Roman past is common throughout the county. Forts, villas, roads, settlements — to judge by the lack of signs and 'heritage interpretation' one could think that the Roman Empire had a day off between Leicester and Lincoln.

In modern Nottinghamshire, the Fosse Way now mostly lies under the A46, entering the county from the south near Willoughby-on-the-Wolds, passing through Newark and exiting the county north of Brough. Along the route there are five known Roman settlements including *Margidunum*. These communities were spaced between 11 and 21km (seven and 13 miles) apart and it is Roman accuracy in measuring distance which has helped modern historians match up modern place names with the ancient Roman settlements. The most relevant document on the issue is the possibly early 3rd century *Antonine Itinerary*, a list of 225 road routes in the Roman Empire, with starting and finishing points, stopping places along the way and mileage between. It is only the last section that concerns Britain, with the Nottinghamshire section of the Fosse Way — although not so named — taking its starring role in *Iter VI* and *Iter VIII*, London–Lincoln and York–London respectively. Antiquaries used to contort themselves trying to identify Roman place names on these routes with

The lonely Highways Agency notice board opposite Brough on the A46 and (below) a Fosseway road sign in Car Colston.

communities such as Farndon, Southwell, Collingham and Mansfield. But the firm consensus now, based on archaeological evidence, is that if one had reached Leicester, on *Iter VI*, the next Roman stopping place would have been *Vernemetum* (near Willoughby-on-the-Wolds, 13 Roman miles away) followed by *Margidunum* (near East Bridgford, another 12 miles further), *Ad Pontem* (Thorpe, 7 miles) and *Crococolana* (Brough, 7 miles). For some unknown reason *Iter VIII* omitted *Ad Pontem*, suggesting a drag of 14 Roman miles (or 15 modern miles) between *Margidunum* at East Bridgford and *Crococolana* at Brough.

There has been speculation that most of the Fosse Way must have fallen out of regular use by the time that the *Antonine Itinerary* was drawn up. This is based on the absence of any other Roman settlements on the Fosse south of Leicester on the British road routes. However, this really is speculation; indeed, nobody can be certain exactly when the *Antonine Itinerary* was drawn up or even whether all the published routes were contemporaneous. However, whichever of the two published *Iters* you followed along the Fosse, the next and final stop after *Crococolana* would be Lincoln. Thus Lincoln, which was for a while the conquering army's most northern military base in Britain, was at the top end of the Fosse Way and just 14 Roman miles from Brough in modern Nottinghamshire.

The fortress was home to Legion IX *Hispana* until around 71, when it moved to the new legionary fortress at York. The replacement at Lincoln was Legion II *Adiutrix*, a supporting formation, until perhaps 77. Typically for Roman legions, both would have been made up of soldiers from across the Empire. Tombstones found in Lincoln, for example, tell us that Legion IX's ranks included men from modern-day Spain, Italy and Macedonia. Men from Legion II included those from Lyons in Gaul and the Danube frontier in modern Hungary. So we can speculate that it would have been these multinational forces, marching up the Fosse Way, who would have impressed on the people of ancient Nottinghamshire the nature of the new world order. Likewise, the locals would have needed little reminding that the same soldiers were only a day's march away in the event that 'pacification' work was required.

Few of the Roman legions have attracted as much myth and speculation as Legion IX (or VIIII, as the soldiers sometimes wrote it). This has been due to the belief that it was mysteriously wiped out in Scotland in around 120. The story was popularised by Rosemary Sutcliff's 1950's novel *The Eagle of the Ninth*, which was filmed as *The Eagle* in 2011, this following another film dealing with the alleged fate of the same legion, Neil Marshall's full-blooded *Centurion*, in 2010. However, stamps on clay tiles made by legionary soldiers found in the late 1950s and early '60s suggested that the Ninth was in Nijmegen around the time of its supposed annihilation. Yet even discounting the myth of the 'lost legion', the men of the Ninth suffered badly in Britain. According to Tacitus, it was the Ninth that marched out of its camp to help the Roman forces besieged in *Camulodunum* during the Boudican revolt. Led by their *legate* Petillius Cerialis, the infantry was wiped out by the rebels and only the cavalry and the *legate* escaped back to their fortifications. This base is now thought to have been the 10.9 hectare fortress at Longthorpe, just outside Peterborough. An adjacent 4.4 hectare fort has been interpreted as evidence that the survivors, reduced in number, were forced to quickly build a smaller defensive position. The fort complex was soon abandoned and the legion moved to Lincoln to build a new fortress. The trail of the legion's tile stamps and bricks show that its soldiers were later at Templeborough, Old Winteringham, Malton, Aldborough, York and Carlisle. It later served in Scotland under Agricola in the 80s, when it was attacked at night and was described by Tacitus as 'then the weakest of the Roman army'.

How long did it take to build the Fosse Way? What would it have looked like? When did work first start on it? These questions have possible answers, but nothing is known for certain. The building of the Fosse Way, or an earlier track that preceded the paved road, may have accompanied or followed in the steps of the army. If the early track was built when the Britons were still potentially hostile, then common sense and some expert speculation suggests that a vanguard Roman military force would have appeared first, with a rough 'tactical road' being constructed one or two days behind the advance. A proper metalled road would then have been developed on top of this embryonic highway. Reviewing Ivan Margary's Roman road books, Sir Ian Richmond, one of Britain's most eminent 20th century Roman archaeologists, summarised the process thus: 'the military pioneers' trail, then the track, and lastly the road'.[5]

The Jewish historian Josephus gave an admiring description of an advancing Roman army column, included its road builders, in his history of the Jewish revolt against the Romans in Judea between 66 and 70.[6] The column was a particularly large force led by Vespasian, the general who had commanded a legion in Britain and became Emperor in 69. The native Britons must have seen something resembling the forces described by Josephus when the Roman army marched on to *Corieltauvi* turf. First, said Josephus, came a screen of lightly armed auxiliaries and bowmen; then fully armed legionaries on foot and horse; then soldiers carrying the surveying equipment who would mark out the night's camp; then came the 'roadmakers' to 'straighten out bends in the highway, level rough surfaces, and cut down obstructive woods so that the army would not be exhausted by laborious marching'. Next was a cavalry force with the commander's baggage, followed by Vespasian surrounded by the best infantry and cavalry; then legionary cavalry, followed by artillery and battering rams with the components loaded on mules. Behind all these came the generals and senior officers with the Empire's sacred eagle banner, and legionary banners, held aloft by soldiers titled *signifers* and *aquilifers*. After these, trumpeters. Next came the full legionary infantry force marching six abreast, kept in line by centurions, followed by servants looking after the baggage. The rearguard was made up of mercenaries and more Roman infantry and cavalry. Josephus also briefly described how soldiers and cavalry were sent ahead to level a stony mountain track so the army could advance. They took just four days to build a 'broad highway', which shows how quickly soldiers could build new roads in hostile territory.

In modern times, author and former soldier John Peddie conducted a study with the Royal Engineers to find out how long it would have taken legionaries to do the construction work for a levelled tactical road.[7] The study applied to the road built from the possible Roman invasion landing site at Richborough to London, but the figures can be applied elsewhere. According to the Royal Engineers, it would have taken 1,056 men 15 weeks to build a road from the coast to Westminster — or a distance of 119km, or 74 modern miles, including the crossing at the Thames. These figures involved clearance of all trees and scrub on either side of the road with a levelled carriageway marked by timber kerbs. The distance between Leicester and Lincoln along the Fosse Way is 85.6km or 53.2 miles, which suggests that a stretch of the early Fosse Way could have been built between these two points in less than three months assuming the same muscle power.

As a supply and military route, the finished Fosse Way would then have been fully engineered with the full benefit of camber, drainage ditches and a weather-proof metalled surface. This Roman road surface has occasionally been found in recent decades. Excavations of the site thought to be *Vernemetum* in the 1960s found a road surface of 'large cobbles up to about 250mm long occurring singly and in patches, and smaller rounded pebbles'. Media reports of excavations of the A46 when it was being widened near Newark in 2002 quoted officials as having seen 'tightly packed cobbles, the material used to construct the road and even the ruts made by Roman carts'.[8] In the same year local newspapers reported that excavations revealed a Fosse Way surface 'in near perfect condition'.[9] But who would enjoy riding or walking over large cobbles? However, the original road surface was probably finished in fine gravel, long-since washed away. The 18th century antiquary William Stukeley, arriving in Brough while following the Fosse Way, noted that local people didn't even think that the great road was Roman. 'The country people have a notion that the Foss Road is the oldest in England, and that it was made by William the Conqueror,' he wrote in the 1720s.[10]

Ivan Margary put the maximum width of 'important' Roman roads at 9 metres (30ft), with 7.3 metres (24ft) being often found. These widths, though, include the maximum extent of the underlying raised bed, or *agger*, on which the roads sat. The *agger*, the most obvious physical evidence for Roman roads at ground level, probably served the purpose of aiding rain water run-off and helped make a noticeable 'Roman' zone through the countryside. An intriguing detail on the historic perception of the Fosse's *agger* in east Nottinghamshire was given in a mid-19th century history of Collingham by E.G. Wake, who wrote: 'Its raised construction is conveyed to us by the Saxon word *Rampart* — a term generally applied to it in this part of its course.'

Excavations of the Fosse Way itself in or just beyond Nottinghamshire have placed the width of the metalled road surface at 10 metres (33ft) (Willoughby-on-the-Wolds, 1964–68) and 12 metres (39ft) (near RAF Swinderby in 2002). The average width of the Fosse Way's road surface has also been examined by Hugh Davies, a former highway engineer who has brought a modern technical eye to the issue.[11] His study of hundreds of road excavations indicates that Roman roads varied widely in width but that the *average* breadth of the metalled surface of the Fosse Way was 5.2 metres (17ft); its average metalling depth was just over half a metre. This, though, meant that the Fosse Way as a whole was still one of the narrowest of the main Roman highways. According to Davies' number-crunching, Dere Street, which ran from York to the Firth of Forth, averaged 7.7 metres (26ft) in its surface width while Watling Street, which ran from Dover to Wroxeter in Shropshire via London, averaged 10.1 metres (34ft). With outer marking ditches added, the complete maximum width of a Roman highway could be as much as 25.3 metres, or 83ft. These figures mean that the Fosse was, on average, half the width of Watling Street. Davies thought that Roman roads may have been built wider to reflect their greater military use and that roads were generally wider in the north, which remained a militarised zone throughout the Roman period.

But who travelled on the roads such as the Fosse Way? A list of road users in Italy was compiled by French historian Raymond Chevallier from Roman literary sources. He listed: military leaders and their forces, Emperors and their trains, dignitaries and their staff, envoys, messengers from the *cursus publicus* mail service and private citizens. These last included merchants in search of supplies or fairs, itinerant craftsmen such as masons, sculptors and mosaicists, gangs of seasonal farm workers, theatrical performers, teachers and lecturers, litigants, poets looking for patrons, the sick on their way to drink healing waters or breathe healthier air, pilgrims seeking holy places, VIPs looking for oracles, strolling priests, tourists, people on their way to see a play or games at an amphitheatre, courtesans and people in funeral processions. Then there were commercial travellers such as people transporting food to the towns from the countryside, wares from local workshops, and those driving waggons of grain destined for the army's granaries.

Milestones, in the shape of tall cylindrical stone columns, accompanied Roman roads throughout the most distant reaches of the Empire and two examples from the Fosse Way in the East Midlands survive today. Both are from Leicestershire. One is from Thurmaston, just north of Leicester. Dated to 119/120, it is dedicated to the Emperor Hadrian and marked 'A RATIS M II' — or 'two miles to Ratae'. Another milestone was found at

Thrussington on the Fosse Way further north but bears only a brief fragment of a dedication. Another three Roman milestones from the region are from Lincolnshire, one of which appears to mark the distance of 14 miles from Lincoln to Littleborough (*Segelocum*) in Nottinghamshire. Since carving in stone took some time, the Romans used a form of abbreviation which bears comparison with modern text messaging. So, the inscription on the Littleborough milestone, dedicated to the 3rd century rebel Emperor Victorinus 'the fortunate, pious, unconquerable', ends with the shorthand ALS MP XIIII — or (L)indo (S)egelocum (M)ille (P)assus 14. The distance agrees with the distance of 15 modern miles between Lincoln and Littleborough in *Iter V* of the *Antonine Itinerary*.

As for the Fosse Way's famed straightness: this, like the straightness of Roman roads everywhere, was long regarded as the expression of the Roman's efficiency at getting from A to B. Davies and other analysts, on the other hand, propose that building in straight lines, rather than curves, was a direct consequence of the Romans' sophisticated surveying and planning techniques.[12] In this theory, the known existence of equipment such as elementary theodolites and right-angle measuring devices like the *groma* — sometimes seen today at modern Roman 'living history' camps — would have helped teams of surveyors and engineers to plan roads on maps first, before transferring precise route information to the terrain. Such maps have not survived, but their existence has been assumed. Important in the surveying of unknown ground was the availability of good views from high points, and one notable high point along the Fosse Way in Nottinghamshire is found at Cotgrave, or Owthorpe as this part of the road is sometimes called. A quick look at any road map shows that the Fosse Way in the county isn't entirely straight, but is routed along straight stretches, with a long section between Lincoln and Cotgrave being affected by only minor realignments. These help the road curve gently towards a more southerly direction. However, at Cotgrave Gorse (or Owthorpe), the road turns south by a relatively abrupt 30 degree bend. This noticeable change of direction, said to be the sharpest bend in the road's entire length, occurs on high ground and must have aided the Roman surveyors in their road planning. The curve in the road is obvious today and the view from the ridge gives motorists a good view of the Fosse Way's direct route northwards. G.M. Boumphrey, a radio broadcaster who wrote a gentle 1935 travel book titled *Along the Roman Roads* ('a book for the knapsack and the fireside'), jested lightly that the course change appeared to have been made 'as if to avoid Nottingham'. He added: 'Looking north from this old sighting point, the road dropping away in front of you, there is a fine view along the valley of the Trent, and the low-lying ground to the east, and you see the Fosse Way cutting through it almost straight for Newark.'

It's sometimes said that after the end of the Roman period no *new major* roads were built in Britain until the first turnpike roads were constructed in the 17th century. This seems incredible. Yet it wasn't as though no new roads at all were constructed. After all, all towns and cities that were founded after the Roman period (such as Nottingham, Oxford and Coventry, all founded in the Saxon period) had to be reached by new rudimentary transport routes. Perhaps the salient point is that the durable Roman network remained the best option for rapid long-distance travel overland even into the medieval period, and that was despite the roads not being maintained. Local evidence, again from excavations on the Fosse Way, suggests that one reason for this lack of maintenance, apart from loss of the required skills, was that traffic on sections of some Roman roads simply came to a halt after the Romans left Britain.

In the 1960s, looking for ancient *Vernemetum* near Willoughby-on-the-Wolds, archaeologists found the cobbled surface of the Fosse Way — except that it was 90 metres (295ft) to the west of the A46. How could its original alignment have veered so much from the modern road? The archaeologists' thinking on this reflected their finding of an Anglo-Saxon cemetery alongside and directly on top of the Fosse Way (jewellery and other Anglo-Saxon items recovered from the area are on show in Nottingham Castle museum). Some of the Anglo-Saxon graves were sunk to the level of the cobbles on the Roman road surface. From this evidence, the archaeologists theorised that the Fosse Way must have fallen into disuse after the Roman period, with road traffic reduced to a trickle or ceasing altogether. The archaeology report doesn't specify why the road would have become abandoned after the Roman withdrawal, but we can speculate here that it was because the Anglo-Saxon sense of society was very different from the Roman one. The orthodox view is that England under Anglo-Saxon domination broke down into a system of distinct kingdoms that eventually congealed into the Heptarchy of Northumbria, Wessex, Mercia and so on. Inward looking, and with no sense of national unity, the most important roads to the Mercians who inhabited the East Midlands region were the roads that went to the nearest market. In which case, there would have been little use for a road passing across rival kingdoms. With the road out of use, ploughing and the accumulation of soil and debris began to impinge on the Fosse until eventually the layer was so deep that the Anglo-Saxons regarded the land near *Vernemetum* as suitable for burial. A folk memory of the road's existence may have lingered on in the use of its alignment as a local boundary (the modern county border runs straight up the middle of the Fosse Way in this area). At some point, however, traffic picked up again. The Fosse Way was in demand once more. Except that now horses, carts and pedestrians couldn't get through at this point because there was a cemetery in the way. So gradually road users developed a new route, veering away slightly to the east of the original Fosse Way — and it is this short alignment which became part of the modern A46, 90 metres away from the original Roman road. Or so the theory went. Oliver Rackham's general description of how ancient roads changed course is apt for this section of the Fosse. Quoting G.K. Chesterton's poem *The Rolling English Road*, he said: 'The straight course of most Roman roads is more obvious on the map than on the ground. Ancient roads, of whatever origin, usually have a course which on the small scale consists of a series of wobbles. Over the centuries travellers have had to go round fallen trees, sloughs, holes, muckheaps, purpestures [encroachments on common land], dead horses, and all the things that people put or allow to remain on the highway; and they have often continued to go round after the obstruction has disappeared. The resulting small diversions come to look as if indeed "the rolling English drunkard made the rolling English road".'[13]

The Stations of the Fosse

It is often said that Roman civilisation in provinces such as Britain was essentially an urban phenomenon. It was the Romans who first brought planned towns to the island and it was from these concentrations of new wealth, with their street grids, town houses, markets, forums and statues dedicated to Emperors and gods, that Roman culture and ideals of civic virtue percolated into the surrounding countryside. In this sense, the most influential sources of Roman culture in the territory of the *Corieltauvi* must have been Leicester and Lincoln. Leicester, with its forum, temples, market, bath house, aqueduct and slave-owning town house residents, was the administrative capital of the *civitas*. But Lincoln must have been even more impressive. The legionary fortress alone, with fortifications and gateways, enclosed 16.5 hectares (41 acres) of land. And it was in the reign of Domitian towards the end of the 1st century that the fortress site then became one of the province's new *coloniae* for the settlement of army veterans. New stone defences up to 1.2 metres (4ft) thick were added plus four stone gateways, of which one part, the Newport Arch, remains standing. There was a grid of streets, buildings with colonnades and heating, an aqueduct, statues, an Imperial cult and, down the hill, an enclosed 'new town' which may have had a high proportion of Britons among its population. Beneath the streets, Lincoln's wide underground sewers washed the people's waste away.

But although Leicester and Lincoln may have been the true powerhouses of Roman culture in the region, it is interesting to speculate how Roman ideas — as well as the latest news and gossip — must have spread to Nottinghamshire, with its string of small roadside towns, via travellers moving up and down the Fosse Way. The Romans developed many small settlements such as these along their main roads and in modern times they have traditionally been referred to as 'stations' — a word so vague as to both deaden the imagination and allow it to run riot. The Roman communities along the Fosse in Nottinghamshire are probably best regarded as minor towns or, in a less prepossessing phrase, 'loosely planned road-side settlements'. Archaeologists have sought to define such places by finding common features among them. They were obviously smaller than Roman cities and chartered towns; they covered a core area of 1.6–4 hectares (4–10 acres); life in such places was usually connected with the life of the countryside nearby; and they generally lacked the public buildings and grid street pattern found in planned Roman cities and larger towns. Some small towns had defences, others did not, but the presence of walls and ditches did not necessarily mean that they had an important military purpose anyway. Some might also serve as 'walled posting-stations', a phrase used by the archaeologist Sir Ian Richmond in the classic blue-bordered 1955 Pelican *Roman Britain*. These posting-stations, called *mansiones* by the Romans, were situated about 19km (12 miles) apart and had facilities to change horses and put Roman travellers up for the night, including official Imperial messengers and postal staff. In Richmond's view, the fact that these facilities were fortified didn't suggest that they suffered constant attack; rather, that 'critical points' in the Roman administration should be guarded against the possibility of attack. According to these criteria, the Fosse Way settlements would have to be thought of as minor towns. One other suggested common characteristic of settlements was that they usually had villas nearby, probably connected to the life of the town. This is true of *Margidunum* (villas nearby at Newton, Car Colston and Bingham), *Crococolana* (villa at Norton Disney), *Ad Pontem* (villa debris nearby) and Redhill (probably a villa, plus two nearby at Barton-in-Fabis and Lockington). The spacing of these settlements along the road suggests that some or all of them had facilities to act as *mansiones*. But except for *Margidunum*, no archaeological evidence has been found so far showing that the Fosse Way towns had the buildings to provide this service.

Vernemetum

A site in a field near Willoughby-on-the-Wolds has been identified with *Vernemetum* in the Roman road itineraries for hundreds of years. The Elizabethan scholar and traveller William Camden observed in *Britannia*, his survey of the kingdom, that there was a place of note in this area called '*Vernometum* or *Verometum*, whereof Antonine the Emperour hath made mention' and that such a site was 'twelve Italian miles' from Leicester. Camden hesitantly named the site as being 'Burrowhill or Erd-burrow' and said the ground in his day was used for arable farming — and wrestling by local youths. But, for him, the main evidence for a Roman presence was that there was a steep hill, at the top of which were 'expresse tokens of a towne destroyed, a duple trench, and the very tract where the wals went, which enclosed about eighteene acres of ground within'. The site was included in *Iter VI* (as *Verometo*) and *Iter VIII* (*Vernemeto*) of the *Antonine Itinerary* and has also been identified with *Veratino* in the *Ravenna Cosmography*, a document listing 300 place names in Imperial Roman Britain including Leicester and Lincoln. However, it was the 18th century antiquarian William Stukeley who first had the confidence to identify these names with the site near Willoughby recognised today. Although Stukeley mistakenly called the site *Margidunum*, he left a detailed and valued description of the terrain near Willoughby that he saw:

> *Here they said had been an old city called Long Billington. 'Tis often called the black field in common discourse from the colour and excellent richness of the soil, so that they never lay any manure upon it. Here is a place called Thieves, and on the other side of the valley a place called Wells, but the city was mostly on the Willoughby side, for the land on the other side in Broughton is poor, whilst this is luxuriant to the last degree so that they affirm a farmer once happening to let his sheep-fold here, it rotted the corn upon the spot, and often he has been forced to mow the blade before it spindled (in their way of talking). The soil is perfectly black, though all the circumjacent land be red, especially north of the valley upon the edge of the hill, and where most Roman antiquities are found; which certainly was the true place, whence the Roman name signifying a marly hill. Richard Cooper, aged 72, has found many brass and silver coins here; there have been some of gold. They have a notion of great riches being underground, and a vulgar report that one balk or mere [i.e. a division between the ploughed fields] has as much money under it, as would purchase the whole lordship. But people have been frightened from digging it by spirits, and several pleasant stories are told thereupon. They have likewise a tradition that the city was destroyed by thieves, perhaps from the place so called. Many mosaic pavements have been dug up; my landlord, Gee of Willoughby, says he has upon ploughing met with such for 5 yds. together, as likewise coins, pot-hooks, fire-shovels and the like utensils, and many large brass coins which they took for weights, ounces and half-ounces, but upon trial found them somewhat less... . At Over and Nether Broughton and Willoughby too the coins are so frequent that you hear of them all the country round.*[14]

A few years after Stukeley, the historian John Throsby, who was researching a revised version of Dr Robert Thoroton's *Antiquities of Nottinghamshire,* passed the same way and duly noted that, 'the eminence overlooking Willoughby brook, the supposed site of the station, makes a little bend from the Foss Road (one of the signs of a station)'. Although the site 'is not now so easily to be traced', he concluded the place had to be *Vernemetum* on the basis that no writer of any importance had offered an alternative.[15]

Usefully for modern archaeologists, Stukeley also provided a sketch of the area showing Willoughby, Willoughby brook and the misnamed *Margidunum* on a hill near the Fosse Way, which is depicted as a raised road between two parallel ditches. The Roman site Stukeley sketched isn't named on the modern OS Explorer map of the area. It was marked on the first one-inch Ordnance Survey map of the area in the 19th century and on early 20th century OS maps, the latter pinpointing *Vernemetum* to the field immediately east of the Fosse Way, south of the Broughton Lodge crossroad with Back Lane that leads to Willoughby itself. That the modern OS map doesn't include this location is probably explained by the fact that the Roman site is now buried by an embanked link road connecting Back Lane with a bridge over the A46. Indeed, it was the need to excavate *Vernemetum* before it disappeared under the road, as part of an A46 widening project, that led to the site being excavated between 1964 and 1968 by a team led by Malcolm Dean, then mathematics teacher at Rushcliffe Boys' School.

Apart from the Anglo-Saxon cemetery and the section of Fosse Way already mentioned, the team concluded that *Vernemetum* 'may have extended up to 2km along the road, and probably contained at least one colonnaded building'. Other 'more humble structures' of timber and possibly stone, as well as drainage ditches, were also found. Speculation over the colonnaded building was based on the recovery of part of a column base. This, and the name *Vernemetum*, translated as some variation on 'very sacred grove', suggested that *Vernemetum* may have had a temple. Camden had used complicated etymological analysis to come to the same conclusion about the site four centuries before, writing that 'there stood there some great Temple of the Heathen Gods'. Another of the great 18th century Romanists, John Horsley, in the early 1730s, said the name had generally been interpreted as 'great temple' but added this sensible thought: 'But how uncertain are these conjectures, and how easy it is to find out and adapt an etymology to almost any name and place? This station has hitherto passed for *Margidunum*; and all other antiquaries have gone quite off the way to seek for *Vernometum*, and thereby lost both themselves and the station. If we keep close to our guide, the Fosse, it will conduct us safely to *Margidunum*.'[16]

Digging in the right place 230 years later, Malcolm Dean's finds included the very basic remains of an oven which may have been used to dry or roast cereal grains; 63 coins dated between 194 and 402; 7.6kg of pottery and 3.2kg of sherds of *amphorae*. Dean concluded that while there had been some presence at *Vernemetum* in the 2nd century, the principal occupation had been in the 4th.[17] Significantly for the old Fosse Way 'fortified frontier' theory, Dean found no evidence of a military presence at *Vernemetum*. However, typically for archaeology, the report on the excavation hedged its bets by saying that a military use 'could exist undetected'. Dean, who also lectured in archaeology at Newark Technical College and led the excavation of the Anglo-Saxon cemetery in Newark, was to die in a car crash in 1970. A magazine article published the following year described him as 'an archaeologist with tremendous courage, organisational ability, a trained engineer and with continuing enthusiasm to "carry" his band of volunteers'.[18]

The big excavation of 1964–68 was preceded by some smaller efforts in the same area. One of these took place over 1947 and '48 and concentrated on a feature called the Crosshill Tumulus, located on a prominent ridge near the original Broughton Lodge crossroads. Led by Dr F.M. Heichelheim, of University College, Nottingham, this work also took place because the tumulus was about to be flattened by the A46. Heichelheim found the remains of what he thought had been a watch tower, a stone-floored building, a ditch and pottery dated between the 1st and 4th centuries. But he also found five skeletons, one with a slab on its chest and another with deformed joints and an unusually thick skull. These were later diagnosed as evidence of Paget's Disease, a bone condition. But this didn't prevent the *Nottinghamshire Guardian* newspaper from having fun with the findings, reporting the deformed 'Willoughby Skeleton' under the headline 'Thick Skull Amazes Nottm. Geologist'. The article began: 'Was there a strange race of people living in Notts nearly 2,000 years ago of whom we have no knowledge — a race with skulls nearly half-an-inch thick, lower jaws having two sharp points, one on each side, and thigh bones much larger than those of normal human beings?'

By the way, the answer to this is 'probably not'.

An earlier report on the excavations by the same newspaper, carrying a headline 'Light on Ancient Notts. Folk', reported that the excavations also unearthed a silver signet ring bearing the words 'Ioves Bret', believed to indicate *Jupiter Brittanicus*, a local cult dedicated to a British form of Jupiter. No mention of this ring is made in the excavation report. However, despite these weighty matters, the *Nottinghamshire Guardian* began its report on the excavations with these words: 'Anybody who thinks of archaeology as the pastime of bearded ancients will be surprised if he peers through the right hedge, for the diggers are mostly cheerful young men and women.'

Ad Pontem

With modern archaeological techniques providing a firmer basis for identifying the locations of Roman communities on the Fosse Way, it can be easy to forget the cloud of unknowing in which the early antiquarian enthusiasts operated in the 18th century. And of all the local Fosse Way names mentioned in the *Antonine Itinerary*, perhaps none provoked as much discussion and uncertainty — and for so many years — as *Ad Pontem*. Stukeley thought it was at East Bridgford. Magistrate William Dickinson considered *Ad Pontem* to be 'the post of difficulty', but was so certain that Southwell had been the location that he added the words 'The Ad Pontem of the Romans' on the title page of his *History and Antiquities of the Town of Southwell*, published in 1787. John Throsby, for his part, repeated the theory of a 'Gentleman of high respectability' who had fixed *Ad Pontem*, by a process of mathematical logic, at 'Thorpe-bar'. Confused? It got worse, since Throsby also quoted John Horsley. And Horsley, using the distances stated in the *Antonine Itinerary*, placed *Ad Pontem* not unreasonably at Farndon, since the mileages placed the Roman town 'two or three miles from the middle of Newark' and the Trent comes close to the Fosse Way where there could have been a bridge. He reasoned that if *Ad Pontem* was at Farndon, then Newark itself must have been built from the ruins of *Ad Pontem* on one side and *Crococolana* on the other. But if so, where was the bridge over the Trent implied in the very name *Ad Pontem*? Horsley went to look for suitable ground 'and did not think the situation or appearance very unpromising'.

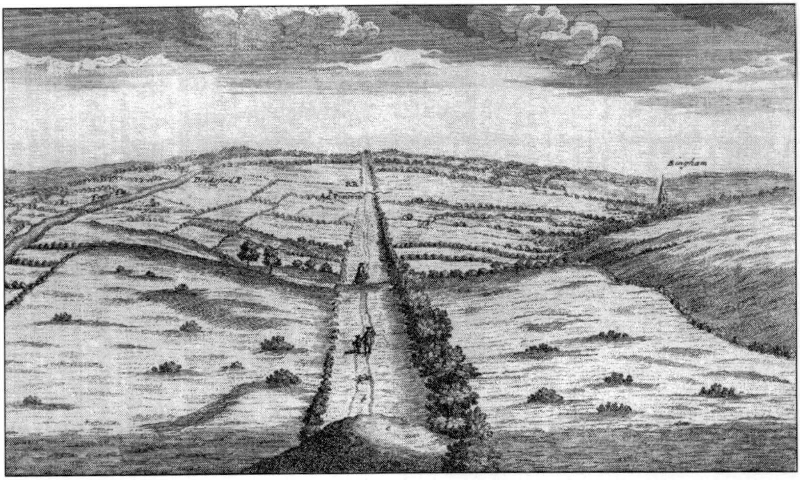

View along the Fosse Way, with Bingham on the right and a misnamed *Ad Pontem* at centre. From William Stukeley's *Itinerarium Curiosum*.

Just under 200 years later historians were still twisting themselves into knots to firmly identify the site of *Ad Pontem*. H.B. Walters, the author of the Roman chapter in the *Victoria County History*, published in 1910 and today still an important source of knowledge on local Roman matters, began his telling of the tale with the words 'the theorizing has been endless' and ended it two pages later with 'the fact is that we waste time thus torturing the sense of the Itinerary and the probabilities of the case'. The debate finally ended when excavations by Adrian Oswald over the winter of 1937–38 finally established *Ad Pontem's* location at the hamlet of Thorpe, or Thorpe-by-Newark, just north of East Stoke. In truth, Thorpe had long been one of several favoured spots for *Ad Pontem*; coins had been found here since at least the 18th century and the nearness of the Trent suggested suitability for the name *Ad Pontem*, which is translated as either 'at the bridge' or 'to the bridge'.

However, further debate over the exact nature of *Ad Pontem* was now to begin. Later excavations and aerial photography in the 1950s and '60s appeared to show beyond much doubt that the Roman site here had first supported a small military fort, superseded by two larger civilian settlements surrounded by walls and ditches. But, in the late 1930s, Oswald didn't have the advantage of aerial photographs and his digging and scraping — which he could only do on Saturdays — revealed a complex history which he divided into six periods of building development starting in round 60 and ending in the middle of the 4th century. In most phases the rebuilding was motivated by destruction by fire. The site was complicated by the fact that stone had been taken away, which meant that Oswald found many concrete building floors but hardly any walls. Oswald also said he could find nothing on the site which suggested military use. This view was later to be revised, but based on what he found Oswald wrote: 'The excavations here described gave the impression of a poor civilian settlement rather than a military camp.'

Like *Margidunum*, the settlement at *Ad Pontem* had developed ribbon-fashion, with building taking place north and south of the main site along the Fosse. Oswald found a large amount of pottery, including two complete vessels, but concluded: 'The absence of small finds of luxury objects, of wall plaster and of well-founded walls implies a poor standard of life and a humble settlement in the area excavated.' Oswald concentrated his digging in the fields fronting on to the eastern side of the Fosse Way adjacent to the Thorpe and Farndon parish boundary. However, surface finds of coins and pottery had been found spread over 30 acres in the nearby fields and despite Oswald's seemingly infallible conclusions about *Ad Pontem's* location, there was still doubt. In 1942, Oswald got into an argument in the letters page of the *Nottinghamshire Guardian* with a correspondent who insisted that the bridge of *Ad Pontem* had been at Gunthorpe, across the Trent from *Margidunum*. Oswald firmly told this tiresome personage that there had been too much speculation on Roman Nottinghamshire based on 'unsatisfactory documentary evidence' which was unrelated to the evidence on the ground. With a seeming exertion of authority, Oswald signed his letter, 'Adrian Oswald, Capt. RA, MA, FSA (Scotland).'

Yet understanding of the Thorpe site was to deepen and become substantially modified in the 1950s, aided by aerial photography which revealed the outlines of at least three overlapping structures — two rectangular, one oval — surrounded by a complicated maze of ditches. These were all located in a field called Wharf Close, on the eastern side of the Fosse. These aerial images were among a large body of photographs of ancient British sites taken by a geology professor called Dr J.K. St Joseph in a project co-ordinated by Cambridge University. St. Joseph was hardly the first to recognise the value of aerial photography to archaeology. O.G.S. Crawford, the former Royal Flying Corps observer who modernised the Ordnance Survey's archaeology mapping, used aerial photography of ancient sites in the 1920s and pilots such as Major G.W.G. Allen also contributed aerial studies of southern England in the 1930s. But the programme initiated by St Joseph and Crawford in 1939, and resumed in 1945, was national and systematic, the photographs being taken at low level from small RAF aircraft on training flights and eventually covering most Roman sites in Britain. Derrick Riley continued the tradition over Nottinghamshire and in the 1990s the county was included in the extensive National Mapping Programme of aerial photography. Aerial photography has had a significant impact on the modern study of ancient sites, allowing archaeologists to see the outlines of ancient structures and revealing hundreds of new sites in landscapes previously studied only from ground level. It has also enabled wider perspectives across large areas of ground, suggesting how ancient sites related to their landscapes.

In 1952, guided by new aerial photographs, digging on both

Aerial photograph of *Ad Pontem*. The outline of the larger, later defences can be seen to the right of the A46. The same outline is shown in R.R. Inskeep's drawing of the site below.

sides of the Fosse at Brough was started by R.R. Inskeep. The excavations were limited but the upshot was his tentative suggestion that there had been a primary area of defended settlement measuring 109 metres by 174 metres (360ft by 570ft), covering 1.8 hectares and protected by a 2.4 metre (8ft) thick wall backed by an earth rampart. Inskeep also found what he believed to be the foundations of a timber gateway or tower, while smaller finds included roofing stones. Inskeep's characterisation of the settlement gave it life. 'Such discoveries, combined with the position of *Ad Pontem*, astride a main road, and adjacent to the river, give the impression of a busy and important, though not necessarily highly civilised, small provincial town; the inhabitants, probably entirely Romanised Britons, engaged in industry and farming, and receiving travellers and raw materials both by road and by river,' he wrote.[19] This was certainly an advance on Oswald's 'poor civilian settlement'.

However, *Ad Pontem* wasn't finished with archaeology and interpretation of the site was to undergo further revision in the second half of the 1950s and 1960s when St Joseph's aerial photographs were reinterpreted and new excavations took place. This new analysis of *Ad Pontem*'s development concluded that there had first been a small fortlet with rounded corners, sur-

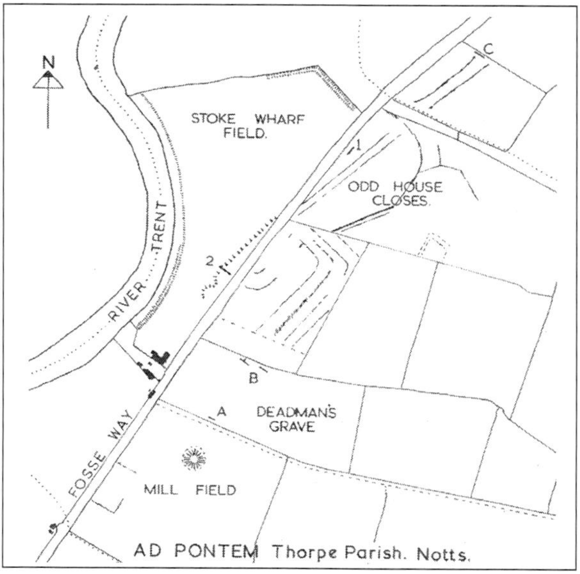

Inskeep's drawing of cropmarks showing the Roman settlement at *Ad Pontem*.

rounded by two ditches, built in the 1st century. This was the small oval structure seen in the photographs and it may have acted as a 'small road-post garrisoned only by a detachment'. The fortlet was succeeded in the 2nd century by a larger civilian settlement surrounded by a ditch around 6 metres (20ft) broad. Then, in the 3rd or 4th century, this was succeeded by a much larger enclosure surrounded by a stone wall, 2.6 metres (8.5ft) thick, with rectangular corners, surrounded by two more ditches, later formed into a single wide ditch. The outline of a rectangular building around 30 metres (98ft) long, and around six metres (19.5ft) wide, was seen at the north end of this enclosure. It was end-on to the Fosse Way and had a narrow room or passageway in it. An east–west running street, perhaps with a central drain, was also seen. St Joseph and Sheppard Frere in their book *Roman Britain from the Air,* published in 1983, speculated that it might continue further east and lead to the Roman town of Ancaster in Lincolnshire.

But there was still a separate polygonal, or kite-shaped enclosure, north of the settlement which couldn't be explained. This can clearly be seen north of the original route of the Fosse Way in the aerial images. Excavated in 1965, it was seen to be made up of two ditches, the larger one four metres (13ft) wide. St Joseph and Frere didn't know what it was for, but speculated that it could have been part of a supply depot for the fortlet. After its military role came to an end, *Ad Pontem* was expanded into a larger civilian settlement. The enclosed size of the initial military fortlet was put at 0.5 hectares. The defended civilian settlement which came next measured 150 metres (492ft) north to south and may have covered 1.5 hectares. The second and larger defended civilian settlement which replaced this measured 170 metres by 128 metres (557ft by 420ft), covering 2.1 hectares (5.2 acres).

According to all this, then, *Ad Pontem* did have a minor military role in the first century of Roman occupation. And if it did have a garrison, the soldiers would probably have been auxiliary troops rather than the regular soldiers of the Roman legions. Although auxiliaries had a definite place in the Roman battle line, in pacified territory they were also used in a static garrison and policing role that left the legions free to mobilise when required. Unlike the soldiers of the legions the auxiliaries were not Roman, being foreigners recruited from lands conquered by

Rome. These foreign units were posted far away from their native lands in the belief that this would make them less likely to become a danger to Roman power if they became hostile. Reflecting the heterogeneous nature of the Roman Empire, auxiliary units posted to Britain were a suitably exotic assortment and included Syrian archers on Hadrian's Wall, *Frisians* in Derbyshire and *Thracians* in Colchester. Particularly prominent in the conquest of Britain thanks to frequent mentions in the written histories were a bunch of hardcases called the *Batavians*, from an island between the Rhine and the Waal, whose speciality was swimming across fast rivers and broad stretches of water beside their horses while fully armed. It is the *Batavians* who are believed to have crossed the Menai Straits to Anglesey, defeating an army on the shore that included outraged women with 'dishevelled hair' and Druids shouting terrible curses, their hands raised to heaven. Units of British auxiliaries also served with the Roman army, including a cohort of 1,000 men which served in *Dacia*, modern Romania, in the 1st century. This unit included a soldier called Marcus Ulpius Novantico, son of a man from Leicester called Adcobrovatus. An auxiliary's reward for 25 years' service included Roman citizenship for himself and his children, and the right to marry.

So that's *Ad Pontem* — apparently. But where's the bridge? The fact that the remains of a Roman bridge over the Trent have not been found at Thorpe has led to speculation that a bridge was never built here. Perhaps it was really the case that since the ground here is so close to the Trent, and was actually 'four to five feet' lower in Roman times than the present day (according to Adrian Oswald), then there was some kind of raised track over the potentially boggy ground here. 'It is also the point at which the river flows nearest to the road, and is probably the only spot between Newark and East Stoke which, under present conditions, remains just above water at high flood level,' wrote R.R. Inskeep. One of the chief proponents of the 'raised track' theory was Oswald senior, Felix, who also searched for a bridge on the river bank at Thorpe but 'without any tangible results such as pottery, coins, building stones or wooden stakes'. Short of evidence, Oswald F. theorised that the low-lying land at *Ad Pontem* may have been traversed by a 'corduroy road' composed of tree trunks, serving a similar role to the matting laid by British 'bobbin' tanks on the soft sand of the Normandy beaches on D-Day in 1944.

However, Oswald's influence for this idea wasn't the war, but his travels as a commercial oil geologist where he noticed how roads of tree trunks had been laid through 'the dense, dank forests' of the Caucasus. His other inspiration was the writings of Tacitus, who spoke of *pontes longi*, or long bridges, being used by troops over boggy ground during the Roman campaigns in Germany. 'These constituted a narrow pathway... through the bleak marshlands, and apart from that there was nothing but a bog of thick, heavy mud, intersected by streams that rendered it hazardous,' wrote Tacitus.[20] Oswald said: 'In this manner the low-lying plain between East Stoke and Farndon, still frequently liable to flooding, was effectively stabilized by *pontes longi*, whilst the higher and solid ground at East Stoke, flanked and protected on the west by the river Trent, became a secure encampment for troops to guard the engineers whilst felling trees and laying the tree-trunks.'[21] Oswald's suggestion probably deserves more attention than it has received since traces of several Roman wooden roads over wet terrain have been found in western Europe. And as is described elsewhere in this book, a wooden road was also built over wet ground next to the river Idle in north Nottinghamshire, so there is sound local evidence for the practice.

Yet there has also been speculation that the bridge referred to in the name *Ad Pontem* was one that may have crossed the Trent at Gunthorpe. Another theory places a probable crossing point just to the west at Fiskerton, where the Trent makes another loop in its course. A third suggestion is that the bridge was at *Ad Pontem* but was destroyed by an eastward migration of the river channel, which ate into the edge of the Roman settlement. In the most recent thinking, the favoured location for the bridge is also back at *Ad Pontem* in order to connect it to the fort at Osmanthorpe, which seems to have a road pointing back to the riverside settlement. Clearly, a bridge *somewhere* in the area would have been necessary for there to be a connection between the two.

The best-known finds from *Ad Pontem* are discussed in Chapter 4. However, since the excavations of the 1960s *Ad Pontem* has continued to bring up small Roman finds. A bronze head of a mule, measuring just 23mm long, was found in the nearby fields in 1979. And in 2003, south east of the town, fragments including mosaic *tesserae* and a part of a central heating flue tile were brought to the surface. These items suggest a villa may also have been nearby.

Crococolana

Unlike the uncertainty that lingered over the identification of *Ad Pontem* with Thorpe, observers have long been confident that the hamlet of Brough, on the A46 immediately to the south of the border with Lincolnshire, was the same place as *Crococolana* in the *Antonine Itinerary*. Stukeley said that Brough was the 'undoubted *Crocolana* [*sic*] of the Romans' and both he and John Horsley in the first half of the 18th century bought locally found Roman coins when they visited (the *Newark Advertiser* was surely mistaken when it reported, in 1955, that a gold coin from the reign of Emperor Nero found stuck to the mud of a farm cart in Brough was the first Roman coin found 'in the Newark area'). Aerial photography has shown that *Crococolana* was a small, roughly rectangular town defended by deep ditches, 6–10 metres across (19–32ft), enclosing around seven hectares (17 acres). Only two metalled streets inside the town have been identified, one heading east, the other west to some kind of compound. A possible third street has been seen at the southern edge of the town. Apparent arrangements of paddocks and small fields suggest that the town had a minor agricultural and market role. A military presence has not been identified here. However, unlike Thorpe, Brough has not been explored by modern excavation.

The first and so far only time *Crococolana* has been subjected to a thorough dig was in 1903–05 when T. Cecil Smith Woolley found the remains of a house and unearthed a large amount of pottery, *amphorae*, bones, iron tools, ornaments and more than 130 coins dating from the 1st to the late 4th century. However, his most eye-catching find was the copper cheek-piece of a ceremonial cavalry helmet. Smith Woolley, who was a professional land agent from a long-established Collingham family, speculated that *Crococolana* had covered an area of 16 hectares (40 acres) stretching up and down both sides of the quiet road that now passes through the hamlet. He added, 'and the objects which have been turned up by the spade clearly show that the place was much more than a mere soldiers' barracks'. Here, as usual in Nottinghamshire, the archaeologists were exploring a site where there were no visible Roman remains left standing above ground. It was the same in Stukeley's day. 'At Brough no Roman tokens visible... the city has been most perfectly levelled by the plow, so that the mark of ridge and furrow remains in the very road...' he said. A decade later Horsley also noted that 'the ramparts at Brugh are levelled by the plow'. But despite the absence of overground remains, there was plenty to unearth below the ground.

Stukeley's account continued:

> *...there have been many Roman coynes dug up here and all the way between it and Newark. I bought a large brass Faustina junior* [a Roman coin], *lately found in the cornfield over-against the alehouse. In digging too they found great foundations for half a mile together on either side of the road, with much rusty iron, iron oar and iron cinders, so that it's probable here was an eminent Roman forge. Across the road was a vast foundation of a wall, and part still remains. Out of one hole they showed me has been dug up 10 or 15 load of stone, so that it should seem to have been a gate. The stones at the foundation are observ'd to be plac'd edgewise, and very large ones, but not of a good sort. This was the method the Romans justly thought the most convenient, in this springly soil, for the springs rise here all about, within two foot of the surface. They told me some very large copper Roman coyns have been found here, and silver too, and many pots, urns, bricks etc. They call the money Brough pennys.*

Horsley said that the old man he bought the Roman coin from told him that 'they often struck upon ruins in plowing or digging, and had a tradition of an old town formerly standing there'.

When Smith Woolley came along in the early 20th century he lamented that medieval and modern builders and road menders had removed so much stone from both above and below ground that reconstructing the Roman settlement at Brough was 'almost pure guesswork'. However, he found the foundations of a wall 1.5 metres (5ft) thick almost at right angles to the Fosse. This, and the remains of the fallen upper structures, led him to believe that he'd found a Roman house with mud walls. Plaster and vivid paintwork could still be seen. The roof had been made of red pantiles similar to those seen in Tuscany and, he said, Collingham. Elsewhere, said Smith Woolley, the meagre evidence suggested that other structures here had been made of timber.

Initially at least, enough of the finds were taken back to Smith Woolley's home in Collingham that his house was likened to a small museum. However, like items excavated from *Ad Pontem*, Smith Woolley's finds at *Crococolana* were subsequently loaned to Newark for public display and they are currently stored in Newark and Sherwood District Council's Resource Centre as part of a collection of 60,000 local historic objects. After his main excavations, Smith Woolley's enthusiasm for the site was such that he purchased a nearby field in Brough where he continued digging.

A deeply religious man whose many activities included educational welfare and work for Southwell Diocese, Smith Woolley died in 1913 when he was cycling back to Collingham on a February evening. He collided with a pedestrian, fractured his skull and died the following morning, his only spoken words after the collision being 'oh dear'. His obituary, which filled an entire broadsheet page in the *Newark Advertiser*, reported that this pillar of the community 'did much to [re]move the reproach which had lain long against Notts. antiquaries that they had done so little to bare the history of Notts. during the Roman occupation'.

Later, aerial photography of Brough, by J.K. St Joseph, appeared to confirm the impression that *Crococolana* had been one of Roman Britain's 'loosely-planned road-side settlements'. St Joseph saw 'a maze of pits, drains, post-holes' in the sub-soil on the western side of Brough and he also identified the defensive ditches. But overall 'little sign of planning appears' and *Crococolana* seemed to be 'a straggling settlement grown up beside the Fosse' which had not been bound by its defences. In 2001, further excavations took place in advance of the construction of the A46 bypass at Brough. Many of the finds were Iron Age, but the work did identify traces of Roman-period agriculture and a single cremation burial. Other Roman ditches and pottery suggested occupation over the late 2nd century to the mid 3rd century.

Anybody who watches the TV series *Time Team* may remember the episode where Tony Robinson and colleagues excavated the fields around Ancaster and found a coffin bearing the name of a local Roman god. However, the initial suspicion that the coffin may have had lead in it prompted serious health concerns. The archaeologist Mick Aston was warned that if he wanted to open the coffin, he would have to don contamination suits because of the risk of lead oxidation. Did he want to continue? Did he have the suits to protect him and others from the risk of contamination by airborne lead particles? If not, the opening of the coffin would have to be delayed. But, oh for the days before 'elf and safety, when people didn't make such a fuss over potentially fatal risks like lead poisoning. Because if they had, there would have been a lot of standing around doing nothing when *Crococolana* produced an unmarked lead coffin, unearthed in a farmer's field just 40cm under the soil. This was 1940. Because the field had previously been ploughed by a heavy steam plough, part of the coffin lid had been bent and it was this which was seen sticking up above the soil. No doubt because this was war-time, the farmer reported the find to the police with the words, 'Believed unexploded bomb in field near church farm, Brough'. A police sergeant subsequently arrived and discovered the coffin. A 1.7 metre (5ft 8in) skeleton was found inside. Arthur Smith, of Newark's library and museum, recalled the moment with this cheery description: 'The remains of the skeleton existed in a conglomerate and decomposed mass on the bottom of the coffin and extremely few bones were removed complete; even these crumble to dust if touched with anything but the lightest pressure.'

In 1971, two more coffins were found by a teenager called

Now, just where did I put those Roman coffins...? The three Brough coffins in storage in Newark. The one in the foreground also has its skeleton on display inside.

John Hart using what the *Newark Advertiser* described as a '£40 metal detector'. The first was found in a sugar beet field at Little Danethorpe Farm, just off the A46 immediately south of Brough, and was reported to have been '100 yards' from the 1940 coffin. The skeleton of a man was inside. 'The coffin is only 5ft 8ins long and it looks as though his head was chopped off to fit him in a coffin they had handy at the time,' the *Advertiser* merrily reported. Then, later in the year, Hart found another coffin. This time the newspaper declared that it was a '1,650-year-old lead coffin containing the skeleton of a pagan settler!' No doubt about that, then. Hart also found the decorated handle of a Roman skillet in 1972. Bearing a vine-leaf motif, and coloured blue, green and red, the handle attracted scholarly interest because of the rarity of objects decorated in this style. As well as the items such as the copper cavalry helmet, cheek-piece and face jars, described in Chapter 4, finds at *Crococolana* included metalwork such as a delicate and finely worked silver 'ear pick' — an item whose role is now performed by the contemporary cotton bud.

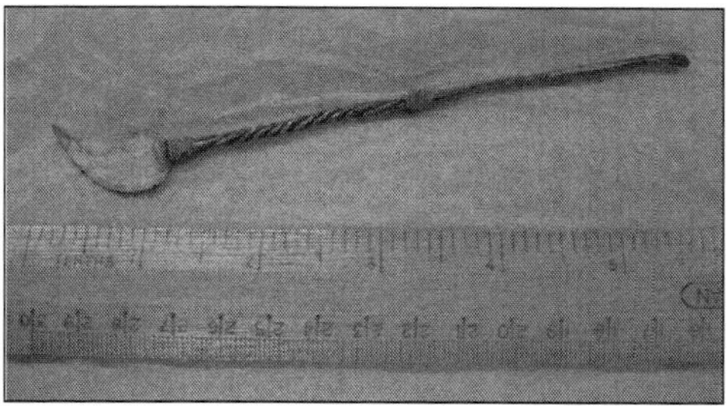

Silver ear pick found at Brough.

One other impressive find from the area is the detailed copper alloy statue of a male rider on a horse. This statue, found by a metal detectorist, was acquired by the British Museum in 1990 and is described as that of a warrior god. The site of the find was just over the Lincolnshire border, near Norton Disney, where the villa was excavated by Adrian Oswald in the 1930s. In Roman times the people of *Crococolana* and the villa must have regarded each other as neighbours. Today, the two locations are separated by the county border, which runs down the middle of the Fosse Way for a distance. The border's dog-leg shape puts Norton Disney on the Lincolnshire side, but leaves a Roman track called North Scaffold Lane, which must have led to the villa to the east, on the Nottinghamshire side. Just 2.5km (1.5 miles) to the west of Brough, at Holme, Roman troops also constructed a temporary camp but it is not known whether it had any relationship with

Statue of horse and rider found at Norton Disney. The rider is missing a spear, shield, left hand and leg.

the settlement at Brough.

About Newark

One of the antiquarian William Stukeley's stranger if forgiveable ideas was that Newark had been the site of a Roman town called *Eltavona*. In fact, the name was pure invention, being based on arcane etymological procedures of the kind that antiquarians of the 18th and 19th centuries revelled in. One other such local reveller was William Dickinson, who repeated the fiction in his *History and Antiquities of the Town of Newark,* published in 1816. But Stukeley also believed that Newark was 'certainly raised from the neighbouring Roman cities' of *Ad Pontem* and *Crococolana*, suggesting he thought that the very stone used to build Newark had been taken from those Roman settlements. Given his own observation that the people of Newark lifted stone from the Fosse Way to mend their own streets, this isn't so far-fetched. Indeed, Newark's name, originating as 'new work', suggesting a fort, seems to distinguish it from the 'old work' of other defences, perhaps those of *Ad Pontem* or *Crococolana.*

Meanwhile, other 18th century scholars wrongly put Newark forward as the site of *Ad Pontem*. This seemed to be confirmed by Dickinson's report of the discovery of the stone foundations of an 'immense bridge' across the Trent downstream near Cromwell during the dry summers of 1792 and '93. Here at last was the long-lost Roman bridge over the Trent everyone had been looking for. Dickinson argued that the bridge proved that a Roman road had crossed the Trent in a straight line from Southwell to Brough via Mickleborough Hill, near Upton. Over a century later, in 1884, the same bridge foundations were found during dredging. However, these were removed to improve the navigation of the river and archaeologists have since demonstrated to their own satisfaction that the bridge dated from the Saxon era in the 8th century. Despite this, it's understandable how historians could think Newark had Roman origins given the modern town's straddling of the Fosse and its location approximately mid-way between Nottingham and Lincoln. In fact, despite wrong turns over *Eltavona* and so on, the antiquarians weren't wrong in the substance of their belief; modern archaeologists have since produced evidence that Newark was a 'substantial' Roman roadside settlement with the Fosse Way, running through modern Millgate, Castlegate, Bargate and Northgate, perhaps being the 'earliest man-made feature present in the modern topography', according to one report.

This certainly marks a change in perception from that prevailing for at least the first half of the 20th century. In 1955, for example, historians writing for the Thoroton Society said: 'At Newark there is evidence for no more than some casual squatting, and perhaps some industry of a rural nature, at what was in Roman times a road junction of local importance.' The road junction referred to was that of the Fosse Way with Sewstern Lane, which runs for 18.5km (11.5 miles) north west from Thistleton on Ermine Street towards Long Bennington and then up the Great North Road to Balderton, immediately south of Newark, largely following county and parish boundaries. Much of this track is now marked as the 'Viking Way' and can be followed easily using OS Explorer 247. There's a tradition of assuming that Roman Newark developed where it did as a result of the junction of Sewstern Lane and the Fosse. Further proof of Sewstern Lane's importance in this regard has been the claim that the Anglo-Saxon name for Balderton's main street was *Beauverestrete,* with *strete* usually indicating a paved Roman road. Ivan Margary accepted that Sewstern Lane had been a prehistoric trackway, but thought that only part of it bore evidence of Roman engineering. Whatever the case, although Sewstern Lane was marked as a probable Roman road on the 1955 OS map of Roman Britain, it was omitted when the latest version came out.

Although Newark didn't merit mention in the various Roman itineraries, it is now thought that it had two phases of Roman settlement, the first having a 'high status or military character' in the 1st and early 2nd centuries, associated with the period of invasion and conquest, the second in the late 3rd and 4th centuries. Cornelius Brown's *A History of Newark-on-Trent*, published in 1904, devoted several pages to Roman history and described the many Roman coins and pieces of pottery that had been found in the town, especially in the Spitals. According to Brown, a quantity of grey earthenware, arranged in a kiln, had been dug up a few years before. He said these had identical mouldings to the pottery found at Brough, but were 'unfortunately broken' and most of the pieces were thrown away before their value was realised. Coins were also found on nearby land and a complete urn was unearthed on a site 'now occupied by the maltings of Messrs. R. Bishop and Sons'.

A handful of excavations in the 20th century turned up numerous other Roman finds and established that there had been a Roman settlement around the Fosse in Northgate. In 1978, a gardener in the Northgate Allotments found a 'plaster floor and tumbled wall matter' (sounds like many other allotments in that sense). In 1988, Roman pottery was found under the rampart of Anglo-Saxon town defences less than a kilometre from Northgate. Then, in 2003, an archaeological 'strip and record exercise' also took place in Trent Lane ahead of a new store and parking development. The site was 25 metres (82ft) from Northgate and next to what was described as the 'important and extensive Romano-British small town'. Trenches were dug that revealed archaeology dating from both the Roman and the English Civil War periods. The Roman finds dated from the 3rd and 4th centuries and included a skeleton with a bone hair pin and copper alloy jewellery. More than 16kg of Roman pottery sherds were also unearthed. Four post-holes suggested that there had been a raised granary inside some kind of enclosure, marked by ditches. The burial was found inside this enclosure and may have been part of a wider cemetery. What did the existence of this skeleton suggest? Since it was normal Roman practice in the 1st and 2nd centuries to burn the dead, the burial suggested that the body had been placed in the ground in the 3rd or 4th century when customs for the disposal of the dead had changed. But, secondly, its location within a settlement area suggested that the Roman settlement at Newark itself was shrinking, since previously occupied ground was now being used for the burial. 'What is perhaps most striking is that the burial seems to indicate a change of land use as a result of a declining population in the late 4th century,' said Richard Cuttler and Eleanor Ramsey, who led the dig. The settlement continued to contract and eventually, towards the end of the 4th century, it reverted to woodland.

Yet whatever was left of Roman Newark, it cannot be a coincidence that the Germanic immigrants who followed the Romans into the East Midlands also saw good reason to settle in the area. Again, perhaps the junction of roads and river was an attraction. The large Anglo-Saxon cemetery at Millgate, excavated in the 1960s and '70s, was found to contain 400 cremated remains in urns, four of which were Roman — 'possibly salvaged from the settlement on Northgate', said archaeologist Gavin Kinsley. Finally, some debate has taken place over whether the line of the Fosse through Newark is the Roman one, since the modern road veers away from a straight line through the town. In 1968, when the bridge over the river Devon, at the southern entrance to Newark, was being built, the discovery of timber piles in the river bed and an almost intact Roman pot suggested, at the very least, that the Roman road had entered the town at the same place as the modern road.

Tracing the Roman Fosse Way today

It was after the First World War that aerial observation began to help transform the Ordnance Survey's hitherto hazy mapping of Roman antiquities into the accurate form we know now. This development seems particularly apt for the Fosse Way, since travelling along the length of the modern A46 by air has to be far preferable to driving along it. Margary's road 5f is fast, busy and noisy with the constant thunder of HGVs. The road is a wide dual carriageway in its northern and southern portions and another major section between Newark and Widmerpool was being dualled at the time of writing. This was due to open in the summer of 2012.

According to the Highways Agency, the Widmerpool–Newark

section carries 16,200–25,300 vehicles per day, of which up to 15 per cent are heavy goods vehicles. Meanwhile, pavements along the A46 are a rare surprise. Walking along the verge cannot be recommended. And crossing the road may involve making a risk/benefit calculation. The double irony here is that the very use of the road by modern traffic which has helped preserve the route chosen by the Roman surveyors has helped to undermine or destroy the sense of it being an ancient Roman highway — except, that is, in its width and its very straightness. But of course this straight quality is not unusual, since straight Roman roads can be seen across Britain. And there are examples of Roman highways where original features such as the raised *agger* or road surfaces with kerbstones can be seen. But these are not features associated with the Fosse Way in Nottinghamshire. So is there anything Roman left about the A46? Sort of.

Firstly, as has been mentioned, excavations have revealed that the original Roman road exists under the modern tarmac in places. In 2002, dualling work revealed the cobbled ghost of the ancient highway between Winthorpe roundabout and the junction with the A1133 Collingham road. The occasion was marked by a press release from the Highways Agency, the communiqué adding: 'The new road will be built over it, preserving it for future generations.' Which, you might say, is a nice way of saying that nobody will see that part of the original Roman road again for decades to come. But it is interesting that the Highways Agency has also helped revive the name *Margidunum,* the name it routinely uses today for the roundabout that was built over the fort's southern defences in the late 1960s.

For modern Fosse Way hunters, though, potentially more exciting than any of this is that the ancient road does not follow the line of the A46 exactly. Look at OS Explorer map 246 and you can see a dotted line veering away from the A46 across private farmland between Willoughby Fields Farm and Lodge Farm near the Nottinghamshire border with Leicestershire. This is the straight line of the Roman road that was projected, following the excavations in the 1960s at Willoughby, when the Fosse was found to be 90 metres west of the A46. This line of the Fosse was established by the excavations and subsequent 'probing'. Alas, the surface of the Fosse found here was all covered over again years ago and there's no sign of the old road on the

Approximate beginning of the projected route of the Roman Fosse Way heading north between Willoughby Fields Farm and Lodge Farm. The A46 is over the hedge on the right.

ground today. At least not here.

Further north, near East Bridgford, the ridged remains of the earliest line of the Fosse Way are said to be present running north from *Margidunum*. The feature is now very faint and described as being visible only in certain light. However, in the past it has been described as a low ridge running parallel and 140m west of the A46, and was consequently known locally as 'the hump'. Felix Oswald noticed it during his excavations and believed it marked the original course of the Fosse before it was straightened in the early 2nd century. Oswald said the original road leading into *Margidunum* came from the south west. An aerial photograph published in 1939 appears to show the north-bound road as a faint track running across the fields, with the road to *Margidunum* from the south entering at an angle of the defences. Another aerial photograph shows the north-bound track running across fields opposite Flintham Park. The course of this ridge was subsequently traced as far as Kneeton.

Sections of 'the hump' were excavated by Maurice Barley at Kneeton and Syerston airfield, recording what seemed to be clear evidence of a rounded road profile. Then, in 1966, when the ridge was showing particularly well on the surface of the fields, new air photography was taken and sections of the road were excavated at the southern and northern boundaries of Syerston airfield, the latter location where the ridge crosses the east–west running Longhedge Lane, itself an ancient track pre-dating the Romans. Malcolm Todd helped excavate the ridge at these two points and found the Roman road surface to be 3–3.5 metres (10–12 ft) wide, with perhaps two successive surfaces. The road surface was made of skerry (sandstone) slabs laid on beds of gravel and marl at one cutting, and a mixture of gravel and small stone fragments at the other. Todd observed that the road seemed to be 'remarkably narrow' but speculated that the earliest Roman roads, laid out in freshly conquered territory, were not always the finished article.

If all this is correct, then 'the hump' would seem to mark the early course of the Fosse Way that may have been constructed during or soon after the Roman army's advance into what is now modern Nottinghamshire. Todd added: 'Any extension of this length of road northward is conjectural, but it is worth noting that, unless there was any marked deflection to the north-north-east, this alignment would meet the A46 precisely at the south defences of *Ad Pontem* in the parish of Thorpe.'[22] However, an archaeologist involved in the latest A46 dualling scheme revealed to this author that, despite extensive recent excavations along the length of 'the hump', no evidence of a Roman road has been found anywhere. Where this leaves the feature investigated so assiduously by Barley and Todd is open to debate.

For the sake of clarity it should also be mentioned here that one of the other roads Oswald believed he had found at *Margidunum* in the 1930s was the *via Principalis*, the main Roman road running south east–north west through the heart of the town. Extended north westwards, Oswald said this road became Bridgford Street and crossed the Trent. Continuing northwards, he said it would have passed close to the villa at

The bridlepath running towards East Bridgford from *Margidunum*.

Mansfield Woodhouse and proceeded towards Chesterfield. It was speculation. However, today the approximate course of the Roman road heading west out of *Margidunum* towards East Bridgford and the Trent is thought to be preserved by the bridle-path that runs along the bottom of fields parallel to the A6097 Lowdham road.

Further on, Bridgford Street exists as a lane running into East Bridgford and another bridleway runs off it down hill to the Trent, presumably also preserving the route of the Roman road. Over time the track from the Fosse has variously been named as Bridgford Street, Burrows Road and Newton Street or Lane. However, a map of 1612, reproduced in a history of the village, gave an earlier name for this route as Street Way. This seems to suggest its Roman origins. The same track was said to have been in use as a packhorse route at the end of the 18th century. An information sign in East Bridgford pointing out the existence of the track to the Trent is one of the few public notices in the county which acknowledges local Roman heritage.

But where did the road from *Margidunum* go when it reached the Trent? Gunthorpe lies on the opposite bank and it has long been believed that a Roman bridge here linking *Margidunum* with the west side of the Trent was the bridge implied in the name *Ad Pontem*. According to at least one 19th century archae-ological sleuth, Frank Miles of Bingham, an old road called Newton Street was marked on the OS map coming down to the

Public notice in East Bridgford.

Trent on the Gunthorpe side. In 1910, the *Victoria County History* noted: 'It is known as Newton Street or Bridgeford Street... The writers who placed *Ad Pontem* here naturally saw in this the Roman road leading to the supposed bridge.' But no ancient bridge here has been found. An alternative is that the Trent was crossed by a paved ford here and local lore has it that there was a ford near the site of the old toll bridge, which was opened in 1875 and replaced by the present road bridge in 1927. A ferry also crossed the Trent here and was marked on the first one-inch Old Series OS map of Nottingham in the 19th century. In summary, there's a long history of the Trent being crossed one way or another at the place where a Roman road from *Margidunum* came down to the river. Indeed, in his history of East Bridgford published in 1932, the Rev. Arthur Du Boulay Hill said that wagons had forded the river here within his memory. It has been speculated that a road also led south east from *Margidunum* towards Bingham and the Vale of Belvoir. One of the findings of the *Margidunum* excavations carried out as part of the most recent A46 dualling was a 3–4 metre (10–13ft) length of road heading east from the Fosse.

Further north, just before Thorpe, the Fosse Way 'appears rather winding and distorted' (according to Ivan Margary). Then, at Thorpe itself, an older route of the Fosse, running north east of the A46, can be seen as a cropmark in aerial photographs of the site. This early route of the road was probably straightened out early in the Roman occupation as the settlement evolved. Certainly, old maps of Thorpe (such as a manorial map of 1712 in the Nottinghamshire Archives) show the Fosse Way following the same course as the modern A46. During excavations at Thorpe in the 1930s Adrian Oswald thought that a 'well marked embankment' running across fields next to the A46 was the line of the original Fosse Way. Although later excavations concluded the bank was post-Roman, another section of road thought to be the real thing was examined by archaeologist John Wacher in the mid-1960s. This road started from the point where the track to Thorpe hamlet meets the A46 and ran north east across the fields to the boundary with Farndon parish (this all makes more sense if you have OS Explorer map 270 to hand). Wacher found gravel had been removed to provide a foundation for the modern road. Only the earliest phase of the Roman road was left intact, a layer of gravel measuring 7.3 metres (24ft) across. Wacher was actually interviewed by the *Nottingham Evening Post* at Thorpe in 1965 and told the reporter that, 'it seems obvious that most of the metalling of the original road has been robbed at later dates, probably accounting for the present deviation'.

North of Newark there is another area where the Roman road and the A46 part company. Or at least they did when Ivan Margary described it in the 1950s. Margary said that in a field on the eastern side of the A46, opposite Langford Hall between Newark and Brough, he saw a length of the original Roman *agger* nine metres long and 0.6 metres high (30ft long and 2ft high), completely free of the modern road. 'As the only piece of the original Foss Way that can be well seen free from modern disturbance for a very long distance this merits strict preservation,' he wrote. J.H.B. Peel, a countryside writer for the *Daily Telegraph*, also saw this feature a few years later. 'Here the main road runs parallel with a grassy tract of the Foss, thirty feet wide, foretasting the pleasures that lie ahead,' he wrote in *Along the Roman Roads of Britain*, published in 1971. 'Excavations revealed two roads on this sector, more or less side by side. The older course was ten feet narrower than the newer.'

Sadly, Margary's call for preservation went unheeded as no terrain feature of his description is to be seen in this area today. In the 1970s, the remains of the road here were described as 'a ridge about 2 feet high in a farmer's field'. But it has all now completely disappeared, eroded by ploughing and finally eaten up by the construction of this section of modern dual carriageway in 2002. "It's now underneath the north-bound carriageway," one local archaeologist told me. Despite this loss, anyone searching this area for remants of Margary's and Peel's Fosse Way remains — as I did — will quickly appreciate just how relatively quiet the A46 must have been in their day. Today there is nowhere 'to stop and stare', as J.H.B. Peel wrote, since there is no safe place to park on the eastern, southbound carriageway. Two metal barriers between the carriageways also dissuade you from walking over from the other side of the road. To get a look I had to park up in Thorpe and walk back down the road verge. Take great care if you want to do the same.

Margary said the Fosse Way where it reached Brough was 'considerably distorted', possibly describing the ripples its course follows as it leads up to the hamlet. However, this section of the road has at least been left relatively intact since a bypass now takes A46 traffic past the village. Indeed, according to local newspaper reports in August 2002, one of the reasons the Highways Agency built the bypass was so that heavy traffic would avoid the Roman site. Before this, in 1979, two laybys on either side of the A46 were built near Brough which revealed a small section of the Roman road. Excavations for the modern road went down to 70cm, with the top of the Roman highway being seen 65cm down under clay. The width of the Roman road was around 9 metres (29ft 6in), the road being made of rammed gravel over 30cm deep, beneath two layers of limestone paving. Gravel lay on top of the paving. The double layer of paving was interpreted as evidence of resurfacing. When William Stukeley came here in 1722 he sketched the view along the road but said that the Fosse Way at Brough was actually ploughed over.

The Fosse undergoes a slight course change on the high ground at Potter Hill a little further north of Brough before exiting the county for Lincoln. Here, Thomas Codrington wrote: 'The road appears to have been fenced in 20 to 30 yards wide, and to have since been encroached upon in many places, by which the general straightness is disguised.' The track called North

View south along the Fosse from Potter Hill just before the road leaves Nottinghamshire for Lincoln, from William Stukeley's *Itinerarium Curiosum* in 1724. The tower in the distance is Newark. Brough, or 'Crocolana', is marked at A.

Scaffold Lane runs west to Collingham near here and is marked as a Roman road on the OS map. There's also a Romanstone Plantation and a Villa Farm, next to the site of the Roman villa at Norton Disney.

Roman well found near *Margidunum* in 2009.

The dualling of the A46

A long-delayed project to improve the safety and capacity of 28km (17 miles) of the Fosse Way in Nottinghamshire began in the spring of 2009 and is due to be finished on 19 April, 2012. This large scheme between Newark and Widmerpool, with an estimated cost of £322m–£409m, has involved constructing a new dual carriageway, new bridges, roundabout improvements, new junctions (one at *Margidunum*) and a bypass for East Stoke and Farndon. The scheme, which was approved by the then transport minister and Ashfield MP Geoff Hoon, was expected to improve safety on the Fosse Way while cutting 20–25 minutes off an average peak time journey. According to Highways Agency figures, between 2001 and 2005 there were 13 fatal, 56 serious and 222 slight accidents on the existing A46. This dangerous record stems in part from the fact that the road follows the largely straight but narrow and undulating Roman route beneath. Or as the Highways Agency puts it: 'This can make safe overtaking difficult and it is made worse by many junctions and accesses to fields, farms and houses.'

In addition to the safety improvements, a report commissioned by the due-to-be-abolished East Midlands Development Agency concluded that the scheme will deliver £21.7m in productivity gains to the region by 2017. So it's a win-win situation. Or is it? One impact that has been little commented on is that the full widening of this part of the A46 means that long stretches of it will finally lose almost all their remaining semblance to the Roman road underneath. 'Already the dual carriageway has crept as far north as Widmerpool and you can be left in no doubt, as you drive along the rest of the modern A46, with all those heavy lorries, that from a motorist's point of view, it is a dangerous road which cries out to be widened. When that happens the Roman Fosse Way will be lost forever.' So wrote the authors of a short BBC guide to the road, back in 1976.[23] Although their timing estimate for further dualling of the Fosse was premature, their fear that people would no longer be able to see 'anything approaching its ancient imperial splendour' is being largely borne out. While this is a concern that is always going to be outweighed by the scheme's claimed safety improvements, the new road's detrimental impact on the Fosse Way's historic character may be remembered when future generations lament the creeping loss of Britain's ancient landscape features. During the construction of the road the Highways Agency has also been criticised for the loss of natural features such as ancient woodland.[24]

On the other hand, extensive archaeological studies of land along and adjacent to the A46 route, carried out as part of the scheme, have revealed or investigated many new previously unknown or suspected Iron Age, Saxon and Roman features. The contract for investigating and monitoring this aspect of the road project went to a private archaeology partnership, Wessex Cotswold Archaeology (CWA), which was a collaboration between two practices, Wessex Archaeology and Cotswold Archaeology. The two firms have since merged. Investigations into the potential impact of the road on the Fosse's archaeology were carried out from the early 1990s onwards but work carried on into new assessment reports after the main contractor Balfour Beatty was appointed in 2004. For the Roman period particular interest focused on *Ad Pontem* and *Margidunum*, both of which are Scheduled Ancient Monuments. Some details of the *Margidunum* excavations were revealed at a public meeting in March 2010 and these are mostly detailed in Chapter 3. In the summer of 2009, as a result of the surveys, a Roman well was also found near *Margidunum* roundabout. The well, or least the top metre of it, was dismantled and donated to the Bingham Heritage Trails Association which intended to reconstruct it and put it on display — finally giving Nottinghamshire an intact, if small, Roman structure. The discovery was widely reported in local media. According to Nottinghamshire County Council senior archaeology officer, Ursilla Spence, the well further modified opinion on *Margidunum*. "The fact that the well was found outside what we thought were the boundaries has opened our eyes to the size of the town," she was quoted in the *Nottingham Evening Post*. "The well was found underneath a Roman road so we have to deduce that the Romans would have covered over the well to provide access into a high status residence." But although a public summary of the full findings along the A46 is expected to be published, it is doubtful whether a full detailed report will be released to the public.

Scheme maps show how the new A46 will deal with the Scheduled Ancient Monuments at *Margidunum* and *Ad Pontem*. At the former, the new road swings clear of the site to the west of the Fosse Way; at the latter, the new road bypasses the site to the east. However, one ancient feature, the pre-Roman trackway Longhedge Lane, which crosses the Fosse Way at Syerston

Top: Longhedge Lane with Syerston airfield to the right and the Fosse Way ahead plus the usual fly-tipping and (bottom) the notice that used to read 'Longhedge Lane' amid the signs of impending dual carriageway construction

airfield, is being blocked off and diverted to a new bridge. Since Longhedge Lane is the southern fork of Sewstern Lane, which links the Fosse Way with Ermine Street in Lincolnshire, it plays a part in the local Iron Age/Roman road network and its further bisection by the new road has to be regretted. The new junction means that the ancient route is being divorced from its original junction with the Roman road for the first time in two thousand years.

Late flowering red campion *Silene dioica* on Longhedge Lane leading to its crossing of the Fosse Way on its eastern side in November 2009. The ancient byway at this point was officially off-limits to all traffic including pedestrians due to construction work on the new dual carriageway, which meant walking here to take this photograph was illegal. This crossroads of the ancient trackway and the Fosseway no longer exists.

Notes

1. *The History of the Countryside* — Oliver Rackham. Phoenix Press, 2000.
2. *Roman Britain and the English Settlements* — R.G. Collingwood and J.N.L. Myres. Oxford University Press, 1937, 2nd edition reprinted 1975.
3. *Roman Roads in Britain* — Ivan D. Margary. Two volumes. Phoenix House, 1955 and 1957.
4. *Archaeology of the Fosse Way, Volume 2. Implications of the Proposed Dualling of the A46 between Newark and Widmerpool* —

D. Knight and G. Kinsley. Trent and Peak Archaeological Trust Report, 1992.
5. Review of Ivan Margary's *Roman Roads in Britain, Vol. II, North of the Foss Way–Bristol Channel (Including Wales and Scotland).* The *Journal of Roman Studies* 48, 1958.
6. *The Jewish War* — Josephus. Penguin Classics, 1981.
7. *Invasion: The Roman Conquest of Britain* — John Peddie. Guild Publishing, 1987.
8. *The Dukeries Advertiser* 19/3/2002.
9. Ibid. 19/4/2002.
10. *Itinerarium Curiosum, Or an Account of the Antiquitys and Remarkable Curiositys in Nature or Art, Observ'd in Travels thro' Great Britain* — William Stukeley. Printed for the Author, 1724.
11. *Roads in Roman Britain* — Hugh Davies. Tempus, 2002.
12. Ibid.
13. *The History of the Countryside* — Oliver Rackham. Phoenix Press, 2000.
14. *Itinerarium Curiosum, Or an Account of the Antiquitys and Remarkable Curiositys in Nature or Art, Observ'd in Travels thro' Great Britain* — William Stukeley. Printed for the Author, 1724.
15. *The Antiquities of Nottinghamshire* Vols I, II and III, edited and enlarged by John Throsby, originally published in 1790 and 1796, reprinted by EP Publishing Ltd in collaboration with Nottinghamshire County Library, 1972.
16. *Britannia Romana or the Roman Antiquities of Britain* — John Horsley. Originally published 1732. Frank Graham, 2nd edition, 1974.
17. *Excavations on the Romano-British Settlement and Anglo-Saxon Cemetery at Broughton Lodge, Willoughby-on- the-Wolds, Nottinghamshire 1964–68* — M.J. Dean and A.G. Kinsley. Nottinghamshire Archaeological Monographs 4, published by Department of Classical and Archaeological Studies (Archaeology Section), University of Nottingham, 1993.
18. Holme Pierrepont — D.G. Bilton. *Nottinghamshire Countryside* 32 1, 1971.
19. Excavations at Ad Pontem, Thorpe Parish, Notts — R.R. Inskeep. *Transactions of the Thoroton Society of Nottinghamshire* 69, 1965.
20. *The Annals* — Tacitus. Oxford World's Classics, 2008.
21. The Roman Station of Ad Pontem, now East Stoke; its Origin, and the Derivation of its Name — Felix Oswald. *Transactions of the Thoroton Society of Nottinghamshire* 55, 1951.
22. The Early Course of the Fosse Way: Kneeton to East Stoke — Malcolm Todd. *Transactions of the Thoroton Society of Nottinghamshire* 70, 1966.
23. *The Fosse Way in Nottinghamshire and Lincolnshire* — Trevor Dann and Keith Train. BBC Radio Nottingham, 1976.
24. Wildlife Trust in Complaints over A46 Habitat Loss. *Nottingham Evening Post*, 13 October, 2009.

Chapter 6

To the ford at Littleborough and the temple at Redhill

Those seeking a less life-threatening Roman road experience than the modern Fosse Way should head for the relatively unspoiled stretch of road linking Littleborough with Bawtry in the top north east corner of Nottinghamshire. Mostly quiet and satisfyingly straight, travelling this road also means making a visit to the hamlet of Littleborough which, marking as it does a Roman crossing point of the Trent, resonates with the unseen presence of ancient ghosts in transit. And somehow, despite the visual intrusion of the two huge power stations nearby, Cottam and West Burton, Littleborough also manages to remain one of the most tranquil and disarming locations in the whole of Nottinghamshire.

The 51km (32 mile) Lincoln–Doncaster road on which the Romans built their little town of Littleborough, called *Segelocum* (also *Segeloci or Ageloco*), perhaps within ten years of the invasion of Britain, is thought to have been a later addition to the road network in the region, providing a method of accessing the route to the new legionary fortress and Roman northern capital at York, *Eboracum*. The road has been described as a territory-holding road, meaning it was meant to define territory newly occupied by the Roman army, in contrast to penetration roads such as Ermine Street which facilitated the direct march and supply of the legions. Before the Lincoln–Doncaster highway was built, travellers going north from Lincoln would have had to head straight up Ermine Street and risk a ferry crossing across the Humber estuary. Instead, the new road struck straight west from a junction with Ermine Street 5.5km (3.5 miles) north of Lincoln and continued directly to the Trent. At Littleborough on the western side of the river the road veered north west to Bawtry, then to Doncaster, called *Danum* by the Romans, then to Castleford and Tadcaster. 'This route involves crossing the rivers Trent, Don and Aire, but avoids all other considerable rivers, and though somewhat longer than the Ermine Street route is yet very direct,' wrote Ivan Margary.[1]

The Lincoln–Doncaster road was included in the *Antonine Itinerary* in Itineraries V (London–Carlisle) and VIII (York–London), the latter routeing travellers up the Fosse Way to Lincoln before turning off for Littleborough. The milestone putting the distance at 14 Roman miles is described in Chapter 4. The Littleborough–Bawtry route was mapped as a Roman road in the late 18th century, being marked as such on a County Map of 1789 by Noble and Cary. However, decades before this, the antiquarian John Horsley had suspected there was a Roman road here. 'The military way between Littleborough and Doncaster... is but obscure,' he wrote.[2] 'I have oftener than once enquired and sought for it, but could neither see nor hear any thing of it that was certain... .' Horsley thought he could discern a Roman road at the Doncaster end and added: 'However, there is no doubt but a military way has gone from Littleborough to Doncaster...the distance of sixteen computed miles from Littleborough answers to 21 in this iter, for the distance between Segelocum and Danum.' Strangely, the Elizabethan traveller John Leland, in the 1540s, had no trouble finding the same road and described crossing the Trent from the Lincolnshire side and following 'Watling Street' as the 'public route to Doncaster'.[3]

Today, much of the Roman road to Doncaster can be followed or projected on OS maps. Margary numbered this road 28 and while the Roman route is swallowed up by the old Great North Road after Bawtry, following the Bawtry–Littleborough section makes for a good day out on a bicycle (if you can handle one steep hill). The road can be followed easily in either direction, but travelling towards Littleborough has the bonus of finishing the journey at the Trent on a very straight section of quiet narrow road on which it is possible to envisage Roman travellers moving to and from what was an important river crossing. Indeed, T. Cecil Smith Woolley — he who excavated *Crococolana* — was moved to remark that Littleborough was 'one of the more important points of the great Roman Empire, so far, at least, as regards its splendid dependency of Britain'. It is easy to agree with him. This tiny hamlet, now supporting only a farm, some cottages and a small Norman church, was important enough to merit inclusion in two of the travelling routes of the *Antonine Itinerary*, a document which covered road travel in the Roman Empire as far east as Jerusalem. Littleborough guarded the key river crossing on the most direct route between the *colonia* at Lincoln and the new military base at York; if the Trent crossing had been lost to hostile forces these two Roman cities would have been cut off from one another or have been forced to communicate via the Humber. Belying its bucolic tranquillity, Littleborough could arguably be considered as one of the most strategically important Roman sites in the county and region.

Today, the fast wide main Bawtry Road/A631 heading east out of Bawtry and across the river Idle doesn't bear any resemblance to the quiet roads up ahead. Margary noted that the main road 'shows signs that it had the same wide verges noted previously on this route', but its real point of interest is that it gives a view over a site immediately to the north marked as a Roman fortlet on OS Explorer map 279. This site is dealt with below. The road then bows south to Scaftworth before turning awkwardly and abruptly south just after Everton village and, after perambulating around Drakeholes and the Chesterfield Canal, assumes a reassuringly straight and distinctly Romanish course all the way to the Trent. According to a 1909 report by the Thoroton Society, many 'relics of the Roman occupation' were found when the canal tunnel here was being cut. After Drakeholes, modern travellers heading towards Littleborough follow a mostly straight road which passes the estate of Wiseton Park and Clayworth village. Margary said the Roman road 'may indeed be visible as a wide ridge in the roadside copse' of Wiseton Park. Further on, from the top of Haughgate Hill, once known locally as 'Awkward Hill' (try cycling up it), you get a fine view of the Roman highway stretching onwards to the Trent.

The view along the Roman road towards the Trent from the top of Haughgate Hill.

The road gets slightly lost through the next villages of North and South Wheatley but its approximately straight route seems to follow a footpath joining the two communities. An upper portion of a Roman tombstone, found in 1929, can be seen in the church of St Peter and St Paul in North Wheatley.

After South Wheatley, the route is preserved by Wheatley Road which continues to Sturton-le-Steeple. Again, the straight road has been lost here but projected onwards the Roman road would have bypassed the village at an angle and joined the current road leading directly to Littleborough behind Low Holland Farm. The line of the road seems to be marked by an overgrown hedgerow behind the farm. At last you're on Littleborough Lane, the narrow lane that leads directly to the Trent. Here, near Sturton, Margary perceived the road to be 'raised about 2 feet and about 40 feet wide between the ditches'. Today, the height is more noticeable than this width. The Roman road continues on straight to the hamlet, save for a wobble to the south which seems to avoid an old enclosure, once surrounded by a bank. Most of the Roman finds unearthed during excavations at Littleborough were found within this area and the Roman town seems to have been concentrated here after flooding inundated buildings in the original town. After this wobble you are soon in the hamlet and then on a rough track down to the Trent.

On the opposite side of the Trent in Lincolnshire the Roman road continues as a track called Littleborough Lane to Marton village, proceeding along Till Bridge Lane to a junction with Ermine Street. Turn south here and, just as you could have done from the early 3rd century onwards, you can enter Lincoln under the Newport Arch. It is the only complete Roman arch used by traffic in Britain.

Yet the obvious connection problem with this journey is the clear absence of a bridge at Littleborough. Whichever direction you're coming from, the nearest bridge over the Trent is several kilometres south at Dunham-on-Trent (directly opposite the site of a Roman fortress at Newton-on-Trent). With no evidence of a Roman bridge at Littleborough having been found, the other two options for crossing were ferry and ford. There was certainly a long tradition of ferry use here and indeed it has been a staple of the descriptions of Littleborough to say that the ferry was the oldest in the country, and had been in continuous use since Roman times. Dr Robert Thoroton, writer of the first history of

The quiet Roman road leading to Littleborough (top) and (bottom) the track down to the Trent.

Nottinghamshire in 1677, called the place 'Littleburgh' and said: 'Here was a famous passage over the Trent and near it have been found some old pieces of Roman antiquities, coins, and the like, as I have heard.' A ferry was in use in Camden's time ('there is at this day a Ferrie much used', as he put it) while Leland said the hamlet was known as Littleborough Ferry. The ferry service seems to have gone out of use in the Edwardian era, perhaps 1906, but the necessary winding equipment was left as 'a ruin on the river bank' until the late 1960s. Even this cannot be seen any more. But a memory of the vital service was revived at some point before the Second World War when a resident of the bankside farmhouse, Alfred Barlow, began rowing people across the river.

The evidence for an ancient ford at Littleborough is, like most things buried and unseen under water, murky and intriguing. A raised causeway around 5.4 metres (18ft) wide in the bed of the river was said to have been present until 1820. 'It was then removed, I suppose, for the same reason that led to the destruction of the remains of the Roman Bridge at Collingham in 1884, viz, to improve the navigation,' wrote Smith Woolley in 1909. 'In 1877, Mr Watkin [who had described the causeway] obtained the evidence of an old and trusted servant of the Trent Navigation Company, who had himself helped in the work of the removal, and who said that the ford was paved with rough square stones. On each side of the road piles ten or twelve feet long were driven into the bed of the river, and pieces of timber ran from one to the other giving support to the whole. The timber was black oak, but soon rotted when exposed to the air. This was not the case with oak from the bridge at Collingham. Existing specimens, after twenty-five years' exposure, are still quite sound.'

A similar description of the causeway was given by Thomas Codrington, who added the detail that the stone causeway was supported by oak piles 10 or 20 feet long. The causeway, or its surviving foundation stones, was seen in 1933 when the water was low during a very hot summer. Why not dive down to see if the causeway is still there today? Sheffield University Diving Club tried this in 1955 but the results were said to have been inconclusive. In 1868 sight of 'a portion of the paved descent' down to the river on the Nottinghamshire side was reported. The traveller who witnessed this feature was one Archdeacon Trollope, of Sleaford, who regarded the road as an extension of Ermine Street. Leland, you will remember, had called it Watling Street. Its Roman name, if it had one, is unknown.

However, anyone hoping to walk or drive across the Trent at Littleborough in a normal year now would have to be considered unhinged. The river is clearly far too deep to cross without a boat. That the Romans once used this part of the river as a ford suggests that water levels have changed over the centuries. Given the Trent's historic reputation as a 'volatile and capricious' river perhaps this should not be surprising. The Trent has a history of seasonal flooding and abrupt course changes, and modern environmental analysis now suggests that during the Roman occupation the Trent Valley as a whole became wetter and cooler. This made the Trent more prone to flooding and to abrupt changes in the use of river channels. Evidence for this impact on Roman settlements close to the river was revealed during excavations at Littleborough in the late 1960s, when the remains of Roman building structures were found covered with thick alluvial deposits. Episodes such as this must have been part of a pattern of volatility that led to the river's abandonment of an old channel to the west of Littleborough (now occupied by a drainage ditch called the Mother Drain), so concentrating water flow to the present channel to the east of the hamlet. It may have been this that led to the loss of the shallow ford. The Trent's volatile character was later noted by Shakespeare in *Henry IV Part I* when he made Hotspur complain, 'see how this river comes me cranking in/And cuts me from the best of my land'. Although the Trent's flow is now better controlled by locks and weirs, it's said that there are about 30 locations which show clear evidence of the river's course changes. The last time this happened was in 1792 and 1797 near Gainsborough, downstream of Littleborough, when the Trent cut through two meandering loops and marooned around 40 hectares of Lincolnshire on the Nottinghamshire side of the river. Today a tidal bore, the Trent Aegir or Eagre, flows from the Humber to Gainsborough and spring water levels can change by as much as three metres there. Perhaps it was for some, or all, of these reasons that the Romans named the Trent as *Trisantona*, the trespasser (or wanderer), and why the name for their settlement at Littleborough was *Segelocum,* or 'violent pool'. Nor was Littleborough the only low-lying Roman settlement to be affected by climatic change in the Roman period: Gonalston, Rampton and Ferry Lane Farm at Besthorpe were also among the settlements which were evidently subjected to flooding.

Littleborough

It's been said that *Segelocum* was the largest Roman settlement in Nottinghamshire not built on the Fosse Way. However, the actual crossing of the Trent here seems to have been primarily guarded by a 0.7 hectare (1.7 acres) fortlet at Marton on the Lincolnshire side of the river, the traces of which have been seen as cropmarks. On the Nottinghamshire bank, Littleborough was a 'substantial defended settlement' which was settled as early as the late 50s or early 60s and occupied throughout the Roman period. Prior to modern excavations the site produced its share of finds, including inscribed altars and so many Roman coins that they were called Swine Pennies because pigs used to turn them up with their snouts. Despite this, no Roman stone remains above ground today, unless you count the Roman tiles which went into the hamlet's small Norman church nearby, St Nicholas, now managed by the Churches Conservation Trust. This absence of obvious remains meant that even Camden initially had difficulty finding the site:

> *This town have I heretofore sought for in vain about the Country adjoining, but now I am verily persuaded and assured that I have found it out, both for that it stands upon the old port Highway, and also because the field lying near to it shows express tokens of walls, and besides affords unto ploughmen every day many pieces of the Roman Emperor's coin, which because swine many times rooting into the ground turn up with their snouts, the country people call Swine-pennies.*[4]

Stukeley came to Littleborough by ferry from Lincolnshire, having travelled along Till Bridge Lane, which was in such a poor condition that he joked it needed a Roman legion to repair it. Although Stukeley wrote a long description of the village, including observations on finds, the map he drew of the village, which portrays Littleborough as surrounded by water, is peculiar. 'As usual, after reading his report, one wonders whether Archaeology is the richer or the poorer for his wealth, his wild imaginings, and his credulity,' wrote Smith Woolley.[5] Nevertheless, Stukeley provided interesting detail on some of the larger finds here:

> *In 1718 they dug up two altars handsomely moulded, which are set as piers in a wall on the side of the steps that lead from the water-side to the inn. On one is the remnant of an inscription, LIS ARAM DD., these are of course the coarse grit-stone... . Mr Hardy has a large urn with the face of a woman on the outside. In this same field near White's bridge are great foundations of building. Coins are often found too at the lowest edge of the water, when the tide is gone off, and in dry seasons. On the east side of the river has been a camp.*[6]

Closer to Smith Woolley's own time, traces of the alleged Roman ditch and wall surrounding the settlement were seen in the late 19th century. And according to the Rev. H.J. Griffin, a Roman stone coffin had also been found by a gravedigger in 1860. The clergyman's anecdote recalls scenes from the film *Indiana Jones and the Kingdom of the Crystal Skull*: 'The gravedigger, having cut extra deep, struck the top of a Roman stone coffin, and called in a neighbour to help him to lift the massive stone cover, on raising which the men, for only a few seconds, saw within the coffin the perfect body of a young woman whose funeral garment was clasped by a Roman brooch. After a few moments' exposure to the air, all collapsed into fine dust, to the great astonishment and alarm of the men. This coffin is now in the cloisters of Lincoln cathedral; the brooch is now in the possession of Mr B. Wilmhurst, of Retford...'

20th century archaeology finally came to Littleborough in the 1950s and between 1968 and '70 when excavations were led by John Wade, then of Durham University, now a part-time Latin tutor at Sheffield University. Wade found the outlines of several buildings with clay and stone hearths, an oven and a possible latrine. But everything was covered by a layer of earth, up to nearly a metre thick, that had been delivered by floodwater. Yet, undeterred by inundation, Littleborough's Roman inhabitants seemed to have rebuilt the affected parts of their town since Wade found the remains of newer walls, wall plaster, crop-driers, pottery and coins more or less directly on top of the flooded buildings.

Further west from the river bank, excavations by W.B. Clark in the mid-1950s had unearthed an extensive cobbled service, evidence of a 'substantial building' and the 7 metre (23ft) wide cobbled surface of the old Roman road, in the bank of the Mother Drain. A building resembling a barrack block was found and Wade later wondered if Littleborough had had a military origin, but had to conclude it was more likely that the structures he'd found were civilian. Flooding seems to have caused 'major replanning' of the town, with the focus moving to the slightly higher ground north of the current road (the enclosure area where the road deviates). The flooding process may have begun in around 160, or in the early part of the next century. Based on the town replanning, Wade concluded that the route of the causeway across the Trent was at an 'oblique' angle to the modern bankside track and must have been aligned with the enclosed area back from the river.

Small finds found near Littleborough have included two items of Roman medical equipment: a brass surgical forceps, found in 1989, and an ophthalmologist's stamp found in the 18th century that has since been lost.

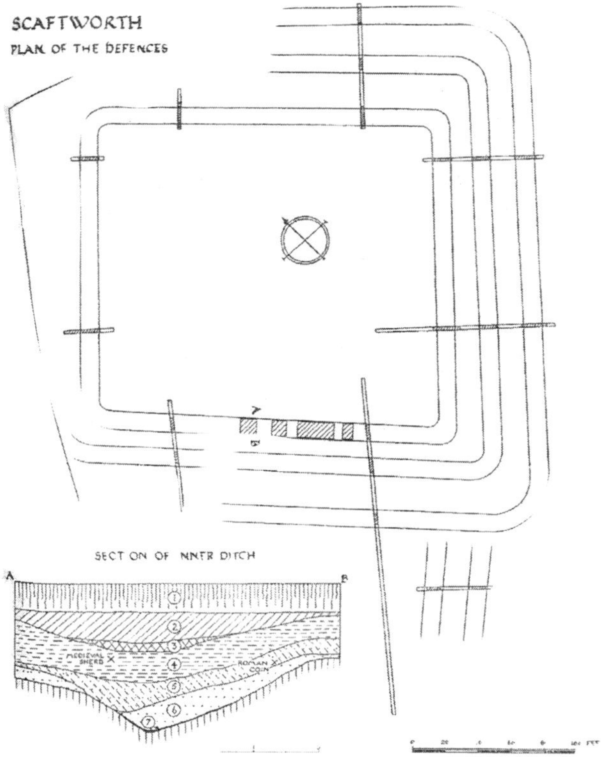

Plan of Scaftworth fortlet's defences.

Scaftworth fortlet

Travellers on the Littleborough–Bawtry road will soon notice the words 'Roman fortlet' marked just outside Bawtry on OS Explorer map 279. This site, overlooking the river Idle, was marked on some maps in the late 18th century and early 19th century. John Cary's county map of 1801, for example, had the fort marked as an 'Ancient Encampment' while the road passing it was marked as the 'Roman Road from Doncaster to Lincoln'. However, the site appears to have disappeared from local maps by 1813 possibly due to ploughing and it wasn't rediscovered until 1944 when aerial photography captured images of a small, almost square, enclosure surrounded by a triple system of ditches. The site was subjected to excavations in 1948 and 1956 when the enclosed area was measured as 62 by 56 metres (205ft by 185ft), or just less than an acre. Finds included small sherds of pottery, fragments of querns and a coin, described as a bronze imitation of a silver piece from the reign of the 4th century pagan revivalist Emperor Julian. One interpretation is that the fort was built in the second half of the 4th century to police the road to York after the northern provinces of *Britannia* had been regained from barbarians by Count Theodosius. 'The Scaftworth fort may have been established because the site was a minor focus of communications by road and water, or else purely as a defensive measure to prevent the river crossing being blocked by hostile forces,' wrote J.E. Bartlett and Derrick Riley in 1958. But if it were built to guard the river crossing, one wonders why the authors failed to mention the implications of the fort's date for the building of the important Lincoln–York road. Does a late 4th century date mean the road wasn't built until then? Or did the crossing of the Idle go undefended until that time? If so, why? Some answers to these questions came in 1983 when two sections of Roman road near the fort were excavated. The later section was a well-preserved timber causeway, six metres wide, unearthed from under half a metre of peat. It ran north west to south east, just north of the fort. The road was set on timbers and strengthened by thick sharpened stakes set seven metres (23ft) apart. Radiocarbon dating of one of the oak timbers placed it in the 3rd century, establishing that the road was built before the fort. Here also was proof that the route of the Roman road near Bawtry differed from the modern road. The earlier section of road, in the wetter area near the Idle, was built of turf and timber and provided a 'floating road' over the boggy ground. There is surely also a reminder here of the 'corduroy road', composed of tree trunks, that Felix Oswald suggested had crossed the damp terrain at *Ad Pontem*.

Other Roman roads

Although Nottinghamshire doesn't possess an abundance of known major and minor Roman roads, what can be seen now is probably only a fraction of what existed 1,600–2,000 years ago. While the main roads seem to be mostly known, there must be many other Roman roads and tracks that have long disappeared from view. As Oliver Rackham wrote: 'The known Roman roads are but a small part of a system that penetrated to every part of

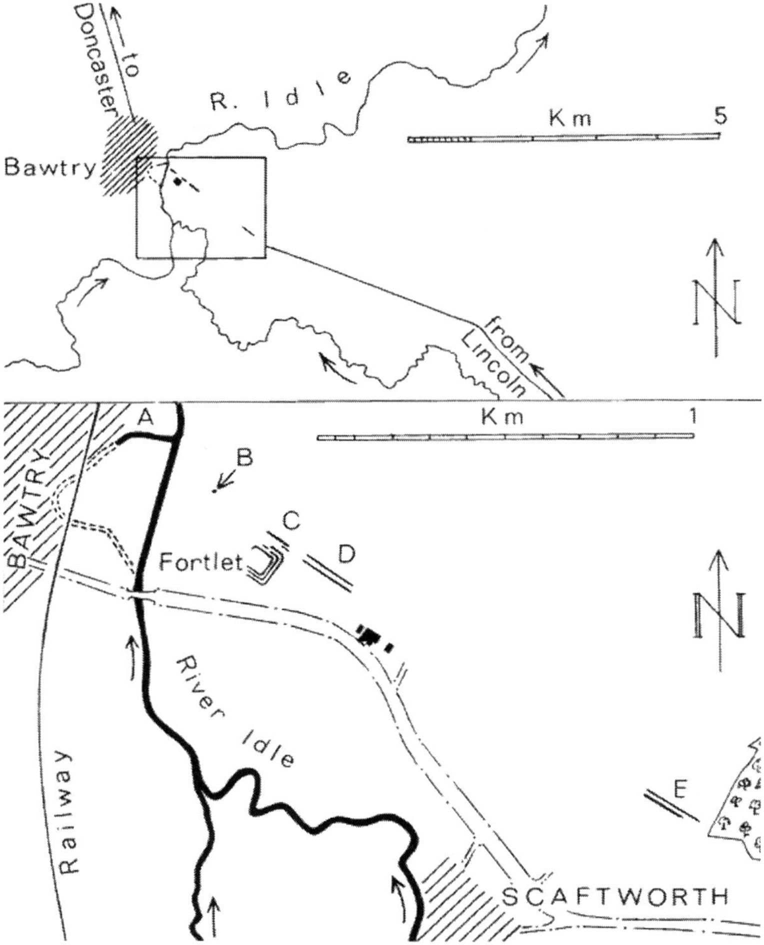

Maps drawn by Derrick Riley showing the route of the excavated Roman road found running north east of Scaftworth fortlet. The modern road to Bawtry is south of the fortlet; the true route of the Roman road is marked by the letters B, C, D and E.

England. They are no more representative of all roads in the Roman period than motorways are representative of all twentieth century roads.' [7]

Two centuries before Rackham, William Dickinson, the 18th century author of the first history of Southwell, employed the delicious circumlocutory prose of his era to describe the missing road situation in Nottinghamshire: 'It has long been considered as a matter of not only pleasant and curious, but even of useful enquiry, to determine the roads, and stations, of the Romans, while they held the dominion of this island. Many of them have been ascertained with indisputable precision; some have been conjectured, subject to much doubt and controversy; and many more remain still entirely undiscovered, to excite the diligence of the antiquary. Southwell *certainly*, Newark *with great probability*, presents a most exuberant field for examination.'

Occasionally, logic and archaeology provide enough critical mass to suggest the likely existence of a long-obscured Roman road — or at least the ghost of a road. Such is the case with the highway that seems to have connected *Ad Pontem* on the Fosse Way with forts to the north west, at least as far as modern Bilsthorpe, and perhaps as far east as Ancaster in Lincolnshire in the other direction. But what about the more minor roads or tracks that must have connected the various villas to the main road network? Some of these tracks may be indicated by ancient boundaries. The *Southwell Charter* of 956, for example, has been subjected to close analysis which plausibly shows that the Anglo-Saxon boundaries of Southwell preserved certain Roman tracks and roads, including part of the route between *Ad Pontem* and the fortress at Osmanthorpe. This excellent synthesis of local history and topographical analysis, published in 1982, was written by the late Philip Lyth, an agricultural author and former principal of Brackenhurst College, near Southwell.[8] Lyth asserted that an 'old paved way' mentioned in the charter marked the route of the *Ad Pontem* Roman road. Another reference to a paved way and a hollow brook was deduced to refer to a track connecting Thurgarton with Holbeck, the area astride the B6386 Oxton road. This track is the bridlepath marked on OS Explorer 270 which runs along the ridge separating Epperstone from Halloughton. Lyth had this down as a 'probable' Roman road, bolstered by an earlier comment by Adrian Oswald, who thought it was 'obviously a work of some age, probably a road and possibly Roman'. Lyth also thought that another cross-country track, which crosses this ridgeway, may also preserve the route of a Roman track connecting the villas at Thurgarton/ Epperstone with Southwell.

If we believe studies like this, as well as the collection of lore and tradition about ancient routes that is found in out-of-print

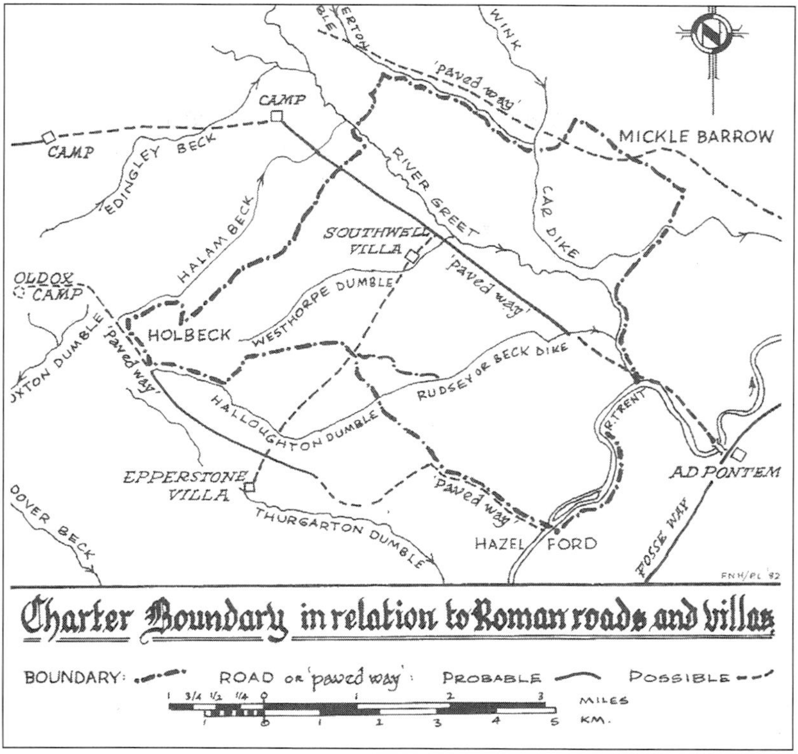

Charter boundary in relation to Roman roads and villas, Southwell.

books and a multitude of battered local history pamphlets, then our current picture of the Roman road network in Nottinghamshire is very incomplete. The subject is ripe for much more research and fieldwork.

The roads to and from *Ad Pontem*

Although no trace of a Roman bridge at Thorpe (*Ad Pontem*) has been found, the evidence for a linking track or road that would have connected with the settlement via a Trent crossing continues to grow. Adding together fragments of physical evidence, this road seems to have run north west up the Greet Valley, past the Roman fort at Osmanthorpe and continued further north west to Bilsthorpe. The evidence includes straight field bound-

Top: the 'possibly Roman' paved way, now a bridlepath, running along the ridge between Thurgarton and Holbeck, near Southwell.

The post in the bottom picture marks the junction with the track that runs downhill to the Epperstone/ Thurgarton villas nearby. Both pictures were taken on 23rd January, 2010 — hence the mud.

aries near the Osmanthorpe fort and a 'band of gravel' described as being 5.3 metres (17ft) wide and '200 yards in length' on a field surface near Camp Hill, west of Kirklington. An article on Nottinghamshire Iron Age hill forts, published in 1963, added this detail: 'Even today, a well-made farm track going east–west

The 'Roman road' heading up to Camp Hill from Kirklington?

in a straight line over the hill, and not more than 20 or 30 yards from the gravel band at its nearest point, is known to the farm workers as the Roman road.'[9]

The road from *Ad Pontem* seems to continue to Bilsthorpe where, at Belle Eau Park, a section of the road was excavated in 2002. The road here was seen on the surface as a 'linear double-ditched cropmark' following aerial photography. Nearby, to the south east, were a mound and a ditch about 100 metres (330ft) from the modern road. 'This mound occurs at the point where the Roman Road would be expected to exist, according to the aerial photographs, and it seems very likely to be a surviving part of the embankment or *agger* of the road,' wrote the archaeologists, Keith Challis, Vicki Priest, Carol Allen and Gavin Kinsley.[10] Two trenches were cut in the road. A metalled surface of dense gravel, with cambered edges and side ditches, was seen in one. The evidence in the second ditch was vague but seemed to suggest a shallow ditch. The metalled width of the road was estimated at 9–10 metres (29–33ft). Further south, the same road was seen in a drainage ditch as a layer of gravel. The surface ridge of the road was once visible but seems to have been ploughed out. Further south still, near Kirklington, the 5.3 metres (17ft) gravel band already noted had been seen on the projected line of the road. Straight field boundaries running towards Osmanthorpe are claimed to reflect the continuing line of this long-obscured Roman road. Since Osmanthorpe was a 'vexillation' fortress, designed to hold a substantial section of a legion probably engaged on active campaigning, the road servicing the fort may have dated to the mid- to late 1st century. Although the general line of the road can be traced easily enough on OS Explorer map 270, Philip Lyth, in his article on the *Southwell Charter*, specified that Lower Kirklington Road and Crewe Lane probably preserved the route where it ran near Southwell. But where did the road go then?

The archaeologists involved at Bilsthorpe believed that, if projected to the south, the road probably led to *Ad Pontem* via a bridge over the Trent. In the other direction, north of Bilsthorpe, the projected road would have run past the Roman camps at Farnsfield and Gleadthorpe. Further north west it may have connected with Ryknield Street, the main Roman road running north–south through the Midlands to Templeborough, near Rotherham, via Derby. From *Ad Pontem* east the road may have led to the Roman town at Ancaster in Lincolnshire. That was St Joseph and Frere's belief when they examined aerial photographs of *Ad Pontem*. Another proposal has been that the road from Ancaster led to Long Bennington, on the Nottinghamshire/Lincolnshire border just south of Newark. Since Ancaster lies on Ermine Street, any such road could have effectively served as another link road between Ermine Street and the Fosse Way.

Bawtry to Ollerton

If the *Ad Pontem*–Bilsthorpe road projection is correct, it may have crossed or met another possible Roman road running north–south to Bawtry. Thomas Codrington claimed he had identified the Roman original of the Great North Road leading south from Bawtry, beginning at 'the lake at Bawtry' which was drained in 1905 and where supposed traces of road were found. The road extended 6km (four miles) further south along a parish boundary which ran along a country road called Roman Bank Lane, just north of Blyth. The name Roman Bank remains on modern maps. However, this has since been explained as an estate boundary, not a Roman road. Codrington then said that there was a 'broad green road with a narrow metalled track in the middle, leading southwards from Blyth to Ollerton... followed by a parish boundary for five miles, except where the road has been interfered with by a canal, and the boundary goes straight on and is rejoined by the road. There seems to be no other signs of a Roman road in this direction.' However, further speculation on the line of this road has been proposed by others, including the claim that it could be traced from the alleged Roman fort at Dorket Head and along Hollinwood Lane at Calverton. The *Victoria County History* further speculated: 'There is indeed from Oxton to Ollerton a "fairly" straight road (the Old Rufford Road) running in a line with the road from Ollerton to Blyth, through the parishes of Farnsfield and Rufford, and it is possible that there is a southern continuation of the latter. But whence it came and whither it went requires further investigation which may or may not establish its Roman origin.'

Whatever the truth of these matters, it was important to Codrington's thinking (and Ivan Margary's) that there was a link between the obscure routes of Roman roads and the traditional boundaries marking parish and old county demarcations. As has been seen, this connection has also been made on the Fosse Way near Willoughby-on-the-Wolds and at Brough. North of Bawtry a parish boundary also follows the Great North Road, which shows off its Roman lineage by running close to a Roman fortress at Rossington Bridge in South Yorkshire. The countryside writer Oliver Rackham wrote in great detail about the way in which roads and tracks, from prehistoric times onwards, have survived in the British landscape through features such as parish boundaries, footpaths, hedgerows, trenches and earthworks.[11] The issue of tracing long-obscured Roman roads is complicated by the fact that the Roman surveyors may have 'Romanised' Iron Age tracks, some of which were in turn kept in use by the Anglo-Saxons and later still adapted by medieval travellers. An example of a Romanised roadway is the Salt Way which strikes east into Lincolnshire from Six Hills on the Fosse Way.

Road 182: *Derventio* to the Redhill temple and curse tablets

The OS Explorer map of Nottingham, no. 260, clearly shows a straight road marked as Roman Road entering Nottinghamshire from Derby via Borrowash and Draycott. The line of the road is projected over Church Wilne Reservoir, built in 1967, and peters out in the southern suburbs of Long Eaton. Project forward with the eye, however, and you can see that it would have led to the confluence of the Soar and Trent at Trentlock. On the other side of the river junction, atop steep cliffs, is an area called Redhill. Although now the location of Ratcliffe-on-Soar Power Station, it has been suspected since the 18th century that some kind of Roman settlement existed at Redhill. In the 20th century a temple was postulated and then the curse tablets began to be found there in the early 1960s. More recently archaeologists have begun to believe that Redhill was probably a more important and larger Romano-British community than previously thought. Located at the junction of two rivers, and on a network of roads connecting it to the Fosse Way and the Roman fort and later town at Little Chester, Derby (*Derventio*), it is now thought that Redhill has been occupied since Mesolithic times and was developed by the Romans into a small busy town covering perhaps 45 hectares (111 acres). Here may have been a place where river freight arrived on barges and was transferred to road transport, overlooked by a prominent temple or shrine above the rivers. Coins and brooches dredged from the river here suggest that travellers made offerings to a river god in thanks for their safe arrival. There may also have been a villa and farm, plus a small military presence.

Where did the road from *Derventio* cross to Redhill? Several sites for a ford across the Trent have been suggested, including near Red Hill Farm and a place called Point Shallows. The straight road from *Derventio* was marked on 19th century maps such as Sanderson's celebrated map of 1835 and it was naturally noted by Codrington and Margary, who numbered it 182. Codrington brought together some old observations about the road, especially on the Derbyshire side, where it was described as having a visible ridge 30 years earlier — that is, circa 1870 — and with a width of about 3.6 metres (12ft). Codrington said that from *Derventio* the road lies 'in a straight line for seven miles to the River Trent at Sawley, except for half-a-mile where the straight line is continued by hedgerows. It points to the steep north side of West Leake hills, twelve miles distant, rising 200 feet above the Trent Valley, but there are no traces in continuation beyond that river.' He continued: 'The Rev S.P. Potter [author of *A History of East Leake*, published 1903] connects a "street way" in an old terrier [a church survey of land] with a road, not in the same line, which he supposes to be a Roman road in the direction of Six Hills on the Foss road, but the identification is not clear.'

Margary added little about the Nottinghamshire road, except to say that the purpose of the road seemed to be to link the fort at Derby with the river for water traffic. He made no mention of Redhill, which is strange considering that a well-travelled surveyor called Tim Armitage, from Trentlock (he was described in one paper as having 'returned from Patagonia'), began investigating the site from 1919 and found coins, pottery, jewellery and glassware dating from the 1st to the late 4th century. Much of this was given to Leicester Museum; other material was sold or lost from around 1946 onwards; a few items of pottery came to the Brewhouse Yard Museum in Nottingham while coins were bequeathed to the British Museum when Armitage died in 1956.

In the late 1950s and early 1960s further excavations undertaken at Redhill by Herbert O. Houldsworth, the East Leake

Archaeological Group and Ernest Greenfield revealed two buildings, traces of a floor, pottery, coins, a bone comb and diamond-shaped tiles. One of Houldsworth's more grisly finds was the burial of a man who seemed to have died from 'a thrust with a pointed weapon through the left jaw'. The work at Redhill in this period was difficult, in part because of erosion of the cliffs overlooking the Trent, which had caused parts of the remains of one Roman building to disappear, and in part because the site was threatened by the building of the new power station. Greenfield's excavations in 1963 were carried out as an emergency measure on behalf of the then Ministry of Public Buildings and Works, and two of the areas he examined were later reported to have been destroyed by building work for the power station. Sadly, one of these areas contained the remains of walls believed to have been part of the temple or shrine. The extent of the damage at Redhill caused by the power station is indicated by a concise report of activity in 1966: 'During 1966 much of the hill was removed to provide infill for the new roadway from the power station across the River Soar.'[12] The 'bulldozed topsoil' included Roman roof tiles and other fragments.

In 1982, all of the existing evidence from Redhill was considered and the opinion was that it could have been a place of 'considerable importance', occupying high ground overlooking a major river junction and suitable for either trading or a temple.[13] Later thinking, taking into account further evaluations in the early 1990s and 2001 and summarised in an assessment by Alan Palfreyman and Susan Ebbins in 2003, estimated that the Roman settlement covered 45 hectares and that it probably extended around 1km further south than the area covered by its Ancient Monument schedule.[14] The many coins found at Redhill, from the reign of Augustus to Constantine III in the early 5th century, suggests long and constant occupation. A handful of small military finds, such as pieces from a cavalry harness and a tie-hook from a legionary's *lorica segmentata* armour, suggested there was a military presence at Redhill, albeit perhaps temporarily.

As at Littleborough, the course of the Trent here changed course and in Roman times the river at Redhill met the Soar further south, close to Red Hill farmhouse. The temple complex was supposedly located on the current edge of the cliff overlooking

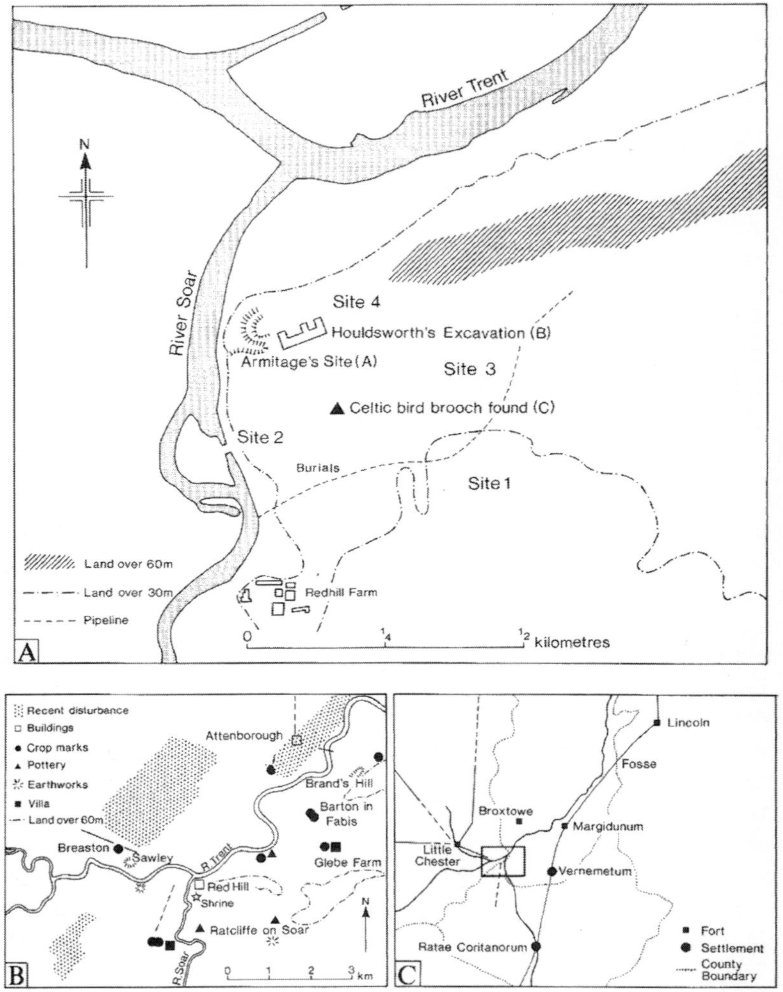

FIGURE 1

A—Sites of excavations at Red Hill.
B—Prehistoric and Roman sites near Red Hill (see appendix).
C—Red Hill with known Roman roads, forts and settlements.

Map of Redhill. The 'Celtic bird brooch' marked at C on the top image is a celebrated item of jewellery found there.

the former confluence of the two rivers; this would have made the temple visible to anybody approaching from either river. Another building existed at the north end of the site, built into the natural slope of the high land. Despite evidence of walls, a doorway, tiles, mosaic pieces, stone paving and remains of a central heating system, the nature of the structure has never been conclusively identified. Suggested uses of this building have included a villa, bath house and *mansio,* which provided official accommodation for officials on Imperial business. A recent study of the land to the east of the site suggests that Redhill also supported a farm growing wheat. This gives credence to the idea that Redhill had a rural villa/farmhouse with a productive estate.

Redhill's location on roads and a major river means it was probably also an important local centre for trade and a road/river interchange for transport of goods including slate from Charnwood and Derbyshire millstone grit and pottery. Trade and transport would have been facilitated by a wharf (not found) used by barges travelling to and from some of *Britannia's* major ports: '...a thriving agricultural, religious and trading centre may have existed when the Romans arrived', said Palfreyman and Ebbins. 'Its essential nature was that of a rural village-type settlement which, due to its position, evolved into a commercial centre in the Roman period.'

Redhill's importance as a trade and transport centre is suggested by the number of tracks which connected it with the more important Roman highways. It was, first of all, almost equidistant between Derby and *Margidunum*, mid-way between the Fosse Way and Derby and between Derby and Leicester. The existence of a Roman trade route serving this latter connection, running south from the west bank of the Soar to Leicester via Kegworth, Long Whatton, Shepshed and Anstey, has been persuasively argued.[15] An Iron Age, later Roman, ridge track from Redhill may also have led south east following Wood Lane to Cuckoo Bush, Court Hill and Costock. From there it could have continued to *Vernemetum* on the FosseWay. A possible route for this track running south east can be worked out using OS Explorer map 246. Two traditional names of local tracks near East Leake, Portway and Streetway, have been cited as evidence supporting the Roman use of these routes.[16] Another track from Redhill may have run to Barrow-on-Soar and connected with the

Salt Way. In addition to these connections, Redhill was close to other Roman settlements including the fort at Broxtowe and villas at Barton-in-Fabis and Lockington in Leicestershire 2km (1.2 miles) to the south west. An earthwork about 1.6km (one mile) to the west of Redhill called Sawley Fort, and known locally as 'the Bull Ring', was thought to be Roman in origin but investigations in the 1960s were inconclusive.

Notes

1. *Roman Roads in Britain I: South of the Foss Way–Bristol Channel* — Ivan D. Margary. Phoenix House, 1955.
2. *Britannia Romana or the Roman Antiquities of Britain* — John Horsley. First published 1732. Frank Graham, 2nd edition, 1974.
3. *John Leland's Itinerary: Travels in Tudor England* — John Chandler. Allan Sutton, 1993.
4. *Britannia* — William Camden. Published in three volumes in the series Historical Cultures and Geography 1600–1750, edited and introduced by Robert Mayhew. Thoemmes Press, 2003.
5. Summer Excursion 1909 — The Rev. Dr. Scott-Moncrieff, Harry Gill, the Rev. A.W.B. Marshall, the Rev. George F. Twycross and T. Cecil Smith Woolley. *Transactions of the Thoroton Society of Nottinghamshire* 13, 1909.
6. *Itinerarium Curiosum, Or an Account of the Antiquitys and Remarkable Curiositys in Nature or Art, Observ'd in Travels thro' Great Britain* — William Stukeley. Printed for the Author, 1724.
7. *The History of the Countryside* — Oliver Rackham. Phoenix Press, 2000.
8. The Southwell Charter of 956 AD: An Exploration of its Boundaries — Philip Lyth. *Transactions of the Thoroton Society of Nottinghamshire* 86, 1982.
9. Iron Age Hill Forts in Nottinghamshire — B.B. Simons. *Transactions of the Thoroton Society of Nottinghamshire* 67, 1963.
10. A Roman Road at Belle Eau Park, Bilsthorpe, Nottinghamshire — Keith Challis, Vicki Priest, Carol Allen and Gavin Kinsley. *Transactions of the Thoroton Society of Nottinghamshire* 106, 2002.
11. *The History of the Countryside* — Oliver Rackham. Phoenix Press, 2000.
12. *East Midlands Archaeological Bulletin 1974* — edited by M.W. Barley. University of Nottingham Department of Adult Education.
13. Iron Age and Roman Sites at Red Hill, Ratcliffe-on-Soar, Nottinghamshire: Excavations of E. Greenfield, 1963, and Previous Finds — S.M. Elsdon. *Transactions of the Thoroton Society of Nottinghamshire* 86, 1982.
14. Redhill Iron Age and Romano-British Site, Nottinghamshire: a New Assessment — Alan Palfreyman and Susan Ebbins. *Transactions of the Thoroton Society of Nottinghamshire* 107, 2003.

15. New Light on a Suspected Roman Road between Ratcliffe-on-Soar and Leicester — Stephen J. Lycett. *Transactions of the Leicestershire Archaeological and Historical Society* 73, 1999.
16. *The Roads, Trackways and Footpaths of East Leake: The History and Origin of their Names* — R. Owen Wood. East Leake and District Local History Group, 1991.

Chapter 7

Forts and other military sites

One of the latest guides to known Roman forts and fortresses in Britain puts the total number at 307 — and that excludes small defended towns, fortlets, watch towers and temporary camps.[1] Since 1997 nine forts, including a large fortress at Alchester in Oxfordshire discovered by aerial photography, have been added to the list. Why were so many large military installations built? In part the list of known forts reflects the sheer size of Roman military power in the new British province over the 40 years it took the army to reach northern Scotland. At its height by the mid 2nd century, the Roman garrison in Britain may have numbered 55,000 legionaries and auxiliaries — a number that has been described as an unusually large concentration of forces for a country of Britain's size. One way this army was able to perform its task of imposing Roman will and policy on the natives was by occupation of intelligently spaced forts, built in different sizes and locations to suit different purposes.

In general permanent forts would have acted as highly visible symbols of power — and as real, unsymbolic sources of armed control, particularly in recently occupied territory. Regularly spaced networks of forts, particularly along major roads which acted as the main routes through hostile ground, seem to have been an aim. Although no such network has been conclusively established along the Fosse Way, such networks certainly existed elsewhere, along Dere Street for example, which reflected the route of the Roman army's march from York into Scotland in the 80s. The largest legionary fortresses were, as the name suggests, constructed to house entire legions of around 5,500 soldiers. These could enclose around 20 hectares (50 acres). The nearest such installations to Nottinghamshire were at Lincoln and then York. Below this size, the army — and it was mainly the army who did the graft — built permanent or semi-permanent defensive installations of different sizes: from small fortlets guarding river crossings to 'vexillation fortresses' of eight hectares (20 acres) or more, which seem to have accommodated perhaps ad hoc 'battle groups' of a few thousand soldiers.

Both of these latter types of forts are represented in Nottinghamshire: at Scaftworth, near Bawtry, and at Osmanthorpe, near Southwell, respectively. The lists of small Nottinghamshire forts may also include Broxtowe, *Margidunum* and *Ad Pontem*. *Margidunum* is a problem for reasons already explored and Broxtowe and Osmanthorpe also present their own difficulties of interpretation. Broxtowe fort seems to have been built in the first 10 or 15 years of the occupation but a housing estate was built over the remains of the site a year after it was found in the 1930s, so preventing any further excavations or interpretation. The best guess for Osmanthorpe, identified only in 1979 through field cropmarks, was that it was built in the first 25 years of the occupation. However, the county's list of forts can be extended if we include another category of temporary camps, of which there are five known so far: Farnsfield, Gleadthorpe, Holme and two on the same site at Calverton. A further four possible temporary camps have been identified through the National Mapping Programme at Hayton, Collingham, Misterton and Ollerton.

A major problem of interpretation with all of these various forts and camps is trying to understand how they may have related to each other, and why they were built where they were. In this sense it helps if one can look at the territory without modern county boundaries, as obviously the invading Roman army did. The wider perspective reveals a cluster of forts along the Trent Valley and in the surrounding area. So, to this early period, within the first 25 years after the invasion, can perhaps be attributed the founding of forts of different sizes at Broxtowe, Osmanthorpe, Newton-on-Trent in Lincolnshire, Rossington Bridge in South Yorkshire and Little Chester in Derby. However, these installations may not have been exactly contemporaneous or used for the same purposes. Broxtowe, although a difficult site to interpret, appears to have been abandoned in the 70s. Little Chester in Derby was also an early fort, built during the reign of Claudius or Nero, but was manned for much longer and eventually became a civilian town. Both of the forts may have been built to consolidate control over territory as the Roman advance moved west from the Trent. The larger forts at Osmanthorpe, Newton-on-Trent and Rossington Bridge have all been tentatively tied to movements of troops north to tackle the

Brigantes. The temporary camps at Farnsfield and Gleadthorpe have also been associated with these campaigns. Another interpretation is that the forts formed a cordon to guard the country from attacks by the *Brigantes*. But theories abound. Nothing is certain.

Nevertheless, by the time the army began its drive north into hostile Brigantian territory in the early 70s, Nottinghamshire and the region were, arguably, already pacified and local forts were either abandoned or reorganised on civilian lines. The demilitarisation of defended small towns such as *Ad Pontem* and *Margidunum* seems to be evidence for this period.

How were forts built? The Jewish historian Josephus gave a

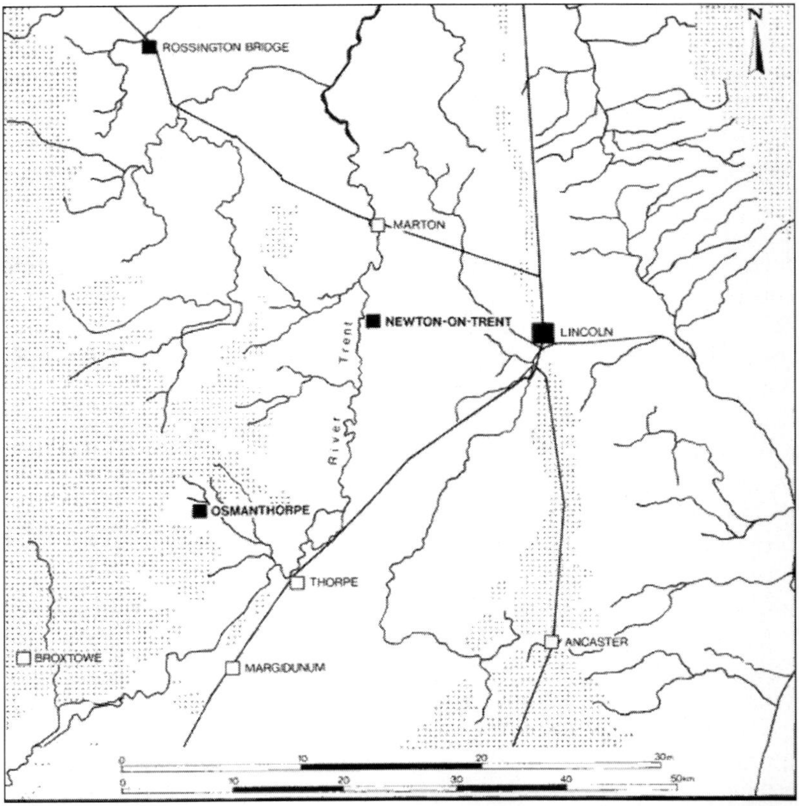

Sketch map showing locations of some Roman forts and fortresses in and around Nottinghamshire.

vivid and awe-struck description of ruthless Roman camp-building efficiency in his account of the Jewish rebellion against Roman rule in the late 60s:

> *if the ground is uneven it is thoroughly levelled, then the site is marked out as a rectangle. To this end the army is followed by a large number of engineers with all the tools needed for building. The inside is divided up ready for the huts. From outside the perimeter looks like a wall and is equipped with towers evenly spaced. In the gaps between the towers they mount spear-throwers, catapults, stone-throwers, and every type of ordnance, all ready to be discharged. Four gates are constructed, one in each length of wall... the erection of the outer wall and the buildings inside is accomplished faster than thought, thanks to the number and skill of the workers. If necessary a ditch is dug all around, six feet deep and the same width.*[2]

Although Josephus' 'rectangle' was no doubt the round-cornered 'playing card' shape of most Roman forts, examples in Nottinghamshire suggest how the army's surveyors were able to adapt to the terrain. Ground often seems not to have been levelled, for example. One end of the Osmanthorpe fort is truncated, or cut short, possibly to accommodate steep ground which was better left outside the defences. The outlines of the five known temporary camps in Nottinghamshire also show that surveyors sometimes chose terrain which appears to be less than ideal defensively. In all, 130 of these temporary camps have been identified in England by the Royal Commission on the Historical Monuments of England (RCHME). Its official-ish definition of them is this: 'A Roman camp was a lightly built but effective defensive enclosure constructed to accommodate highly mobile troops "under canvas" or, more accurately, in tents made of leather.'

Camps of this type, which varied in size from around 0.2–1.6 hectares (0.5–4 acres), were built by soldiers at the end of each day's march and included a perimeter of a defensive ditch and low bank made of the turf dug out of the ditch. Wooden stakes, of which two were carried by each soldier, could be inserted into the bank. Such camps could have been built for many local tactical reasons but are obviously associated with active military campaigning. If so, the camps in Nottinghamshire probably dated from the first three or four decades after the invasion in 43. The slight temporary nature of such camps means that remnants of only a few seem to have survived the toll of two millennia. The 130 plotted by the RCHME showed the highest concentration in Northumberland, Cumbria and Shropshire. Outside these areas, the highest numbers are found in Staffordshire, North Yorkshire and Nottinghamshire. However, this concentration pattern is thought to reflect not the number of camps that were built, but rather the local extent of modern aerial photography. In Nottinghamshire, all but one of the five known camps were identified by Derrick Riley using aerial photographs of cropmarks. These are the surface results of changes in sub-soil caused by the digging of ditches or building of walls, and are best seen in dry weather on sandy soils. Surface features such as defensive earth banks have usually not survived.

Where, as a Roman surveyor, would you locate such camps at the end of a day's march? Common sense, and military instruction, meant that the army surveyors chose sites that were not overlooked by enemies and had access to fresh water. The Roman writer Vegetius, usually ascribed to the late 4th century, said as much in a handbook of military rules and advice. 'Camps — especially when the enemy is near — should be built always in a safe place, where there are sufficient supplies of firewood, fodder and water, and if a long stay is in prospect choose a salubrious site,' he said. Avoid building near high ground that could be used by the enemy. And do not choose a site at risk from flooding. He added that camps could be square, triangular or semi-circular, but that the main gate should face east, towards the enemy or face the direction in which the army was to march. The locations of the temporary camps in Nottinghamshire show the extent to which some of these factors were accommodated. Roman soldiers were expected to build such camps after a standard day's march of 32km (20 miles), or 38.5km (24 miles) if a forced march. But Roman histories suggest that soldiers could march 48–56km (30–35) miles a day if required. The legionary's normal pack weighed in at 27kg, which is approximately the same full equipment weight as carried by British soldiers today and at the time of the Somme in 1916.

The fort at Broxtowe

In 1937 workmen digging the foundations and drains of the new Broxtowe housing estate in north west Nottingham found three Roman coins. Further digging revealed the floor of a building described as a 'large hut, rich with coins and other relics'. But as

Broxtowe estate in north west Nottingham: a Roman fort was discovered here in the 1930s but quickly covered back over to allow the building of the estate to continue.

interesting as this was, nobody yet knew that the people of Nottingham were about to start reading about the discovery of the city's first Roman fort, albeit one that was soon to be covered up again by the housing estate that had revealed it. The terrain the fort was built on had only become an official part of Nottingham five years earlier; the city was growing and the Corporation was building comfortable public housing on the new urban fringe while knocking down the old slums of the inner city. The land that was to become Broxtowe estate, its future street patterns designed in elegant symmetrical ovals and half-moons, was still covered by woodland and the full extent of the site only became apparent as the trees were felled. The coins and 'large hut' were found in Lindbridge Road, in the estate's western half. Work on housing in the eastern section took place in the second half of 1937 and it was here, while drains and pipes for gas and electricity were going in, that a ditch and parapet were found. As the clearance of the woodland continued in November and December, a ditch and a parapet 182 metres (600ft) long came to light. In all, in excavations carried out by the Thoroton Excavating Section, the outline and interior detail of what appeared to be a fort had appeared, its southern long edge just south of the line of what was to become Fenwick Close, and with an apparent entrance at the junction of Alwyn Road and Firsby Road. It was indeed 'a very important and unexpected discovery', as it was described.

A drawing of the camp, bordered at the northern end by 'natural fortifications' formed by an incline dropping 29 metres (95ft) to a valley, was made by the director of excavations, George Campion, a passionate but amateur archaeologist whose CV included studying Nottingham's sandstone cave system. As work continued at Broxtowe into 1938, boys of the HM Borstal Institute at Maythorpe were loaned to help with the digging.

In all, 20 boys a day worked for six weeks and moved 600 tons

Borstal boys help with the digging. From the *Nottingham Journal*, 15th February, 1938.

of earth. Many artefacts were found at the Broxtowe site, later described in an article published in the *Nottinghamshire Guardian*. These included an 'amazing' amount of pottery, mostly in fragments; more than 30 brooches 'of which no two are exactly alike'; numerous coins, the latest dated to the reign of

Vespasian and struck in 71; ivory dice; two parts of a quern for milling corn; sickles; and several iron and bronze pieces including knives, razors and an impressive bronze skillet, stamped with the name Albanvs, which is now on show in the University of Nottingham Museum.

Despite all this, the construction of the housing estate carried on and the site was quickly built over the following year. Yet despite the large number of Roman finds at Broxtowe, the site offers many problems. For a start, there was disagreement between Campion and one of his chief excavators, F. Hind, over the nature of the site. Campion said it had been a Roman fort; Hind, who thought it was too far from the Fosse Way to be a Roman fort, concluded that it was a native British settlement, a point he made in the article he wrote for the *Nottinghamshire Guardian* titled 'Report on the Late Iron Age Settlement'. Hind said that after the initial finding of Roman artefacts the site proved to be 'a British hut settlement, such as existed in all parts of Britain prior to the Roman conquest, in what was known as the "Early Iron Age" Culture.' This view seems to have been based on the remains of 20 'huts', which were usually rectangular and measured 5.4 metres × 2.4 metres (18ft by 8ft). A small number were round and one seemed to have been used as a workshop since it contained 'remains of furnaces, hearths and much iron slag.' Although Hind concluded that the site had not existed before the Roman invasion of Britain in 43, and that it had ceased to be used from 71 or 72, the evidence of ornaments and utensils still suggested to him that the Broxtowe site had been the product of a 'British culture supposed not to extend north of Northamptonshire'. He added: 'Is it a likely assumption to look upon this settlement as being made by refugees from further south, who fled before the Roman arms in 43 AD, and crossing the Trent felt safe, and founded a new home, but bringing the culture of the south with them? They again fled, 28 years later,

Bronze skillet found at Broxtowe Roman fort in the 1930s.

before their foes, leaving Broxtowe deserted.'

Although the consensus today is that Hind was wrong and that the large number of Roman finds at Broxtowe proves it was clearly Roman, there is still the problem that its odd, irregular outline mapped by Campion does not fit the usual 'playing card' shape favoured by the Roman army for almost all their forts.

The problem of identifying it as a fort is compounded by the

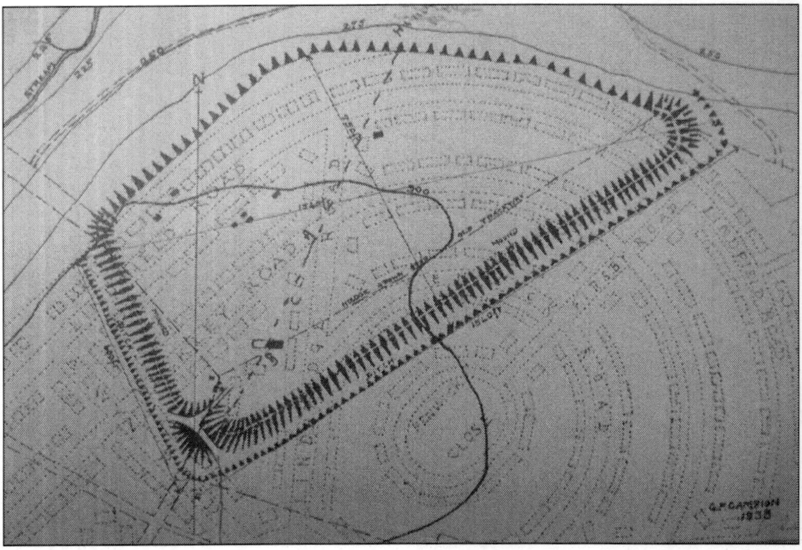

George Campion's plan of the Roman fort at Broxtowe, superimposed on the street plan of Broxtowe Estate.

probable unreliability in Campion's 1930s excavation report and the inability of contemporary archaeologists to re-examine his records.

These problems were highlighted in 1964 when a ditch was found and excavated on the estate, revealing some metalwork, pottery and a piece of lava quernstone dated to 55–75. In his brief account of this work, archaeologist Don Mackreth explained that Campion and Hind had produced different explanations and plans of the site, but that the latest ditch didn't fit in with either. There was not enough evidence to suggest how the different ditches seen by all the excavators related to each other. Mackreth ended by expressing the ambition that all of the surviving pre-war excavation records from Broxtowe, and the

1964 report, would shortly be published together. But this never happened and today nobody seems to know where Campion's 1930s records have gone. In 1955, when Campion died, they were left to his son-in-law Herbert O. Houldsworth, of West Bridgford, but they then disappeared after Houldsworth's own death.

The tale is closely tied up with Campion's own status as an amateur archaeologist in an era when archaeology was not yet on a professional footing (another example of a passionate amateur at this time was Felix Oswald, working at *Margidunum*). Campion was a director of the Campion Motor Cycle Company but took early retirement to pursue his lifelong passion for archaeology. As well as Nottingham's caves and Broxtowe, he investigated Lenton Priory and helped rescue two Bronze Age canoes from the Trent. However, a short biographical sketch of Campion, written by a fellow member of the Thoroton Society, casts doubt on his reliability as an interpreter of archaeology: 'He was a genius at finding artefacts, particularly complete medieval Nottingham pots, though his interpretation of the finds often left a good deal to be desired.' A strange medical condition must also be mentioned. 'Pre-war, Campion had excavated a medieval plague pit where he contracted a serious illness resulting in him losing all sense of taste and smell,' the biography added. A further detail to this story was added by another member of the Thoroton Society: 'He told me that when he excavated a burial pit, the smell and gases were so awful that he lost his sense of taste and smell.' Many photographs of the Broxtowe excavations are to be found within the eight boxes of Herbert O. Houldsworth's papers that were deposited in the Nottinghamshire Archives in 2005. A jumbled and largely untapped mass of private letters, jottings and typed articles covering several periods of local history and archaeology, Houldsworth's papers also include many of Campion's own delicate colour drawings of Roman artefacts recovered from Broxtowe. But the eight boxes do not harbour Campion's records of the excavation.

But where does all this leave the Broxtowe site? Mackreth, in the mid-1960s, said that Broxtowe was 'almost certainly a fort', although probably one that was altered several times by successive army units. The consensus today is that the structure was an early Roman fort, constructed in around 50 (Malcolm Todd

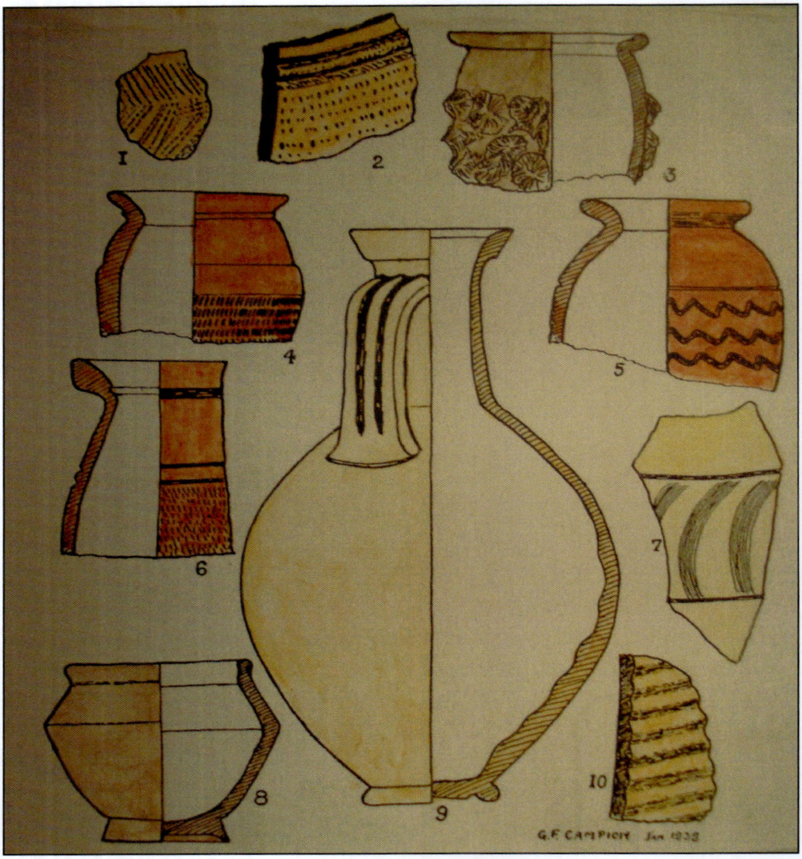

George Campion's own drawings of artefacts recovered from the Broxtowe excavation, dated 1938.

said around 60) and abandoned as the Roman military front line moved north in the 70s. Although not re-excavated, Broxtowe has been tentatively defined as one of several regional strong-points designed to strengthen the Roman position north of the Trent at a time when the Brigantian territory to the north of *Corieltauvi* territory was still unconquered. Today, Broxtowe is regularly included in lists of certain or possible Roman forts in Britain and is marked as a fort on the latest OS map of Roman Britain. However, with the housing estate above it quite obviously not going anywhere, no further investigation of the site is possible. Very occasionally Roman finds are still found in the estate, a reminder of what lies beneath. This happened in 1978, when another coin from Vespasian's reign was found in the garden of a house in Lindfield Road, the estate's outermost road.

From the *Nottingham Journal*, 11th May, 1938.

Osmanthorpe

In the dry summer of 1979 cropmarks on a hill a few miles north west of Southwell were firmly recognised from the air as the remains of the defensive ditches of a hitherto unknown large Roman fortress. Osmanthorpe fortress, between the villages of Kirklington and Edingley in the valley of the river Greet, enclosed nine hectares (22 acres) and was therefore immediately categorised as a 'vexillation fortress' — a term coined to indicate a substantial fortress smaller than one housing an entire Roman legion, but bigger than a temporary camp. The word derives from *vexillatio*, which was a detachment from a legion. Archaeologists have come up with various theories as to what such fortresses were for. But, faced with an absence of confirmation one way or another from the ancient world, perhaps the best one can say is that fortresses of this type were large, perhaps semi-permanent and that their size suggests that the Roman military machine was quite prepared to split its legions and deploy units from them in large tactical concentrations — or 'battle groups' as modern commanders would call them.

An obvious contender for the legion using the fortress is Legion IX *Hispana*, which is believed to have been deployed among three sites, including Lincoln and Longthorpe in Cambridgeshire, before it was moved to York in around 70. The candidates for the legion's third fortress have included Broxtowe, Newton-on-Trent, perched on the eastern bank of the Trent in Lincolnshire, and Osmanthorpe. The fortress's proximity to other Roman camps and settlements in this part of Nottinghamshire suggests there was a clustering, or concentration, of Roman military might in this area established in the

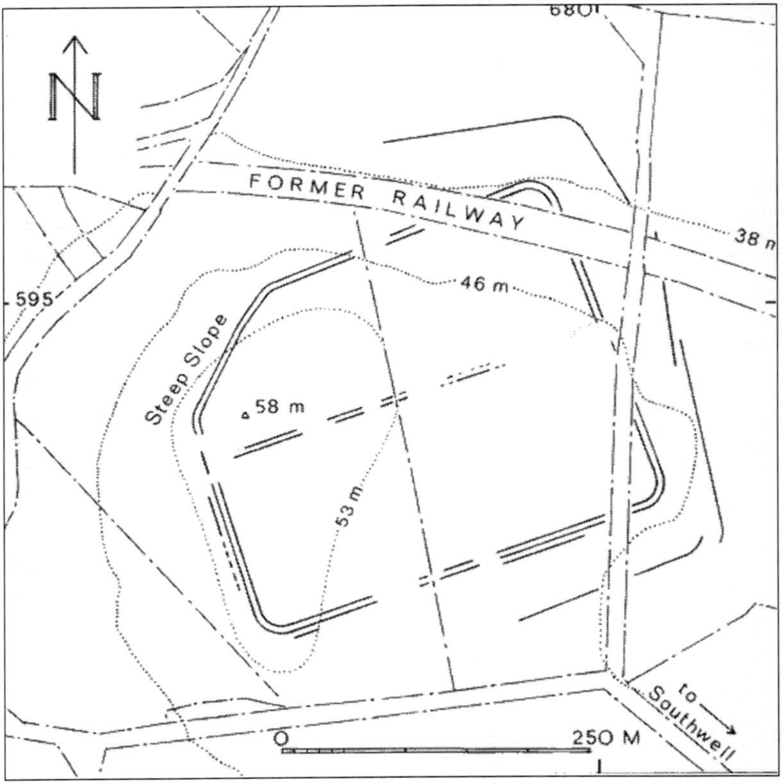

Plan of the Osmanthorpe fortress based on cropmarks noted by Derrick Riley.

first three decades after the invasion. There were temporary camps to the north west at Farnsfield and to the east at Holme, although it is not known if they were connected. The evidence also strongly suggests that Osmanthorpe was connected to the Roman town at *Ad Pontem* on the east side of the Trent. It has been speculated that Osmanthorpe could have been used to help guard against the Brigantian tribes to the north; or was used as a concentration point for troops about to head north to take on the *Brigantes* in the 70s. Finds of pottery sherds, coins and brooches close to the fortress suggest there may also have been a civilian settlement linked with it, while the recovery of isolated Roman finds in Farnsfield, Halam, Edingley and Camp Hill also testifies to the presence of Roman culture in the Greet Valley, perhaps centred on the large villa at Southwell.

Cropmarks showing three parallel ditches were first seen at Osmanthorpe in 1977 and the site was subsequently investigated by Derrick Riley after he photographed two sides of the fort's roughly rectangular shape in 1979. Riley put the distance between the northern and southern defences at 280m (918ft), and 300m (984ft) between the eastern and (unseen) western sides. The fort lies on a prominent hill, two corners of its defences being cut across by the modern Southwell–Kirklington road and the Southwell Trail, which follows the route of a Victorian railway line. No public footpath cuts across the site but the entire hill can be circumnavigated in about 30 minutes on foot following minor roads (but bear in mind that there are no pavements on these). In doing so it becomes quickly apparent why the hill would be a sensible choice for defence since it gives clear views across the surrounding terrain, a point also noted by the Ordnance Survey, which placed a trig point at the summit. For Roman soldiers there would also have been source of fresh drinking water nearby at Edingley Beck.

Further investigations in 1984 confirmed that the fort was defended by double ditches, with a third ditch on the southern and eastern sides. The north west corner of the defences was also found to be truncated. The north east England-based archaeologist Mike Bishop, who led this later study, reasoned that this truncation may have reflected a logical decision to keep the terrain at this corner outside the fort because the hill's very steepness meant it was 'dead ground'. Bishop also saw a line of double ditches running east–west across the centre of the fort and staggered ditches 50 metres (164ft) from the fort's eastern side, this latter feature being interpreted as outer defences. Although Bishop could not definitely identify the fort's gateways, it has been suggested elsewhere that the southern entrance was aligned to the road from *Ad Pontem*. Unfortunately, finds from the Osmanthorpe fort since the 1960s have been relatively meagre, with pottery sherds, a few coins and a saucepan handle turning up in one of the four fields covered by the fort. Sherds of *samian* pottery were dated to the mid to late 1st century, which fitted in with the assumption that the fort dated from the first decades of the Roman occupation. Bishop dug two trenches in 1984 to shed more light on this assumption and, based on this work and other evidence, concluded that the fort dated from the Roman occupation's first 25 years, that is up to 67 or so.

Bishop, incidentally, never used the word 'vexillation' to describe Osmanthorpe, preferring *castra*, meaning fort or fortress. Bishop's problem was that 'vexillation' was not a word used to describe fortresses in antiquity and that the variety of sizes and possible uses of Roman military installations meant that it was difficult to define them using blanket terms. Furthermore, and importantly, Bishop pointed out: 'the way some have imagined that these sites were used has, in turn, affected how they see the early years of the Roman occupation unfolding'.[3] In fact, the archaeological evidence at forts such as Osmanthorpe, or rather its scarcity, meant it was difficult to tell what their precise purpose had been. Were such installations used as winter quarters? As summer quarters? As temporary accommodation for units on 'search and destroy' missions? There were no firm answers to these questions. Bishop concluded: 'It is, we hope, clear... that there is sound evidence for supposing that there was a sizeable pre-Flavian military site at Osmanthorpe. However, in the absence of more extensive excavation, it would be unwise to comment further on the exact appearance of the establishment, or its internal layout. Furthermore, it is impossible to reflect profitably on the politico-strategic significance of the site and the historical context leading to its foundation.'

Temporary camps

There are four (or five) known in Nottinghamshire: Calverton (two camps), Farnsfield, Gleadthorpe and Holme:

Calverton

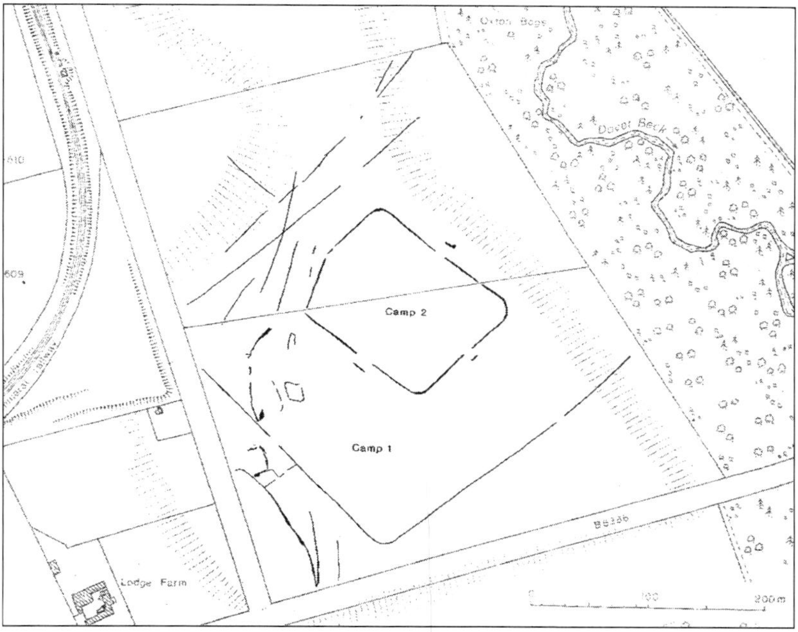

The two Calverton camps.

Two temporary camps at Calverton were identified from aerial photography taken by Derrick Riley in July 1982. His black and white image shows the clear outline of a rectangular enclosure, within a much larger rectangular camp which has its north west corner clipped off by Whinbush Lane. This outer camp is thought to be the earlier one and measures 285 metres (935ft) across, covering a probable maximum area of 10.5 hectares (26 acres). Its exact dimensions depend on how far you think its eastern edge extended towards the Dover Beck which runs through wooded Oxton Bogs. The main gate may have been on the south east side. The smaller camp inside encloses four acres and has a truncated northern end. Here, entrances can be seen at all four sides, with a defensive feature, called a *titulum*, in front of each. These short ditches and ramparts were intended to help prevent a direct assault on camp gateways and were common features of such camps across Britain. At Calverton, as with other temporary camps, the camps' location testifies to the common-sense decisions of the Roman army's surveyors: the site is 60 metres (196ft) above sea level, giving reasonably good views across the nearby terrain (except where the modern pit spoil heap gets in the way) and is close to fresh water. One unusual feature noted about the larger camp is that the north east ditch would have been at the bottom of the slope near Dover Beck, which may have been a defensive weakness since enemies would have been able to overlook the defences. Riley also observed: 'Beyond the Trent, at a distance of about 8 miles from the camps, is the Fosse Way. It is interesting to note that the valley of the Dover Beck is a natural route through the hills on the north side of the Trent valley, which is followed now by the main road running from the Foss Way near Margidunum to Ollerton and Doncaster.' A combination of fast traffic, high field embankments and private land ownership makes the Calverton camps site a difficult one to get a good look at.

Mention here must also be made of a probable Roman fort at Dorket Head, just beyond the northern edge of Nottingham between Calverton and Arnold. Earthworks on this hill were noted by the 18th century Nottinghamshire antiquarian Hayman Rooke and there has long been a tradition that the hill, known in the 19th century as Hollinwood Hill or Holly Hill, had hosted a Roman fort. Rooke said he discovered 'a considerable part of a very large camp, which probably contained the main body of the Roman army. My informant, an old farmer, assured me he remembers the camp complete, extending a long way into the adjoining field, and he is certain it was twice the length of what is now distinguishable.' Attempts to put the matter to rest one way or another were made by James and Catherine Turner of the Sherwood Archaeological Society. After much difficulty, and 20 years' labour, they concluded that they had found a 'card-shaped rectangular enclosure' which seemed to fit the earthworks noted by Rooke.[4] With its ditches 28 metres (92ft) apart, they thought that this had indeed been a Roman fort enclosing eight hectares (20 acres). An entrance at the north west seemed to have a *titulum*. Such a prominent site, they said in their 1997 report, would have given the Roman army a good position for observation and signalling in the valley of the Dover Beck. Although few Roman artefacts were found, the Turners saw this as possible evidence that the fort was quickly built and little used. In fact, the majority of the finds at Dorket Head were

Iron Age, which suggested the hill's strategic position had also been recognised by the natives long before the Romans arrived. Cropmarks of field systems have also been seen on nearby land at Ramsdale and pottery dated up to the mid and late 1st century was found here in the 1990s.

Farnsfield

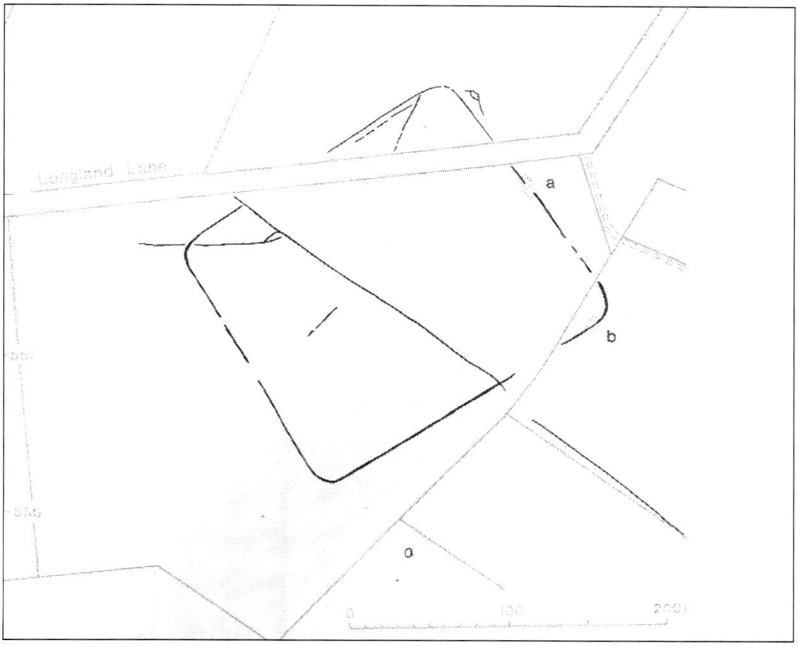

Farnsfield camp.

A temporary camp covering 3.9 hectares (9.6 acres) at Farnsfield was another of the Roman military sites identified by Derrick Riley. Riley saw cropmarks outlining the camp's defences in 1976 and confessed that its discovery was a 'surprise' since he had already spent several previous summers examining the sandstone country of north Nottinghamshire in dry weather — ideal conditions for cropmarks — without seeing it. The camp is a slightly squashed rectangle and is on farmland crossed by Longland Lane, which seems to have obscured the northern gate. A likely attraction for the army surveyors must have been the site's flatness. But while the camp has clear views all around — it may have faced towards the north east — it does not dominate the terrain and there is higher ground immediately to the south. The camp's backdrop also includes the pre-Roman settlement on the hill at Combs Farm, to the south west.

With the Roman fortress at Osmanthorpe 4km (2.5 miles) to the east, and another pre-Roman site to the south at Old Ox, near Oxton, the area provides concentrated antiquity. Luckily, a public footpath passing close to Farnsfield camp and the two ancient British settlements allows you to view all three in one expedition (but only Old Ox is publicly accessible). Was it this path, or another nearby, that was described by Pevsner as 'the ancient trackway between Nottingham and Bawtry'?[5] In the 18th century, thanks in part to the enthusiasm of gentlemen scholars like Hayman Rooke, this whole area was thought to be peppered with Roman camps. John Throsby, in his edition of Thoroton's *Antiquities of Nottinghamshire*, described several 'little exploratory camps' including Old Ox, Combs Farm and one in a field called 'Lovely Grange' near Oxton. The Oxton resident Tom Shipside, in his book of recollections of life in Oxton in the 19th and early 20th centuries titled *I Lived in a Village*, also offered some colourful but fanciful thoughts on the supposed Roman influence on this part of the county. 'The names of rivers and mountains are almost universal, and on them the Ancient British races still speak,' he wrote in the 1950s.

> *Oldox (Oxton) shows old work elaborately carried out against some pressing danger, perchance the Roman invasion of which the three tumuli at Grange Farm, Oxton (on the Lowther Hills) or Cwms (Coombs Farm, Farnsfield) are conspicuous examples. They recall a people exposed to hostile force, flushed with success at having come so far inland, guarding themselves with a widely extended system of strategical defence... There is no Roman place-name in Oxton, for they were a marching not a fireside race, whose only place of settlement was a camp or a grave. You will find an ancient Briton on the bank of a river, but you must seek a Roman legionary on some straight road like that which runs for twelve miles from Lincoln to the Humber.*

Today, these earthworks are believed to have probably pre-dated the Roman invasion. However, air photography did identify the Roman camp at Farnsfield which, because of its complete absence of surface features, would have been hidden to Rooke, Throsby and Tom Shipside. The camp, which measures 182–186 metres (approximately 600ft) across, was excavated in 1978 by Catherine J. Swarbrick and James Turner, of the Sherwood Archaeological Society. They found an entrance 5.7 metres (18ft) wide on the north eastern side (marked 'a' on the drawing). An adjacent excavated defensive ditch was measured at 2.8 metres (9ft) wide and 1.8 metres (6ft) deep, narrowing to 15cm at the bottom. Ancient tool marks were seen in the sides of the ditch. The connected defensive rampart was also seen, marked on its inner edge by a line of pebbles set at a steep angle. A defensive ditch on the camp's eastern corner was also investigated (marked 'b' on the drawing). A handful of Roman pottery sherds were recovered from the ditches.

Gleadthorpe Plantation, Warsop

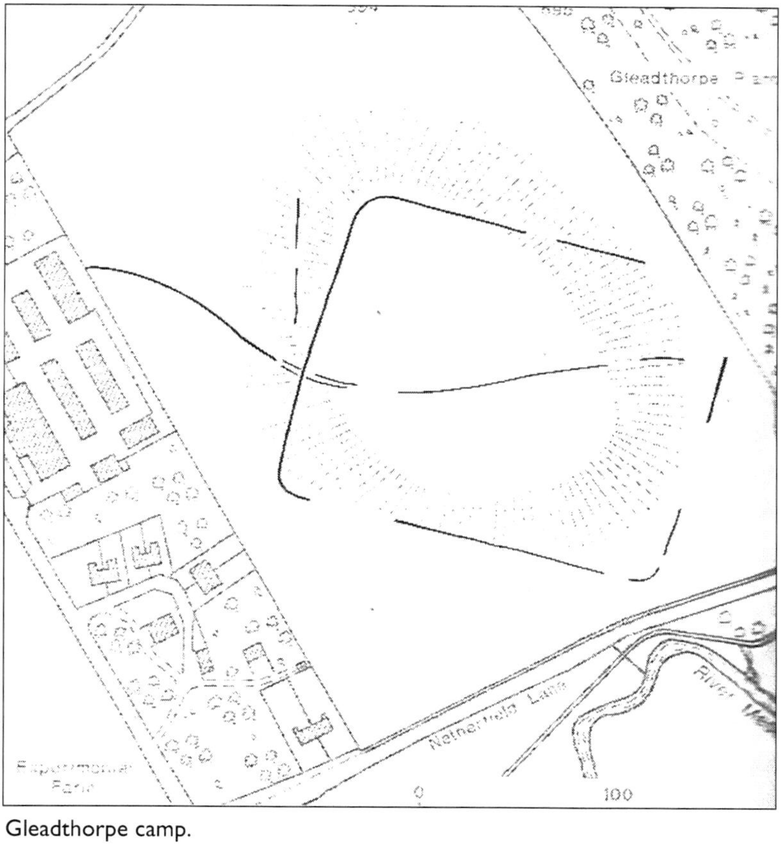

Gleadthorpe camp.

Another Roman camp, similar in size to the one at Farnsfield, was identified by Derrick Riley on a slight elevation surrounded by plantations at Gleadthorpe, north east of Warsop, in 1979. Covering 3.2 hectares (8.1 acres), the camp measures 204m (670ft) across. No entrance gateways have been identified and the site has not been excavated. How much of the Roman archaeology remains intact is debatable. The farmer who owns the sandy land here told me that metal-detectorists regularly asked him for permission to explore the area but all they had found were small pieces of lead. The field itself is called *Tenter* and was under wheat in the summer of 2010. The plantations on two sides of the field are dominated by oak while the camp's water source, the clear, slow river Meden, is immediately to the south.

A comment on the camp by the RCHME said that the site had been disturbed by quarrying, tree planting and the activities of the nearby Government research farm (now ADAS, a department of DEFRA). However, the Roman army's surveyors again seem to have chosen their site well, locating the camp on a rise 60 metres (196ft) above sea level and close to the Meden. Only the slope at the southern corner may have proved difficult for soldiers; the RCHME pointed out that the hill's steepness here may have been unsuitable for tents. Riley also saw traces of pre-Roman agriculture in the same valley and indeed the camp's existence only became apparent when he was examining photographs for evidence of ancient field systems in the area. The

The slight rise on which the Gleadthorpe camp was built.

cropmarks of the camp were distinct, but not prominent, and probably resulted from the filling in of a 'fairly narrow ditch', he said. The Robin Hood Way long-distance footpath passes close to the camp and allows a clear view of the site.

Holme

Holme camp.

Cropmarks outlining the rectangular shape of a large camp a few kilometres north of Newark were first seen from the air by J.K. St Joseph in the early 1960s. Its location next to the Trent, 500 metres from Holme, has always suggested that it was connected to a crossing of the river. With its northern side measuring 410 metres (1,345ft), and the whole camp possibly enclosing as much as 9.3 hectares (23 acres), St Joseph's first reaction was that the camp could have been large enough to house a legion. Three sides of the camp have been identified, the outline of the southern side being obscured by the narrow lane to the A1133 Langford road. Aerial photography has suggested that the southern defences may extend just south of this road. Entrance gateways have not been identified. Walking the length of the camp site today, along the verge of the narrow lane to Holme, it soon becomes apparent that this was indeed a very large camp. However, with the land now divided into fields of rough pasture guarded only by placid cows, it is difficult to imagine hundreds, if not thousands, of legionary soldiers sweating and cursing as they dug the camp's defensive ditch or put up their heavy goatskin tents. Nor is it easy to understand why the surveyors chose this site over any other identical flat area nearby. At just 10 metres (33ft) above sea level, this is hardly dominating high ground. And while it must have been convenient to have the Trent's fresh water so close, why didn't they build the camp even closer to the river? One is left with the impression that the camp perhaps acted as a base for an imminent crossing of the Trent, or was used as a temporary fortress guarding a narrow section of the river when this territory was still being disputed. The small town at *Crococolana* lies on the Fosse Way a short way to the east.

Yes, it's another field. The site of the Roman camp at Holme, now guarded by cows.

Notes

1. *Roman Forts in Britain* — Paul Bidwell. Tempus, 2007.
2. *The Jewish War* — Josephus. Penguin Classics, 1981.
3. Recent Work at Osmanthorpe, Nottinghamshire — M.C. Bishop, P.W.M. Freeman, M.V. Andrews, C.P. Barclay, K. Hartley, D.F. Mackreth, J. Roy, Simon J.N. Tomson and K.F. Hartley. *Britannia* 24, 1993.
4. Dorket Head in Nottinghamshire — James and Catherine Turner. *Sherwood Archaeological Society*, 1997.
5. *The Buildings of England: Nottinghamshire* — Nikolaus Pevsner. Penguin Books, 1951.

Chapter 8

The villas: lives of the rich and famous

'During the month of May this year, Hayman Rooke Esq, of Mansfield-Woodhouse, discovered within a mile and a half of the village, two Roman villas... .'

William Fowler's painting of the mosaic at the Mansfield Woodhouse villa discovered by Major Hayman Rooke in 1786.

So Thomas Bailey wrote in Volume IV of the *Annals of Nottinghamshire*, in his account of the main events of the year 1786. The short entry for Rooke's discovery was sandwiched between paragraphs describing a meeting of Nottingham shopkeepers at the Flying Horse Inn and an obituary for Admiral Sir John Byron who, as a young Royal Navy midshipman, had been cast away on an island near Chile for five years. Put like that, it is slightly difficult to tell that Rooke had actually unveiled one of Nottinghamshire's — and the region's — greatest Roman decorative treasures, and in doing so ensured that the name of Rooke would be forever intertwined with the story of Roman Nottinghamshire.

Major Rooke, who had retired to Mansfield Woodhouse in 1777 following a largely uneventful career in the British army, first identified as Roman some 'small stone cubes' on the surface of a field and duly set three men to excavate. These cubes were the individual *tesserae* that, arranged in their thousands, make up ornate patterned mosaics or the simpler 'tessellated pavements' in Roman villas and town houses. Just a foot down under the soil surface, Rooke's men gradually uncovered two large Roman winged buildings, almost at right angles to each other: measured at 26 metres (86ft) and 43 metres (142ft) long respectively, the smaller of the two buildings had just under half of a large, ornate mosaic surviving on the floor of the central room. This was assumed to be the villa's dining room. Patterned in red, white, yellow and grey, the size and complexity of the mosaic seemed designed to impress visitors with a display of expensive but tastefully refined décor in the correct Roman style. It was an important discovery for Nottinghamshire and the nation which attracted the interest of a high-ranking Government official. Yet nobody today knows who owned the villa near Mansfield Woodhouse. Indeed, nobody knows who owned any of the 600 or so known and suspected Roman villa houses in Britain. Some villas seem to have been relatively simple farmhouses, clustering around towns which must have been the main recipients of their agricultural produce; others were large luxury homes with courtyards, central heating, bath suites, Mediterranean gardens and outhouses that suggest they may have been both country retreats for wealthy people and the centres of large productive agricultural estates. Several Nottinghamshire villas, including the two largest known examples, at Southwell and Mansfield Woodhouse, possessed some of these internal features and one or two have also left evidence of their agricultural role as well. The owners of the larger villas must have been wealthy Romano-Britons who were perhaps keen to show how well they were doing in the Roman establishment. They were the 'local bigwigs' or the 'the rich and famous', as one Nottinghamshire archaeologist has informally described them. Other owners may have been very rich and mostly absent Roman property owners who owned estates in several countries. Yet the fact remains that, despite the ink expended on theories of villa development and how their rise and fall related to the larger economic welfare of the province, no names can be attached to any villa building in Britain; indeed, only a very few individual features such as decorative mosaics and tile stamps have yielded identifying marks of any kind.

Another problem with villas as a whole is one of definition. Variations in their size, form and evident use means that, unlike 'fort', an instinctive encompassing sense of what a 'villa' was remains just out of reach. The word 'villa' also suffers from contamination by modern usage in possible newspaper sentences such as 'the tanned Russian oligarch flew back to the French Riviera only to find his young former mistress had changed the locks at the villa they recently shared'. However, a plotting of villa locations shows that by far the densest concentration of villas was across the English south west and south eastern counties, with particular densities in Gloucestershire, Wiltshire, Oxfordshire and Dorset. In fact, when villa locations are plotted on a map it can be seen that most were built in the southern 'lowland' zone that runs diagonally across England from the south west to the north east — more or less the same line that was followed by the Fosse Way. North of this line villas became thin on the ground. The relative scarcity of villas in Wales, the West Midlands and northern England may have reflected a relative lack of large towns possessing ready markets for villa goods in the so-called villa economy. It is tempting to think that the north's status as a permanent military zone could also have made it an undesirable area in which to invest money in villa construction. But villas were built in the north — the most northerly suspected example in the entire Roman Empire being at Durham — and like villas in the south they were not defended properties. Their presence anywhere suggests that the people who lived in them believed they were living in peaceful times.

Adrian Oswald thought he had found a rare defended villa when he excavated at Norton Disney, a short distance from the Fosse Way's northern exit from Nottinghamshire, in the 1930s. But the ditches around the house he found have since been interpreted as drainage ditches.

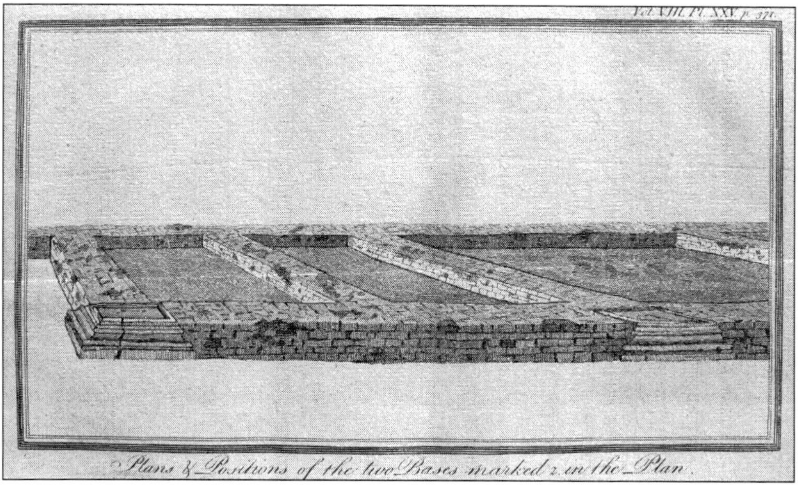

Drawing from the Mansfield Woodhouse villa site by Hayman Rooke.

Within the figure of 600 villas in Britain the number in Nottinghamshire has been put at 48. This figure, though, is difficult to support. Instead, we will venture here that the number of Nottinghamshire villas for which there is good evidence amounts to 13. These are located at: Barton-in-Fabis, Bingham, Car Colston, Cromwell, Flawford, Laxton, Mansfield Woodhouse, Newton, Oldcotes, Redhill, Sibthorpe, Southwell and Thurgarton/ Epperstone. In addition, finds of *tesserae* and other building debris suggest that villas may also have been located at East Stoke, Holme Pierrepont, Langar and Shelton. Evidence for two others have been reported from Willoughby-on-the-Wolds and Stanford-on-Soar, which makes 19. To these you could add the associated villas at Norton Disney in Lincolnshire, which was close to the small Roman town at Brough, and the villa at Lockington in Leicestershire, which was close to the Roman town at Redhill. Clearly, most of the local villas were built in the south of the county, in and close to the Trent Valley and close to settlements and major roads. However, the locations of the villas at Oldcotes and Mansfield Woodhouse, both some distance from any known Roman road or settlement, seem to defy this trend.

The probable villas at Bingham and Newton, close to *Margidunum*, have already been discussed. Another villa associated with *Margidunum*, and one for which a ground plan was fortunately sketched in the 19th century, is at Car Colston. Some of the other suspected villas, such as those at Laxton and Sibthorpe, are known only from scatters of pottery in fields and telling building debris such as wall plaster and roof tiles. Much more is known of the Cromwell villa, since the outline of the building's foundations can be seen as cropmarks amid a complex array of Iron Age and Roman agricultural marks near the Trent.

At least five of Nottinghamshire's villas have ornate mosaics. Or rather, had. Magnificent floor mosaics at Mansfield Woodhouse and Barton-in-Fabis were put on public display soon after they were discovered and were either vandalised or stripped by souvenir-hunters. The Mansfield Woodhouse mosaic was damaged and is now classified as 'lost' while the Barton-in-Fabis mosaic was bodily lifted to supposed safety and then disappeared. Another mosaic in very poor condition was uncovered at Flawford under the foundations of a church, was photographed, and is also regarded as lost. A geometric 'maze' mosaic at Oldcotes, which seems to have had a figure of Theseus in the Minotaur's labyrinth at its centre, was seen when a new Catholic church was being built and was then covered over by the church building. It is, in theory, still *in situ*, even though a former priest at the church ruled that nobody can excavate the villa for 50 years. The large and luxurious villa excavated in Southwell in 1959, estimated at 73 metres by 91 metres (240ft by 300ft) and described as probably the largest villa built in the region, revealed surviving fragments of six mosaics. These fragments were photographed and then covered back over. These, too, should still be intact underground.

In all, there is firm evidence of five Roman country houses in Nottinghamshire whose owners were rich enough to afford the time-consuming skills of mosaic-craftspeople. Most of these houses were occupied into the 4th century, when the mosaic industry appears to have been at its height. Comparisons between styles of mosaics across the country have suggested that four distinct schools of design had evolved by the first decades of the 4th century, when the size and luxury of British villas were at their zenith. The existence of mosaic schools was first suggested in the 1950s by David Smith,[1] who saw comparisons between mosaic styles in several villas in eastern central England and dubbed the school the *Durobrivan*, after the pottery-producing town of *Durobrivae* (Water Newton) in Cambridgeshire where he believed the school was based. The Mansfield Woodhouse mosaic is regarded as a product of this school, bearing stylistic similarities to mosaics at villas such as Nether Heyford and Great Weldon in Northamptonshire, Scampton, Denton and Medbourne in Lincolnshire and Great Casterton in Rutland. Smith, who also analysed the Southwell mosaics, said the *Durobrivan* mosaics were entirely geometrical with repetitive patterns of stars of eight lozenges accompanied by squares, triangles, knots and other motifs. These patterns are easily recognised in the early drawings that were made of the Mansfield Woodhouse mosaic.

Although perhaps only a quarter of all known British villas have produced evidence of mosaic decorations, and most of those are in south west England, the large number of mosaics found in Britain — coupled with the time-consuming nature of mosaic installation — suggests that a large mosaic industry was in operation in the 4th century. How time-consuming was this work? In modern attempts to reproduce one of the largest Roman mosaics in northern Europe, the 15 metre by 15 metre (48ft by 48ft) Great Pavement at Great Woodchester villa in Gloucestershire, the pattern was laid down at the rate of 2 sq ft per day. It has been suggested that the 4th century mosaic schools should be thought of as groups of itinerant craftspeople who were in close contact with each other and carrying out commissions over at least 25–30 years. But while floor mosaics tend to be the main aspect of Roman decoration that we bear in mind when we think of villas, they were not the only form of interior decorative décor. Stucco floors and brightly painted wall plaster, such as Rooke saw at Mansfield Woodhouse, also speak of wealth and opportunities to enjoy leisure time. Coloured wall plaster was noted by Felix Oswald at *Margidunum* and 'elaborately painted plasterwork' was seen at Epperstone. At Southwell, the best-known decorative treasure of the villa is the picture of a swimming Cupid that had been painted on the walls above a 7.6 metre by 4.5 metre (25ft by 15ft) cold bath. This was the eye candy for the Romano-British well-to-do when they took a bracing cold water plunge in Southwell's luxurious bathing suite. The large piece of plaster featuring Cupid is on display in Southwell Minster.

The painting of Cupid from the Southwell villa.

Like Roman military installations, many villas defy a neat historical snapshot analysis because they often reveal evidence of successive phases of demolition and construction. Adrian Oswald, who partly re-excavated the Mansfield Woodhouse villa in the 1930s and found Rooke's original 18th century floor plan to have been 'extremely accurate', discovered that the villa site had first been settled with round and oblong timber buildings in the year 80 or thereabouts. After a fire these were replaced by larger wooden buildings, some with tile roofs, in 130. These in turn were replaced by a rectangular stone building, later extended by the addition of wings, in the early 3rd century. Another fire occurred, but the house was rebuilt with a new corridor including a tessellated floor (also seen by Rooke). Another room was connected to the main building by a passageway and new exterior paving was added. But still the builders had more work. In the early 4th century, an entirely new and separate 'basilican' building was added to the east of the first house. Crude buttresses were tacked on to this structure and new projecting rooms, including a bath, were added at one end. All this brought the house up to around the year 350, after which the datable record in pottery and coins went no further. And it was the remains of these two buildings that Rooke had discovered in 1786 — a villa complex of two apparently related structures, with many rooms, baths, ovens, heating and a large ornate dining room floor mosaic, frozen in time at its peak in the mid-4th century. That the villa had gone through so many alterations is perhaps not surprising given at least two fires and 300 years of occupation.

Adrian Oswald also excavated the villa at Norton Disney and, as at Mansfield Woodhouse, uncovered a structure that had started as timber and evolved into a large winged building that housed a *hypocaust*, bath suite, mosaics and had a possible separate entrance gatehouse. Developing over several rebuilding phases, punctuated by fires, the villa had finally enjoyed what he called its 'time of greatest luxury' between 300 and 360. Oswald felt the villa closely resembled the Mansfield Woodhouse villa, even sharing a similar orientation. Amid the debris was evidence of décor including wall plaster that bore 'a kind of Jazz pattern in greens and blacks and yellows'. Drawings of the damaged and robbed mosaics he found at Norton Disney show patterns of knots, leaves and geometric maze shapes.

In a footnote to his excavation report published in *The Antiquities Journal* in 1937, Oswald stated: 'Unfortunately, it proved impossible to remove either mosaic. Newark Museum did not possess the room for them and I was loathe to destroy them in case the opportunity for removal should present itself at a later date.' However, the most dramatic part of this excavation by far was Oswald's finding of three skeletons in the rubble, and his interpretation of how these two men and a woman had met their end here. One of the skeletons had a knife buried just below the right ribs; another lay contorted underneath stones. They all lay among evidence that the villa had suffered a 'fierce fire'. Oswald continued:

> *It is probably permissible to suggest that these people were trying to escape the burning building and that as the man on the wall passed over the threshold of the door the lintel collapsed on top of him, crushing the body into the distorted condition in which it was found. It is also possible that the other two people met their deaths in a collapse of the outer wall... it is difficult to avoid the conclusion that the end of the [villa] occupation was a violent one and that it took place in the troublous times which the country endured in the mid-fourth century.*[2]

A Dr L.H.D. Buxton examined the skeletons and declared that they had been otherwise fit and healthy specimens for their time. However, there was a problem with one of the male skeletons. 'The only abnormalcy was what might be described as his unusual femininity for a man,' said Dr Buxton. However, this was in 1937.

Substantial roof pantiles from Norton Disney villa. Tiles of a similar style can be seen in use across rural Nottinghamshire today.

Although the Norton Disney excavation was financially supported by donors including the Duke of Portland, the Newark Corporation and the Thoroton Society, a public appeal for funds had to be made to enable the work to continue. According to a report in the *Nottingham Evening Post* in June 1935, private donors brought in £75. Newark's reward for supporting the work would be to receive the pottery and 'other relics' and so have 'one of the best collections in the country of pottery from one site covering so wide a period'. Even so, visitors still had to pay a small charge to see the excavation as it progressed. It was this excavation that the writer G.M. Boumphrey described seeing in his amiable book *Along the Roman Roads*. 'When I was there, they had found two pavements and some traces of walls, and were trying to work out the plan of the place to see where to dig next,' he wrote. 'I went and looked at the excavations. It seems absurd to go out in the middle of a field, scrape aside a covering of straw and see a mosaic floor only a few inches down. But there it is.'

Several parts of the villa, including a section of roof tiles and part of a tessellated floor, are now in the care of Newark and Sherwood District Council.

Darkened section of tessellated floor recovered from the Norton Disney villa.

At Southwell, Charles Daniels, who excavated the town's villa in 1959, concluded that occupation of the building had begun in the early 2nd century and lasted until the early 4th century. However, within this period one wing of the villa may have been demolished and rebuilt while other alterations were made, including embellishments of a mosaic pavement. The large cold bath he found in the villa itself told a story. A first bath was built, decorated with a bright portrayal of Cupid and human figures, lined with tiles and stone slabs on the floor and water-proofed with three-inch thick layers of mortar on the sides. This was demolished and a new bath room built. This room was also demolished, the wall and ceiling plaster being thrown face down into the bath below. The whole bath was then filled with more rubble and a new hard mortared floor was built over the top. When Daniels excavated underneath this floor level and into the bath he found the painted plaster where it had been thrown centuries before. This was resassembled to form the painting of Cupid.

Comparisons of villa outlines show that they could take many forms. Many are often classified today into several recognisable shapes such as 'winged corridor', 'aisle' and 'courtyard'. The smaller of the two Mansfield Woodhouse buildings is a winged corridor house since it had two symmetrical extending wings connected by a corridor, with five rooms behind it. Wings have also been found or suspected at Southwell, Flawford, Barton-in-Fabis, Thurgarton, Cromwell and Car Colston. Like Mansfield Woodhouse, the Car Colston house seems to have had its wings connected by an aisle, with rooms behind it, but there was also another room projecting at the rear. Although larger courtyard villas have not been conclusively recorded in the Midlands up to now, the Southwell villa may have been such a one and the villa remains discovered at Newton near *Margidunum* could have been another, since surveys there seem to show structures clustered around an open space. A few local villas also reveal associated structures away from the main buildings. A small round building at Barton-in-Fabis, for example, was interpreted as housing a threshing floor for cereals, while Rooke, at Mansfield Woodhouse, found two graves, one of which contained an urn of ashes and scattered human bones. He found no farm outhouses or stables. These, Rooke thought, must have been destroyed long ago by ploughing since the soil here was thin.

The location of many Nottinghamshire villas close to towns in the valley of the Trent and its tributaries has already been noted. The fact that a few were also built on or close to earlier Iron Age settlements underlines how Romans or Romanised Britons chose to build their villas on already developed sites. The Cromwell villa was evidently built in an area of Iron Age farming on the banks of the Trent, and Iron Age brooches and other remains were found at Flawford villa. At Lockington, just over the county border in Leicestershire, cropmarks have revealed that a 40 metre long rectangular Roman villa was built next to a settlement of around twenty Iron Age roundhouses. The archaeology could not tell whether the Roman and native sites were occupied at the same time.

Christian church-builders appear to have been attracted to some villa sites when the Roman occupation was over. A Saxon church was built over the Flawford villa and there are suggestions in the literature that churches at Langar and Willoughby-on-the-Wolds were founded above villas. A church was also built over the villa at Oldcotes in the 19th century. But the best-known association between villa and Christian place of worship is at Southwell, where the Minster and grounds lie next to the villa site. A piece of exposed tessellated pavement underneath the pews in the Minster's south transept was long believed to be part of the villa, but has also been reinterpreted as the floor of the Saxon church that preceded the Minster. Yet David J. Neal and Stephen R. Cosh, authors of the recent and vast *Roman Mosaics in Britain*, favour a Roman origin for the paving and suggest that the Saxon builders may have incorporated it into their church. The villa site was certainly visited, if not permanently occupied, after the Romans left. Charles Daniels found 'a pagan Saxon urn' in one room and holes in the mosaics suggested that a hut had been built in the villa, which was extensively robbed. Some 30 human burials were also found in or on the mosaic floors and elsewhere human bones were found, including a skeleton with metal studs in one shoulder, an ankle and the chest. All were regarded as Christian interments.

What did people do in their villas? The people who lived at the Cromwell villa, with their paddocks and outhouses, worked the land and it is likely that many of the other Nottinghamshire villas were also engaged in agriculture. The theory that villas may also have churned out industrial products such as tiles and bricks has often been explored. However, at Barton-in-Fabis, excavator F.H. Thompson's attempts to prove that the villa had processed gypsum failed and he concluded that the villa's economy had also been based on farming. The more luxurious villas were clearly also designed for entertainment. For example, it is thought that the gap between the walls and the edge of the large mosaic in the central room at Mansfield Woodhouse was made wide enough to accommodate three reclining couches. Rooke quickly identified this room as the dining room, or *triclinium*. In Italy, at least, the literature suggests that dining was at the heart of villa life, and especially so in spectacular settings. The wealthier houses could lay on acrobats, singers, dancers and singing cooks for the guests, while the outrageous teenage Emperor Elagabalus was reported to have had lions and leopards trained to jump on to couches in the middle of meals. Although there is no evidence for enjoyable extremes such as this in Britain, the evidence of wealth at some villas in Nottinghamshire suggests that owners and guests enjoyed a high standard of living. The lifestyle would have included the Roman habit of regular bathing. Baths have been found at several Nottinghamshire villas, as have their associated *hypocausts*. These were effective heating systems, the heat being produced in small furnaces and circulated under floors and within wall spaces via box flue-tiles. A complete flue-tile, called a *tubulus*, was recovered from *Margidunum* and can be seen in the University of Nottingham Museum. Imitating the customs in Italy, local villas may have had suites of hot, warm and cold baths. A taste of what life was like in larger villas was given by the 1st century lawyer Pliny, who owned an extensive property at Laurentum in Italy. The villa included heated swimming pools and baths. 'If you want more space to swim or warmer water, there is a pool in the courtyard and a well near to it to tone you up with cold water when you have had enough of the warm,' he wrote to a friend. 'Next to the temperate room is a cooling one which enjoys the sun's kindly warmth, though not as much as the hot room which is built out in a bay. This contains three plunging-baths, two full in the sun and one in the shade, though still in the light...'[3]

Although the invaders had also introduced public bath houses to Britain, these would have been difficult to visit for villa owners who lived far from towns. The Jewry Wall in Leicester is the remains of one public bath complex, completed around 160 or so with hot and cold baths, plunge pools, boiler and latrine, all separated from an exercise area that was set apart by the wall, with its two entrance arches, that can be seen today. With services dedicated to exercise, relaxation and cleanliness, such town baths were 'akin to a good club', in the words of archaeologist John Wacher in the early 1970s. A more relevant comparison today might be with a good modern gym offering swimming, exercise, sauna and social areas. Out in the sticks, building villas with their own heated bathing complexes would have given owners and their guests private leisure opportunities while also allowing them to enjoy civilised Roman customs equivalent to those in the town baths. In British winters, villa central heating must also have had its own value. Pliny, again, described the warming effect that a central heating fire had on a bedroom in his Italian villa: 'This room is very warm in winter when it is bathed in sunshine, and on a cloudy day hot steam from the adjacent furnace-room serves instead.'

Mansfield Woodhouse

Mosaic *tesserae* seen in the northern fields of the parish between Mansfield Woodhouse and Pleasley were called 'fairy pavements' by local people in the 18th century, and it was these and some Roman brick that led Major Hayman Rooke to excavate the villa in May and October of 1786. Rooke found two adjacent buildings and gave them the titles *Villa Urbana* and *Villa Rustica*, following names given by the 1st century Roman agricultural writer Columella. The elegant *Urbana* was the smaller of the houses with the large mosaic and it was this building, Rooke supposed, that had been occupied by the 'master' while the longer *Rustica* building had been set aside for 'the cattle and servants that tilled the land'. The two buildings encompassed three *hypocausts*, a bath and several large rooms, some of which still had brightly painted plaster on the walls including stripes of purple, red, yellow, green and 'various colours'. One small room was delicately described by Rooke as a 'necessary convenience'. Rooke provided slightly different accounts of his discovery for *The Gentleman's Magazine* and then the Society of Antiquaries' periodical *Archaeologia*. After Rooke had completed

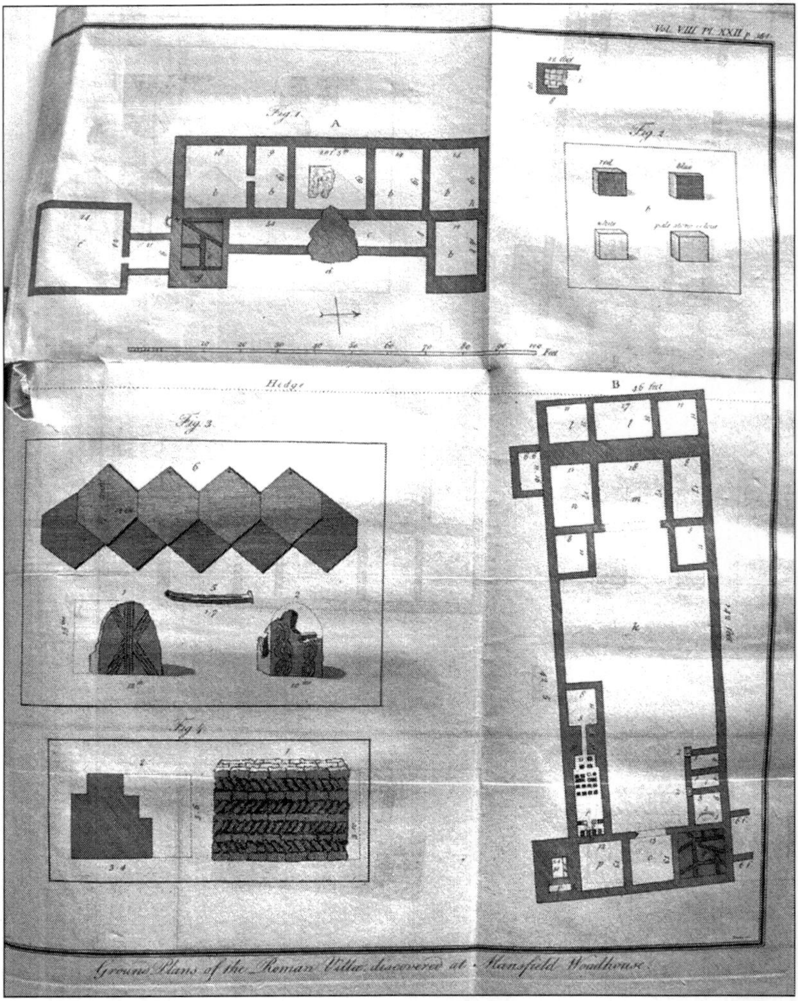

Photograph of an original page of Rooke's illustrations from the Society of Antiquaries' journal *Archaeologia*. The 'Villa Urbana' is the building at the top while the 'Villa Rustica' is on the right.

his study of the *Rustica* building in the spring of 1788 another account of his findings was provided to author William Harrod for inclusion in his *History of Mansfield and it's [sic] Environs*, published in 1801. The scale of Rooke's accomplishment was also underlined by messages of congratulations from Master of the Mint and Fellow of the Society of Antiquaries, the Rt. Hon. George Yonge. The letters grew into a regular correspondence and Yonge eventually visited the villa. He wrote afterwards:

> *Dear Major,*
> *From the view I have taken of the county, and the observations I was able to make, I am of the opinion first, that Mansfield was a station, next, that Woodhouse was also a post, next, that there was also a fort at Pleasley Wood and that the Roman Villa was occupied by some commander...*

The remains of the large mosaic had been found in a room behind the corridor joining the *Villa Urbana*'s wings. The missing half of the mosaic, said Rooke, 'was probably torn up some years ago, when in rooting up some trees and brush wood which covered this spot, several of the small cubes were found'. The remaining half of the mosaic was first drawn by engraver James Basire and then painted by William Fowler, the builder from Winterton in Lincolnshire who went on to create fine engraved illustrations of many Roman mosaics, mainly in Yorkshire and Lincolnshire. The remains of a smaller mosaic were also found near the entrance on the east-facing frontage of the *Urbana*, but had been badly damaged by a lime kiln.

It is fortunate to say the least that the images of the large mosaic were made at the time because without them its complex patterns of *guilloche*, knots, scrolls and star-shaped motifs would have been lost forever. This is despite the fact that the owner of the land on which the villa was found, John Knight, of Langold, quickly agreed to put a protective building up over the mosaic 'for the inspection of the curious,' as Rooke put it. Rooke called it 'the Hut' and provided a painting of the building, showing it as a neat, brick structure with a window and chimney. In his edition of Thoroton's *Antiquities of Nottinghamshire*, John Throsby described the hut as a 'square building, with an outward fence wall, at a little distance.' He added: 'Mr Rook [*sic*] was so obliging as to accompany my friend and me to see the villa and the pavement, with a cheerfulness highly pleasing. The view of them was gratifying to both; but his account of these discoveries, and the accurate manner of his describing the different apartments of the villa, contributed, in a great degree, to the entertainment of a day set apart, in some measure, as a visit to that friendly Gentleman.'

Yet by September 1811 the shelter and Roman mosaic had both been vandalised. A visitor recorded that the door was 'broken open, the pavement ruined and the floor strewed with cubic pieces, the walls written over with ribaldry and its only tenants a mare and a foal, who had taken shelter from the noon tide heat.' And that was how this great example of Roman decorative art came to be lost.

Today, Rooke's entire villa complex at Northfields is discernible only on a map, the words 'Roman Villa' being marked on OS Explorer 270. The land has been returned to farming and the foundations of the villa lie under the soil. 'The field in which they were found has been ploughed... the pavement has disappeared and the larger stones have been used for the repair of fences,' wrote W.H. Grover in his *History of Mansfield*, published in 1894. 'Regrets, however, are vain. The chance of a wonderful show-place for Mansfield, so far as antiquities are concerned, has been lost...' .

Yet, in the late 1990s, an attempt to resurrect the villa was started when a plan was drawn up to build a 'full-scale reconstruction' of the buildings next to Rooke's site. The project involved the universities of Nottingham and Sheffield and attracted nearly £500,000 in early funding from the European Regional Development Fund and English Partnerships. A press release from the University of Nottingham, in January 1997, outlined the plan:

> *The initiative, still in its early stages, will give visitors a real taste of what it was like to live on a Roman country estate nearly 2,000 years ago, helping to put flesh on the dry bones of a vital part of Britain's history. It is hoped that not only will the Nottinghamshire villa become a major tourist attraction, but that it will prove an ideal vehicle for educational visits... The site was an ideal location because adjacent land had fallen derelict so was ripe for development, and the local authority, Mansfield District Council, welcomed the idea as a boost to its plans for economic regeneration.*

Two of the archaeologists involved in the project were Prof. John Wade of Sheffield University and Prof. Roger Wilson of the University of Nottingham. Prof. Wilson, it will be remembered, was the same Roger Wilson who found the 'curse tablets' at Redhill and who later described the last of the *Margidunum* defences in his *Guide to the Roman Remains in Britain*. He is today head of the Department of Classical, Near Eastern and Religious Studies at the University of British Columbia in

Canada. But the idea of the villa project was attributed to John Wade, who was the archaeologist who excavated Littleborough in the 1960s. The villa building scheme was certainly an ambitious project — 'the first of its kind in the UK', as the press release said. Students from both universities would be involved. There was even a personal twist to the tale since Prof. Wilson's original interest in archaeology had started at age 12 when he'd borrowed a book from the library that contained details of the Mansfield Woodhouse villa.

But the plan remained a dream and the villa was never built. Why? Prof. Wade told this writer that the plan collapsed when an application for matching funding from the Lottery was rejected. What would the villa have been like had it been built? Prof Wade says today: "In the context of other reconstructions, such as a Roman gate at South Shields, the turf wall section at *Vindolanda* and at least one bath-house I heard about as a project, together with the publicity and filming which would have accompanied such a project, I would like to think that — given its proximity to M1 junctions — it would have been potentially very successful. But then I have always been an optimist!'

However, a 3D sense of what Rooke's villa might have looked like can still be gained — at least in miniature, thanks to the model that is on permanent display in Mansfield Museum. The model follows Rooke's belief that the smaller of the two buildings was the main house while the larger one was used by agricultural workers.

Another method of gaining a sense of what the villa, and other villas, may have looked and felt like is by walking around the full-size reconstructed Roman villa that was built in 2002/03 at Butser Ancient Farm in Hampshire. The 23 metre by 13 metre (75ft by 42ft) building is based on the foundation plan of one section of a villa excavated at Sparsholt, near Winchester, and comprises six rooms arranged behind a corridor plus a working *hypocaust*. The external walls alone took 200 tonnes of flint and 112 tonnes of lime mortar to build. With the internal walls and fills also requiring 52 panels of wattle and daub, the construction suggested just how resource-heavy even a modest villa must have been. Topped by a stone tiled roof supported by timbers, the building took a team of 5–6 people around 18 months to complete.

It is perhaps fortunate for Rooke that he didn't live to see the destruction of the mosaic at his villa. He died peacefully at home

The villa model in Mansfield Museum.

in 1806, leaving a record of investigation into Roman and British antiquities in Cumbria, Derbyshire, Gloucestershire and Nottinghamshire. His interests extended to meteorology and he also provided detailed accounts of nine 'remarkable oaks' on the Welbeck estate and a sketch of Sherwood Forest. The ancient Major Oak tree there is said to have been named after him. Naturally, he also wrote about Robin Hood. Some of Rooke's observations on various possible Roman camp sites in Nottinghamshire have been mentioned in the text. Although Rooke was inclined to see Roman camps on every hill top that aroused his curiosity, he was an accurate sketcher and recorder of sites of antiquity and he made important contributions to the early study of archaeology in Nottinghamshire and Derbyshire. He was also friends with, or gave his support to, a group of fellow local historians and antiquarians including William Dickinson, William Harrod, John Throsby and the Rev. Samuel Pegge of Derbyshire. As well as his excavations Rooke collected bits and pieces of 'Roman antiquities' in Sherwood Forest and believed he had seen traces of a Roman road running from Newark to Mansfield via Kirklington, Sherwood Forest and Rainworth Water. This road had passed close to his villa, he believed. 'There are many more fragments of these roads in the forest; part of one is plainly to be discerned near the Hut, and others in different parts, all pointing towards Mansfield,' he wrote. Yet the villa's very distance from any known Roman town persuaded Rooke that the owner could afford to live in splendid isolation. In Rooke's words, he or she had been 'some person of great note and consideration' who was trying to imitate the lifestyles of Rome's wealthy — 'as far as the difference of climate would admit.'

A substantial biography of Hayman Rooke would be difficult to write since little is known about his character and only one letter by his hand is known to survive. But short and very helpful biographies about him have been produced, including an article for the Thoroton Society in 1965 and a University of Sheffield dissertation by Pamela McInally. The Thoroton Society article's author was a young and later highly influential prehistorian called Andrew Sherratt, who went on to become assistant keeper of antiquities at the Ashmolean Museum and a professor of archaeology at Oxford University. The Hayman Rooke piece was his first published archaeology article. Today, some of the ancient artefacts found by Rooke in his travels are owned by the Ashmolean Museum in Oxford. These include a Roman chisel and two bone pins found in the villa as well as several Bronze Age spear and axe heads. Derby Local Studies Library also owns a 77-page book of Rooke's drawings of various antiquities while copies of his excavation reports are available at Mansfield Woodhouse public library. William Fowler's painting of the Mansfield Woodhouse villa's central mosaic is in the Society of Antiquaries' Fowler Collection in London.

Rooke's home, Woodhouse Place, also still stands. John Throsby gave a flattering description of Rooke's life in this house. 'This dwelling, which appears to be calculated for retirement and study, is enriched with a selection of things valuable to a mind like Mr Rooke's. This gentleman, cherishing through life a natural propensity to the study of ancient things, luckily took up his residence near a spot, enriched with some of the highest traces of antiquity. The Roman villa, which he discovered in the neighbourhood, and the fine tessellated pavement, near, which he has carefully preserved by an erection over it, must be a pleasing circumstance of his life.'

In his report on his excavation of the Mansfield Woodhouse villa, Rooke included a list of 'Antiquities' he found in the ruins. Reading it now, though, it acts as a kind of ragged and slightly poignant obituary for the fag-end remains of a materially rich Roman lifestyle:

> *Three ivory pins, a top of a lamp, a pair of nippers, a piece of cullender, an iron chisel nine inches long, two fragments of hand mills, two pieces of brass parts of a fibula, part of a circular ornament, with a heart in the centre, which has the appearance of green enamel, with a narrow border of yellow metal, and several coins of the lower empire.*

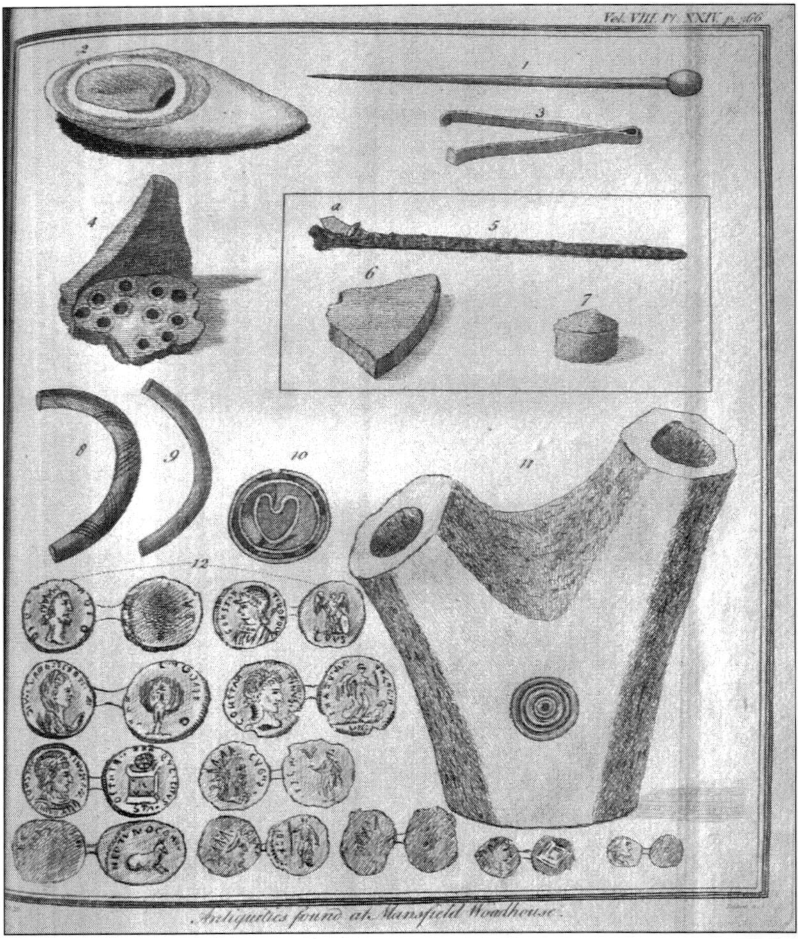

Some of the finds recovered by Rooke at the Mansfield Woodhouse villa, illustrated in *Archaeologia*.

Southwell

Just as the name Hayman Rooke is tied up with the Mansfield Woodhouse villa, so the recent discovery of a large sandstone wall in Southwell has become associated with new concerns about the large villa that was excavated close to the town's Minster in 1959. The wall of broad sandstone blocks was found during excavations at the former site of the Minster School in late 2008 and quickly generated headlines in local media. Archaeologists struggling to explain the wall, and how it may have been connected to the villa, speculated that it could have been part of a temple. Speaking to this author in 2009, Nottinghamshire County Council's senior archaeological officer Ursilla Spence said: "The wall is 30 metres long and up to 1.5 metres tall. It's made of Mansfield red sandstone and cut so that the jointing lines are absolutely perfect. It's a mason's dream of a wall. But sandstone doesn't weather very well and we're pretty certain that they stucco'd it and then painted it red. When I first saw it I thought 'military' but we have no evidence for the military there. So what is it for? All the experts have said 'ah, it shouldn't be there.' The closest thing I've seen to it is the base of a temple building in Pompeii."

Pottery associated with the wall was subsequently found to span the 1st–4th centuries while an adjacent vertical timber pole was carbon-dated to the 3rd century. The wall was, then, clearly from the Roman period and was contemporary with the villa. But what had the wall actually been part of? Nobody knew for sure; proof of a temple remained one theory; another was that it had been the 'imposing boundary wall' of the villa itself. Whatever the truth, the discovery of the wall suddenly made Roman archaeology in the Minster town — pronounced Southwell to those who live there, *Suthell* (a bit like shovel) to everyone else — a live issue again, and the debate about how best to deal with its heritage has been continuing ever since.

Finds of Roman coins, bricks and sections of tessellated paving have been sporadically recorded in the town over the past 300 years and, as has been noted, local historians such as William Dickinson were among those who believed Southwell had been the site of *Ad Pontem*. Richard Shilton, author of a later *History of Southwell*, published in 1819, was less certain, remarking that the 'the accidental discovery of a few scattered coins, or even the ploughing up a pot of the same, ought not to be received as a criterion of the spot having been a Roman station'. Even so, in the 18th and 19th centuries separate finds of tessellated paving, plus fragments of plaster and tile, pointed to the past existence of a villa or other high-status building near the Minster. In 1901 a large expanse of coloured tessellated pavement was found under the soil in the garden of the Dean's Residence. Unlike past finds, this one was recorded by photographs, although the paving was not believed to be Roman at the time.

The villa's existence was finally confirmed in 1959 when Charles Daniels excavated two 'wings' of a Roman building in and just outside the garden of the Residence, the building behind the Vicar's Court quadrangle, east of the Minster.

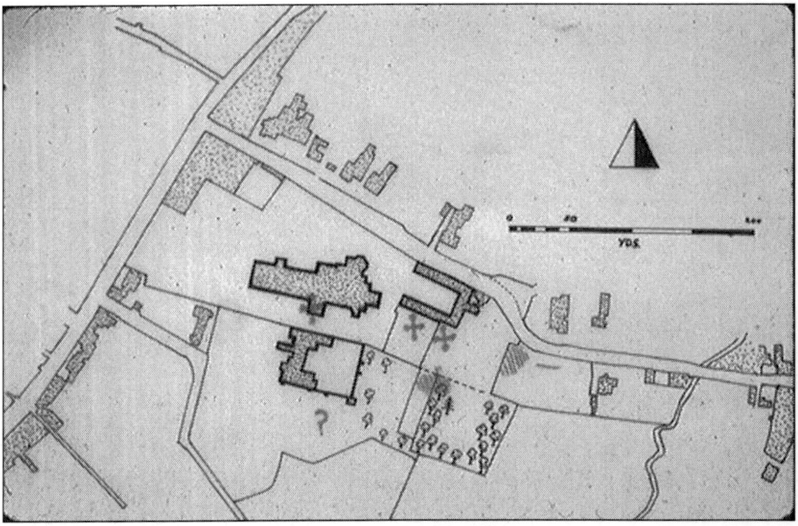

The shaded areas on Charles Daniels' own map shows where he excavated in 1959. The other marks are believed to indicate the previous villa finds.

Daniels' two excavations were to the south and east of the Dean's garden and he duly labelled his finds as the villa's southern and eastern wings. He was confident that the villa extended to the north, and to the west, under the gardens of the Archbishop's picturesquely ruined Palace. An idea of the size of the villa can be gained today simply by walking around the area with a map of Daniels' excavation sites. Daniels believed it had been a courtyard villa measuring approximately 73 metres by 91 metres (240ft by 300ft) — bigger than Mansfield Woodhouse, indeed larger and more elaborate than 'any local villa so far discovered', he wrote. 'In short we appear to have a counterpart of the great country seats most frequently found much further south.' Although Daniels was unable to search for the south eastern corner of the villa because the Minster Grammar School was then being built there, excavations immediately north of Church Street in 2004 by Lee Elliott of Trent and Peak Archaeology seemed to confirm the existence of the villa's northern range and gave the building a total north–south length of around 90 metres. This agreed with Daniels' earlier estimate and confirmed the view that here was one of the region's largest and most luxurious villas, with more possibly to be found under Church Street itself. These later finds included bits of flue and *pilae* tiles (stacks of *pilae* made up the underfloor pillars used in *hypocausts*), painted plaster, and red, white and greyish blue mosaic *tesserae*.

Yet Daniels' original view that the villa was a 'great country seat' wasn't just based on its dimensions; he also took into account the evidence for refined décor that he found in his various excavation trenches. It was, he said, 'a dwelling of some sophistication.' The eastern wing, close to the school, revealed a large room measuring 10.3 metres by 5.4 metres (34ft by 18ft) and the cold bath with the fragments of the 'Cupid' plaster in the bottom. In the southern wing Daniels found six rooms, four of which had floor mosaics. One room, which could have been a corridor, was at least 8.2 metres by 2.7–3 metres (27ft by 9–10ft); another was 8.2 metres by 3.3 metres (27ft by 11ft); a third was square and measured 4.7 metres (14.5ft) on all sides; a fourth was 3.2 metres by 4.4 metres (10ft 6in by 14ft 6in) and had contained the *hypocaust*, which had been all but stripped out. The mosaics in these rooms were all in fragments or had been damaged by drain-layers, grave-diggers and the past insertion of posts. The walls of the rooms had also been completely removed, suggesting that the site may have been deliberately levelled in the post-Roman period. After Roman use of the villa ceased in the late 4th century, the building and then its ruins endured long centuries of occupation beginning with the Saxons. As well as the Saxon urn already mentioned, Daniels found fragments of wares from the 11th to the 20th centuries in the villa debris.

However, the idea that the great Minster, and the early Saxon church that preceded it, were deliberately located where they where because of the villa is an attractive one. The theory is given further credence if the mysterious wall found in 2008 was in fact part of a temple that belonged to the villa. Other villas in Britain are known to have had temples or shrines attached or close to them including Great Witcombe in Gloucestershire and Lullingstone in Kent.

Plaque at Vicar's Court, Southwell, acknowledging the villa's existence.

Mosaic found in the Southwell villa, photographed in 1959.

Another piece of mosaic in the villa photographed in 1959. Note that parts of it appear to be unexcavated.

With the eastern wing of the villa duly declared one of Southwell's two Scheduled Ancient Monuments soon after the 1959 excavation, and the site lying within a larger Conservation Area embracing the entire Minster area, the foundations of Daniels' villa were safe — but underground. Nobody could see the remains (apart from the tessellated paving and plaster Cupid displayed in the Minster), but nobody could damage them either. And that was how the situation remained until the Minster School decided it needed to concentrate all its operations at its second site near the A612 Nottingham Road. The school in Church Street, adjacent to Daniels' eastern wing, was demolished and the land sold to a property company for a reported £2.9m in September 2007. A local housing company, Kean Construction Ltd, subsequently took forward an already approved planning application to build 13 homes on the site and then decided to increase the number of homes to 37. Three archaeological evaluations, including excavation, took place on the advice of Nottinghamshire County Council's principal archaeological officer between September 2008 and May 2009 and it was during the first of these that the sandstone wall was found within a trench.

In the evaluation report the wall was described as 'a substantial stone block-built retaining wall of Late Roman date.' Amid fears that the housing development was too intensive and would damage the Roman archaeology, local groups such as Southwell Community Archaeology Group and the town council now demanded that the villa foundations, including the wall, should at least be protected from any future development. Well-attended public meetings were held in the town and the then Bishop of Southwell, the Rt. Rev. David Cassidy, weighed in with comments about the 'cavalier attitude' of developers towards 'below ground archaeology'. This was all, in its own way, a microcosm of the larger battle that goes on between the values placed on static ancient heritage, all below ground and unseen in this case, and the values placed on development. The passionate feelings the situation provoked in Southwell people opposed to Kean's plans were also great material for local newspapers which reported each new development in the saga. However, as Brendan Haigh, chairman of Southwell Town Council's planning committee, told the *Newark Advertiser*: 'I think because we are a small cathedral town that sometimes we don't get the sort of coverage that other places normally have. If this was somewhere like Canterbury *The Daily Telegraph* would see it as a big story.' He was undoubtedly right. And a story in the *Telegraph* would certainly have been *very* Southwell. However, all the strong feelings on the issue were rendered partly academic when Kean Construction Ltd went bankrupt in early 2009, a victim of the credit crisis. At the time of writing, the land, now protected by hoardings, is still owned by the company that bought it from the school, Caunton Properties (Southwell) Ltd. Meanwhile, Southwell Community Archaeology Group is still pressing for the eastern villa and wall to be protected from any future development. The wall has been covered again.

After all that brouhaha, how did the wall relate to the villa? The suggestion that the wall was part of a temple or shrine remains an option. But Dr Will Bowden, Associate Professor in Roman Archaeology at the University of Nottingham, and a member of Southwell Community Archaeology Group, believes it was probably part of the villa's retaining terrace wall. The wall seems to align more or less with the southern and eastern villa remains found by Daniels in 1959, which would make it part of the south eastern range of the property. Secondly, the neat broad sandstone block construction suggests that it was built to impress. Significantly for this line of thinking, the evaluation report noted that while the wall was 'enigmatic', its 'best quality facing' blocks were presented to the south east, while poorer quality blocks were used as in-filling facing north west, that is, on the inside of the wall. The report also concluded the wall had once been longer, possibly turning towards the north east, and 'presumably significantly higher.' The wall may also have stood in a shallow ditch of water, giving the appearance that it was rising out of water. A kind of water feature, in other words. Says Dr Bowden: "I personally think it was part of the terrace wall from a major villa complex. There is no other evidence of a temple. I could be wrong, but everything points to it being a terrace wall of the villa. The Romans tended to use prestige materials for the facing parts of their buildings, so using large stone blocks would be perfectly okay here. The outside of villas, which would be visible throughout its lifetime, could be ostentatious and I think this was meant to look like a big city wall."

The evaluation at the Minster School site also discovered five human burials, one of which was dated to the 8th century (that is, Saxon). Significantly for the site's Roman importance, the existence of various rubble wall footings also suggested to the excavators the existence of possibly agricultural or industrial processing buildings associated with the villa. Other probable

Graffiti, Southwell-style. This example, on the protective hoardings around the former Minster School site where the stretch of Roman wall was found, is supposed to mean 'Romans Go Home'. But as Monty Python fans know, it's dog-Latin scrawled by Brian in the film *Life of Brian* and should have been written 'Romani ite domum'. A Centurion told Brian to write the correct line out 100 times.

Roman remains in the southern portion of the site included an oven or kiln and a quarry pit. The report added: 'A direct relationship with the adjacent villa may be inferred.' One final observation in the report was that the villa sandstone wall may have remained standing until at least the 12th century — another eight centuries or so after the formal end of Roman rule in Britain.[4]

What about the future for the Southwell villa? SCAG's immediate aim is for the known villa remains to be protected from any future development. The issue of whether the cold bath and associated discoveries could, or should, be permanently exposed for public display as part of some kind of Roman Nottinghamshire visitor centre is not being discussed at the moment. "These things require a huge amount of capital investment and you would also need to demonstrate that it was sustainable from a tourism and business point of view," says Dr Bowden. "But at the moment that is not the aim. It's another discussion. At the moment all we are looking for is to make sure it stays outside development."

Barton-in-Fabis

The story of the missing mosaic pavement from the villa at Barton-in-Fabis is another sad tale of Nottinghamshire's loss of Roman decorative art. This, combined with the villa's excavation history and a later scuffle over efforts to re-excavate the site, provides one of the more colourful chapters in the county's bitter-sweet relationship with its Roman past.

The villa itself, in the grounds of Glebe Farm to the south of Barton-in-Fabis, has been known about since the 19th century and speculation as to the fate of the mosaic pavement can still be heard in the village if you ask around. Briefly, in April 1856 ploughing by the parish clerk revealed a very large 'tessellated pavement' just a foot below the soil. This had followed occasional finds of 'remains of wall', other sections of tessellated pavement and observations of square barren patches on the field surface. Excavations led by the Rev. Wintour soon exposed an area of mosaic some 3 metres by 4.5 metres (10ft by 15ft) which was believed to be just a quarter of the whole pattern. As at Mansfield Woodhouse, a shed was put up to protect the mosaic from the weather. Alas, souvenir-hunters and other thieves then

Fragment of the floor mosaic found at the Roman villa, Barton-in-Fabis, in the 19th century. The mosaic is now lost.

stole so much of the mosaic over the years that it was offered to Nottingham Castle Museum for a few pounds in 1878. The offer was turned down. A plan of the mosaic was then made in 1881 before the whole thing was boarded over the following year. It was subsequently lifted bodily and taken to the village rectory.

And then it disappeared, with no known records to show its fate. At the time it was discovered the mosaic was described as 'bold and elegant' in its design. Wherever it went, there is the possibility that another section of the mosaic still lies under the soil since the other bits of tessellated pavement, found between 1813 and 1832, seem to have been in a different part of the field.

The hut or shed that was put up to protect the exposed mosaic at Glebe Farm. It didn't stop visitors from stripping it for souvenirs.

The villa itself, which seems to lie underneath and adjacent to the modern farm buildings, was partly excavated between 1933 and 1949. The first efforts were made by a team led by H. Martin and Arthur Cossons, the father of former English Heritage chairman Sir Neil Cossons, who was born in Beeston, Nottingham. Cossons senior was a headteacher and local historian, whose publications included the first detailed study of Nottinghamshire's turnpike road system. The villa was partly excavated again in the summer of 1949 by F.H. Thompson and his wife. Thompson admitted that it was impossible to draw up a definite ground plan for the villa because so little had been excavated, but he concluded that it consisted of a single block measuring 55–60 metres (180–200ft) long, with wings at each end perhaps 45 metres (150ft) long. The low mound of a wall joining both wings was seen by Adrian Oswald when he visited in 1937. Another feature noted by Thompson was the foundations of a circular stone structure with a pebbled floor. Thompson thought this structure was free-standing (a wheat threshing-floor, he suggested) and that the pebbles had been part of an open yard. Since the mosaic lay to the south of the round structure, and the mosaic must have been covered by a building, he reasoned that the open yard must have stretched for 12 metres (40ft) towards it. With the nearest wall to the north being 30 metres (100ft) away, he could conclude that he had found a pebbled courtyard 43 metres (140ft) long. The western side of the yard was the same distance away inside a modern farm shed. Thompson also believed he had found the wall foundations of a room with an entrance in the north east corner and, outside the modern shed, the slight remains of another building. He speculated that this may have housed the villa estate's workers. With only small excavation trenches having been dug, Thompson had to confess that his speculation was based on flimsy evidence. Even so, based on the additional evidence of pottery sherds and three coins, he reasoned that the villa had been occupied from the early 2nd century until the middle of the 4th. There was evidence of rebuilding within this time frame, and of some destruction by fire.

Although more than half a century has passed since Thompson's speculations, the Barton villa has not been reinvestigated. However, in 2001, an effort to re-excavate it was made by two Nottinghamshire archaeologists with the agreement of Glebe Farm. A wide trial trench was dug in an open paddock with the aim of developing the site for the training of archaeology students (it also gave this writer his first experience of archaeological excavation). But sharp opposition to the project from Nottinghamshire County Council's archaeology department subsequently brought work to a halt. The argument included face-to-face talks over the trench, one row being described as so loud as to disturb the farmer's bulls.

Why was the villa built where it was? Factors may have included proximity to the Trent and the nearness of other Roman settlements and villas at Redhill and Flawford, with communications served by nearby tracks also leading to the Fosse Way and the road into Derbyshire. Thompson also wondered whether the processing of gypsum found nearby might have been an economic factor. However, gypsum was not found in fragments of wall plaster, which were recovered 12 inches down amid the villa's roughly dressed foundation stones of limestone and sandstone. The Barton-in-Fabis villa used to be marked on Ordnance Survey local maps with those well-known words, 'Roman Villa (Site of)' but this has now disappeared from the modern OS Explorer map. However, the villa is marked on the OS Roman Britain map.

Oldcotes

The remains of a villa in the village of Oldcotes, north of Worksop, were discovered during the construction of St Helen's Catholic Church in 1870. Several rooms and a 2.7 metre by 1.8 metre (9ft by 6ft) area of floor mosaic were found, the latter being described as a labyrinth pattern with a figure believed to be Theseus, in the Minotaur's lair, at its centre. This is the only record of a mosaic in Nottinghamshire which has any kind of figure in it. Yet no part of this treasure is visible today. And nor will it be for some decades. As the official historical record for the villa says: 'The priest of St Helen's states that the church will not permit further investigation/excavation of this villa for 50 years. The published site now falls under pasture and garden.' Ironically, the villa is one of the few in Nottinghamshire to be marked on OS maps as 'Roman Villa.'

At least three rooms of the Roman building were seen in 1870 and described by the new church's architect, S.J. Nicholls. One was a main room six metres long by five metres wide (20ft by 17ft), with an entrance and step down plus a plinth, covered in red plaster, that he thought may have been an altar. This room contained the mosaic pavement. Although Nicholls did not make a drawing of the mosaic, he gave a detailed description of it including the Theseus figure, which was contained within an 80cm square at the centre. The figure was 'unfortunately much injured, but the lower portion of a human figure remains in an attitude of attack; one arm had been extended with a short broadsword pointed downwards, the lower part of the blade remaining, and over the shoulder the outline of an oval shield was evident.' Only a handful of labyrinth mosaics are known in Britain and if the Oldcotes mosaic still survives as it was seen, and is one day exposed for public enjoyment, Nottinghamshire will surely gain a historic treasure that should finally do justice to its Roman past.

Nicholls thought the mosaic he saw was almost identical to one found at the legionary fortress at Caerleon in Gwent, Wales.

But the mosaic wasn't all that he found. Nicholls also described a parallel room, 70cm lower than the mosaic room, paved with grey *tesserae*, and a third unpaved room. Elsewhere, there were more walls, a stone trough filled with hardened lime, bits of wall paintings, roof tiles, broken pottery and a plastered and painted floor. 'More remains probably survive,' says the site's official historical record. The villa was quickly covered back over and it and the mosaic now lie under the priest's presbytery and the adjacent chapel. An area of 'coarse tile/ tesserae' was also exposed nearby. Since then another floor mosaic has been exposed during 'casual excavation' in the garden of the nearby private 'manse.' This one was described as red and white, patterned in squares and scrolls, and bordered by white. This too was covered back over and now lies 10cm down.

Why ban further excavation of this treasure for 50 years? Father Gerry White, the current priest at St Helen's, said it was all news to him and passed me on to the diocesan property department in Sheffield. But Fr White was certainly aware of the villa's existence. He said the large walled grassed area behind the church, which had been used as an orchard during or just before the Second World War, had some ground undulations which may be evidence of the villa foundations underneath. Had

Father Gerry White in the field behind St Helen's Church in Oldcotes.

he found any Roman fragments there? No. Had many people enquired about the villa? No, I was the only person to ask him about it in the five years he had been at Oldcotes. However, the diocesan property department eventually replied to my questions and said that its guess was that the previous priest, dead for some years, had probably wanted to ban further work on the villa for 50 years for one simple reason — he had wanted a quiet life, without intrusion from archaeologists. A spokesman added: "If further archaeological investigation was mooted for the site by a suitable body, I would anticipate that this would be considered by the current parish priest on its merits and provided that the parish was not expected to contribute to the funding of such investigation and it did not cause undue disturbance to the church."

Flawford

There is a flat field on a hill between Ruddington and Plumtree in Rushcliffe which carries a noticeable feeling of absence. A crossroads formed from two roads and two tracks centres on the space, suggesting there was once human habitation here. A few gravestones, standing erect like solitary teeth, point to a history of Christian worship. Indeed, the field is the place where St Peter's Church, Flawford, once stood. Saxon in origin, the church developed into the spacious 'Mother Church of Ruddington' serving four nearby villages, but was demolished in the latter decades of the 18th century due to falling congregations when other churches were built in the surrounding parishes. Only the gravestones were left above soil level as reminders of this rural church's long history.

Then, between 1967 and 1984, members of Ruddington Local History Society excavated the site and revealed the ground plan of the church. But, below the church, they also found the foundations of what appeared to be a Roman building that has been interpreted as a villa, with outbuildings. One of the most significant discoveries was the disintegrated remains of a tessellated floor, found in four places and made up of small grey, white and red *tesserae*, the last made of *samian* pottery. A small eight-inch square of red *tesserae*, which could have been part of a border, was also found. Dating of the *samian* suggested that the mosaic was not laid down before around 160. Other finds included Roman pottery, a comb, roof tiles made of Charnwood slate and a coin of Emperor Tetricus (270–273). Although only a fraction of the villa outline was exposed, the local history group believed the villa had a north–south aligned building with a later east–west lying wing. Foundations to the east suggested related agricultural buildings. Finds of Iron Age pits, pottery and a brooch also suggested that the site had been settled before Roman times, with the villa representing a further phase of occupation up until around 350. Since part of the tessellated pavement was found under the later church nave, it has been suggested that it was ruins of the villa that attracted the Saxon settlers to build their church here too. The demolition of St Peter's Church in 1773 and 1779 therefore seems to have brought to an end at least two millennia of continual human occupation at this site. Today, this long history is marked by a small plaque in the middle of the field that remembers the church but makes no mention of the Roman villa underneath it.

However, the site's location at the centre of a crossroads suggests how the church, and perhaps the villa's occupants before it, compensated for their apparent isolation by being well connected with nearby settlements. Two branches of the crossroad meeting at the site are formed by the minor road, Flawforth Lane, joining Ruddington with the Wheatcroft roundabout. The other two are tracks, one being a lane and footpath running south towards Keyworth and one running east as a bridlepath to Plumtree. It seems possible that these latter two routes fell into disuse over the years. 'There is no archaeological proof that a village ever existed at Flawford, yet old maps show the position to be a commanding one,' wrote Dorothy Shrimpton, an amateur historian and the wife of Ruddington's vicar, the Rev. Canon A.C. Shrimpton, who was involved in the Flawford excavation from the start. She added: 'The churchyard stands at the intersection of roads from Edwalton to Bradmore and from Plumtree to Ruddington, both of which were Saxon, or older, in origin.' So where's Flawford? There is no such village, although there is a Flawford House Farm and a Flawford House. However, Ruddington's local history society reports that the name Flawford translates as 'multi-coloured floor', signifying the ancient local importance attached to the Roman villa here. Several of the Flawford Roman finds, including the bone combs and a small reconstructed section of tessellated pavement, can be seen in the University of Nottingham Museum. A report on the Flawford excavation was written by the late Harry James, of Elston, who was deeply involved with Ruddington Local History Society.

Car Colston

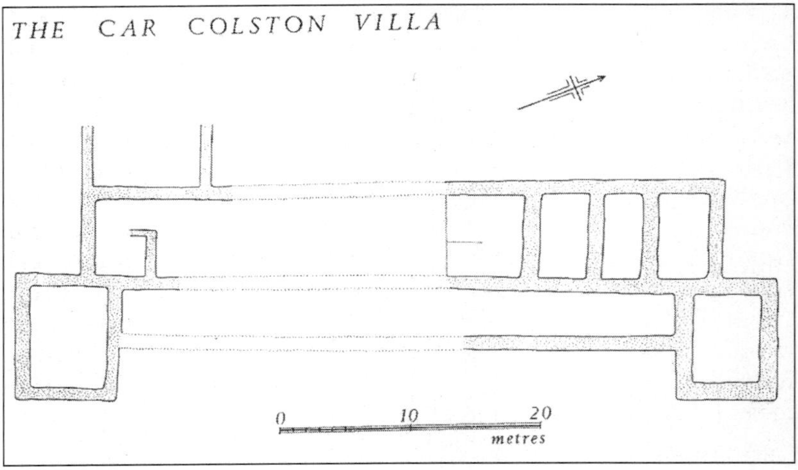

Plan of Car Colston villa, as surveyed from surface indications.

The foundations of a winged house around 24 metres (78ft) long were seen at Car Colston, a village to the immediate east of the Fosse Way, in 1886. In fact, the foundation stones were not only seen, they were actually dug out by one Samuel Burton, owner of Manor Farm, who used the material to build his farm roads. Fortunately, a ground plan of the house, with measurements, was also made by a man called William Martin. The outline of the house, in a large field called Hall Close, was subsequently seen by air in 1963 and tentatively identified as a 2nd century house, similar to the villa at Thurgarton that was excavated in the 1950s.

The Car Colston villa's location, in a large field just south of the village's centre, puts it approximately 2km (1.2 miles) north east of *Margidunum*. 'It is a lovely site, a southern-facing slope looking towards the Belvoir hills,' wrote T.C. Blagg in an article on the villa published in 1970. This farm, and the presence of several other villas nearby, suggests that the countryside here, around the Fosse Way and on the edge of the Vale of Belvoir, was a busy and productive area in Roman times. In 1977, another article on the Car Colston villa, by Colm O'Brien, said that the ground plan of the house was still clearly visible, the removed foundation stones of the wall having made depressions in the grass. The plan shows there were two wings joined by a corridor, or verandah, that was 3.6 metres (12ft) wide. This was backed by at least four rooms to the north. The rooms' widths were put at 5.7 metres (18ft), 3.3 metres (11ft), 5.2 metres (17ft) and 5.8 metres (19ft). The two larger rooms that made the 'wings' were put at 7.1 and 7.8 metres wide (23 and 25ft). Despite the damage done to the remains, O'Brien speculated that the floor of the villa could still survive under ground level. Today a sunken path passing through the centre of the house is visible, being easily seen from a public footpath that crosses Hall Close field. And as Blagg suggested in 1970, it is indeed a lovely site on which to build a house — verdant, with a clear view towards the Vale of Belvoir, and in a field now rich with all kinds of old bumps and banks attesting to hundreds of years of human activity after the villa's occupants disappeared into history. There's even a moat here.

Thurgarton and Epperstone

In 1952, excavation of a 'farmhouse-type villa' with at least five rooms, about 1.6km (1 mile) west of Thurgarton, was begun by C.E. Coulthard and seems to have continued on and off through-

Excavations of the 'Roman villa site' at Thurgarton in 1952. The caption to this image reads: 'Looking upstream from the Sheepwash Bridge and showing a paved way leading down to the Thurgarton Beck, with what appears to be the foundations of a stone bridge discovered by Mr S. Mellor (pictured) and Mr Coulthard in July 1952. Mr M.W. Barley's party made later developments to this site in 1955.'

out the decade. The building had been discovered after 'deep ploughing' and by 1959 a brief note on the work stated: 'No mosaics or tessellation but considerable hypocaust probably in baths. No samian ware but considerable amount found 200 yards further west.' This work was followed, in 1961, by the excavation of a second Roman building 270 metres (or 300 yards, as it was described) to the north of the first. Here, in Epperstone parish, the excavators — volunteers led by S. Revill — found evidence of a higher quality building with 'elaborately painted plasterwork'.

Delicate bronze figure of a 'sphinx' recovered from Epperstone.

The site of one of the buildings, or both, is marked on OS Explorer 260. However, this gives little clue as to quiet drama of the buildings' location, being on an even piece of land at the foot of two hills. Thurgarton Beck gurgles away close by. Did the Romano-British farmers really cultivate their crops in the thick clay soil of these hillsides? A track heading north may have connected the occupants here with Southwell, and with a possible Roman road which crosses it. Revill said the first building, usually described as the Thurgarton villa, was first built of timber and then clad in stone. He gave it a date of around 240–380. The second structure, usually called the Epperstone villa, was built of stone and rectangular in shape. Described in 1964 as being at least 27.4 metres (90ft) long, the villa had a single room projecting at one corner. Extensions, including a heated room and a 'small bath suite', were added later. The whole building had a 'basilican' structure. The house was first built in timber in the early 2nd century, then replaced by one with stone foundations in around 130. The extensions were added in the early 4th century. In 1962, a large number of pottery sherds were also found in fields close to a farm house to the immediate north west. These were dated mostly to the 3rd and 4th centuries.

Looking down at the even site of the Thurgarton and Epperstone villas from the north.

Cromwell

A complex maze of lines and cropmarks in fields outside the village of Cromwell, on the fertile soils of the west bank of the Trent 9km (5.5 miles) north of Newark, was seen from the air in 1946. Almost hidden in the maze, apparently in the centre of a large rectangle of two parallel ditches or walls, is the outline of a villa house with two projecting wings, the walls separating its several rooms clearly visible. There are around six rooms in the main structure joining the two wings. The length of the house was estimated at 25 metres (82ft), while trial trenches of some of the many cropmarks dug in the late 1940s found shallow ditches containing roof tiles and 3rd and 4th century pottery fragments. The size and complexity of the site led Malcolm Todd to describe it as 'a complex of exceptional interest', and one that might provide a case study for the development of mid-sized villa estates.[5] He seemed to imply that such a study would only follow excavation. But this has yet to take place. As J.K. St Joseph wrote: 'Only excavation can make clear the full significance of so complicated a site, but it looks as if the remains are those of a Roman villa or farm, actively engaged in agriculture in a fashion that involved constant changes in the enclosures of its small estate.'[6]

How were the many cropmarks and soil marks around the house to be explained? The large rectangle surrounding the house has been measured at 200m long by 150m wide (656ft by 492ft), its double ditches or walls eight metres (26ft) apart. This is crossed by a long ditch aligned to the Trent. The ditch has been interpreted as a possible earlier boundary ditch associated with a timber house that was here before the villa was built in stone. The timber building's existence was suggested in 1959 when drought revealed a line of post-holes beside the stone villa. Other marks have suggested Roman barns, a small walled

Aerial photograph of the Cromwell villa. The outline of the villa, within the larger rectangle shape, can be seen to the left of the picture.

garden, an ornamental water cistern, paddocks and an orchard. Despite all this agricultural activity, there is little sign of a regular field system. The mass of other lines and marks near the villa have been interpreted as evidence of roundhouses, enclosures, pits and gullies from an earlier Iron Age settlement. The combination of a Roman villa, lying over an Iron Age village, has invited comparisons with the villa site at Lockington, near Redhill. At Cromwell, the juxtaposition of the two cultures produced 'a cropmark pattern of remarkable complexity', in the words of a 1974 article. The Cromwell villa's location on the bank of the Trent meant its occupants would have had easy access to river transport. But they were also close to the Fosse Way, being roughly mid-way between Lincoln and *Margidunum* and within easy communication distance of Roman towns and villas at Brough and Newark.

Notes

1. The Mosaic Pavements — D.J. Smith. In: *The Roman Villa in Britain* — edited by A.L.F. Rivet. Routledge & Kegan Paul, 1969.
2. A Roman Fortified Villa at Norton Disney, Lincs — Adrian Oswald M.A. and L.H.D. Buxton F.S.A. *The Antiquaries Journal*, **17**, 1937.
3. *The Letters of the Younger Pliny*. Penguin Books, 1974.
4. The Former Minster School Site, Church Street, Southwell, Nottinghamshire: *Archaeological Evaluation* Volume 1 Report Text and Figures. Report prepared by JWA Architects on behalf of their clients Caunton Properties Limited by M. Rowe. March 2010.
5. *The Coritani* — Malcolm Todd. Alan Sutton, 1991.
6. Air Reconnaissance of Southern Britain — J.K. St. Joseph. *The Journal of Roman Studies* 43, 1953.

Chapter 9

Hidden wealth: the coin hoards

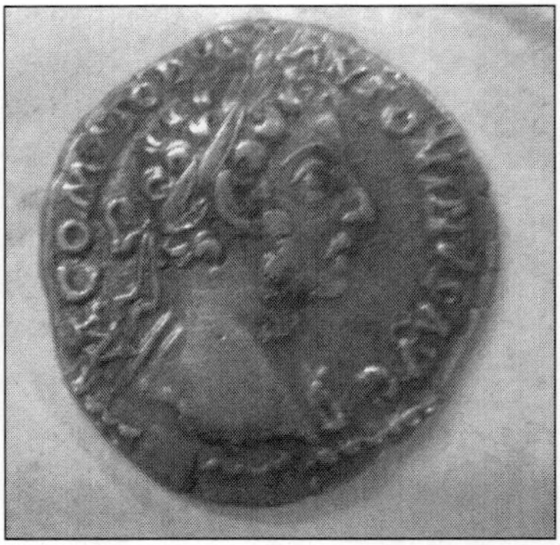

The Emperors of the film *Gladiator*: Marcus Aurelius (left) and his son Commodus (right). In the film, directed by Ridley Scott, Commodus brutally killed his father. In reality stoic Marcus Aurelius died of disease while campaigning against barbarians on the Danube in 180. Both coins were among a hoard of Roman silver coins found in 1992 in Ollerton.

The experience of life for many Britons within the Roman province has been described as impoverished, with people at the bottom economic level eking out a subsistence existence. Nevertheless, the economy of the Empire was a fully monetised system that featured such necessary evils as money lending, credit and debt. Cash, in other words, was the main means of paying wages, buying and selling goods, and paying taxes. Quite how much Roman coinage was in circulation at any time, what it would buy back then, and what its equivalent value would be in today's money, has been the subject of considerable speculation. One argument is that while coins were certainly the main means of exchange for propertied Romano-Britons such as farmers, landowners, shopkeepers and everybody further up the economic ladder, they had little use among the mass of agricultural labourers and peasants except when dealing with authority (to pay taxes, presumably). Yet when Rome decisively invaded Britain in 43, Iron Age minting and coinage systems developed by British tribes such as the *Corieltauvi* were swept away and replaced by a standardised and significantly more numerous Imperial coinage that was, in theory, available for use by people at all levels of society. The value of the coinage was initially based on the Empire's bullion wealth. The highest value coins were made of gold and silver, with the silver *denarius*, for example, being literally worth its own weight in silver.

Some idea of the buying power of a *denarius* in Britain was given by the writing tablets found at *Vindolanda* which indicate that two *denarii* would buy a quantity of pepper but half a *denarius* would buy around nine gallons of (probably native) beer; nine and a half *denarii* got you 21 chickens while 11½ coins bought a cloak. It should also be remembered that, at Redhill, a *denarius* was considered to be sufficiently valuable that its theft earned the thief a ghastly curse in front of the chief god himself, Jupiter. Furthermore, the curser vowed that the return of the coin would earn the god *a tenth* of its value. Clearly, a *denarius* was a coin you didn't want to lose. The gold *aureus,* first regularly minted in Republican Rome by order of Julius Caesar in 46 BC, had a higher value — so high that gold coins seem to have been rarely used for daily purchases. Meanwhile lesser value coins, including the *sestertius*, *dupondius* and *as*, made of brass or copper, were produced by the western Imperial mints in Rome, Trier and cities in Gaul for use in provinces such as Britain.

A huge quantity of coins must have initially come into circulation in Britain to pay the salaries of servants of the Roman state, including its soldiers. The cost of paying the salary of the Roman army alone has been estimated as amounting to more than 22.5 million *denarii* a year in the 2nd century.[1] In brief, coins, *pecunia*, were common in Roman Britain and so it is not surprising that they are the most numerous Roman artefacts found in Britain today after pottery.

Apart from being occasional objects of beauty in themselves, Imperial coins are invaluable in helping to give a date context for the archaeology where they are found because they are stamped with images of the Emperors in whose reign they were produced. Indeed, there are many cases where the presence of coins has been a pivotal factor in the dating of Roman buildings. The evolving imagery on coins also reflected changing social and political ideas emanating from the courts of the Emperors as successive dynasties and rebels took control of the Empire. However, in Britain, which was usually (but not always) far away from the dynastic rivalries which decided the fate of Emperors, money, for those who had it, would have been valued not for its propaganda or artistic values, but because it endowed buying power. It was spent, taxed, saved and hoarded — and occasionally these hoards were hidden away. And every now and then, centuries later, such hoards come to light again. Regardless of their modern financial value to collectors and museums, such hoards tend to exert a fascination over us since we instinctively want to know what circumstances would persuade somebody to hide a large amount of money away — and then not come back to recover it.

When is a hoard a hoard? A quaint analysis in 1932 defined it as: 'Treasure, large or small, deposited by its owner in the safe-keeping of mother earth and never claimed by him or his heirs or assigns.'[2] Approximately 1,500 coin hoards have been recovered in Britain, including dozens found in Nottinghamshire over the past 300 years. However, precisely how many is difficult to say. Nottinghamshire County Council has a list of 33 Roman coin hoards as part of its archaeological Historic Environment Record (HER). But the list has problems: some entries are for coin finds that are too small to be considered properly as hoards and several entries are based on information culled from antiquarian or anecdotal sources that are frustratingly short on detail; some records contain information on two or more finds; four contain no data on the dates of the coins. Nevertheless, the list is the most important single source of information on the subject locally and tells us that the largest individual hoard recovered so far was one of over 3,400 silver and bronze coins found near Babworth in 1988. The northernmost hoard was found near Scaftworth; the southernmost at Stanford-on-Soar; the furthest east was at Meering; the furthest west at Selston. This wide distribution is, at the least, an interesting method of showing how economic activity — or at least hoarding the fruits of that activity — was spread across Nottinghamshire during the Roman period. Yet when all the records are plotted on a map it shows that hoard finds have been densest towards the centre, north and west of the county. This distribution seems to run counter to the distribution of known Roman towns, villas and military sites, which tend to be concentrated in the county's south and east. However, hundreds of other Roman coin finds have been recorded in Nottinghamshire that are too small to be classified as hoards. Including hoards, the total number of Roman coin finds recorded by the county council amounts to 1,048 entries. You have to wonder how the map would look if all of these finds were plotted. Just to complicate this issue, many new coin finds tend to be initially recorded by the Portable Antiquities Scheme (PAS), a scheme set up to record finds by the public. In 2009, 351 finds of Roman coins in Nottinghamshire were reported to the PAS, this making up by far the largest proportion of the 477 total reported finds of non-ceramic Roman items in the county. Most of these coin finds, including 24 silver *denarii* from the reign of Hadrian found in Hucknall, have been made by people using metal-detectors. Although professional archaeologists often feel antipathy towards metal-detectorists, nobody can deny that they have turned up many finds of great historical and financial value. One of the latest Nottinghamshire coin finds, reported in July 2010, was a hoard of 120 Roman copper and silver coins found in a field near Newark by detectorist Maurice Richardson. This was the same man who unearthed Newark's famous Iron Age golden torc in 2005.

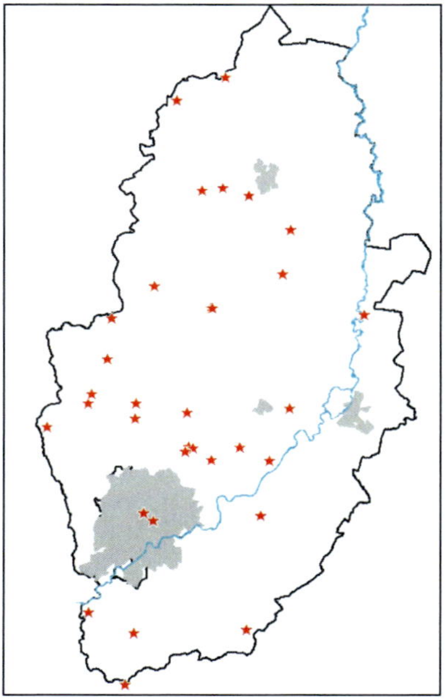

Map showing the locations of coin hoards recorded in Nottinghamshire's Historic Environment Record. The blue line marks the course of the Trent.

The earliest known recording of a Roman coin hoard found in Nottinghamshire dates to the early 18th century when 20 silver Republican and Imperial coins in an urn were turned up by ploughing at Upton, near Southwell. A Mr Lamb, of Southwell, who described the find, said the coins were accompanied 'by several round balls which fell to dust upon ye touch, and a great many round things which seem to be Romish beads, of blew and speckled colours'. Even more opaquely, there was also ‘an entire egg covered with a hard mummy’. In contrast, the latest hoards recorded in the county council’s HER list date to 1990 and 1991. In 1990, 30 coins dated 69 to 166 were found at Kirkby-in-Ashfield while 1,500 late 3rd century coins were found in a pot at Newstead when foundations for a shed were being dug. A second hoard of 298 late 3rd century coins was recovered from another location in Kirkby the following year.

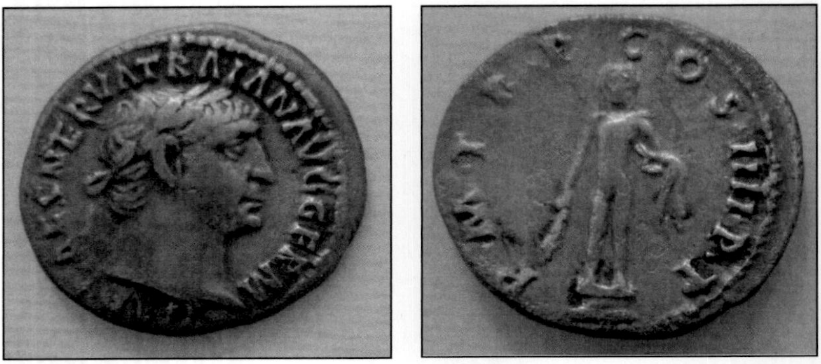

Obverse and reverse of a silver *denarius* of the reign of Trajan found at Kirkby-in-Ashfield.

Some revealing details about the hoards can be picked up from the brief notes attached to each HER entry. A note on the record of the 1990 Kirkby hoard adds that the 30 coins ‘represent about a month’s wages for a Ro[man] soldier, probably concealed for safekeeping’. A note on the Newstead hoard points out that the 1,500 coins were ‘silver washed’, presumably meaning that they were coins made of base metal with a silver coating.

This apparently cosmetic detail points up an important currency problem that began to arise in the western Roman world in the 3rd century and which undoubtedly led some Britons to hoard. When bullion was plentiful, Rome could afford to create gold and silver coinage that had a fixed value based on its actual precious metal content. This bullion wealth had been acquired from treasure and other booty first gained during the Roman Republic’s wars of conquest across the Mediterranean world. Conquest, as well as trade and the state-ownership of precious metal mines, had made the Republic very rich. But as expansion of the frontiers slowed in the 1st century under the first

Emperors, and cash was soaked up by war, the flow of precious metals into the Empire also slowed. By the 3rd century the amount of bullion had dwindled and one result was that the amount of silver in the *denarius*, and its supposedly more valuable replacement, the *antoninianus*, was gradually reduced to make silver go further. Hence the 'silver-washed' coinage found at Newstead. But printing more money, which is what this debasement effectively added up to, led to inflation and further devaluation; these, in turn, led to several major attempts to revise the Imperial currency throughout the period of the Roman involvement in Britain.

One further interesting note on the Kirkby hoard's record states that it contained coins from the reigns of the Emperors 'Gallienus, Postumus, Victorinus, Tetricus'. This dates the coins' production to 260–273, a period during which a breakaway 'Gallic Empire' of western provinces including Britain was set up by Postumus. The provinces were reunited with the rest of the Empire by Aurelian in 275, who also instigated another major reform of the currency. This reminting devalued the old currency and may have led people in Britain to either hoard their old coins or abandon their existing hoards as worthless. Was it a devaluation such as this which led the owner of the 1,500 silver washed coins found at Newstead to hide his money in a pot in the ground? We will never know. However, another reaction to the periodic coinage crises was forgery. An example of a forged Roman coin found in Nottinghamshire is a single 'gold' *solidus*, discovered by a metal-detectorist and described in 1982. The coin, produced in the 4th century, had been coated with gold but damage to the coating revealed the coin to be solid bronze underneath.[3]

One less attention-grabbing aspect of the Newstead find already mentioned is that the coins were found in a container described as a painted and crushed jar. Indeed, regardless of coin content, many hoards seem to have been placed in strikingly unremarkable vessels that have been variously described as urns, pots or jars. 'Flagons' were also used, such as for the hoard of 1,500 coins found buried in sand under the site of Manor Park Infants School in Collyer Road, Calverton in 1959. This was called the Calverton I hoard since another hoard of 225 coins, called Calverton II, was discovered in Crookdale Lane in the village in 1960. Harold Mattingly, who analysed these coins in the early 1960s, said that over two thirds of the second hoard were thrown away by workmen on the basis that they were considered 'useless'. Other coins disappeared into private hands. However, a quantity were later acquired by Nottingham's museums service. With respect to the people of Calverton, coins dug up in hoards have always been vulnerable to mysterious disappearances. In 1825, long before eBay provided a common market for portable antiquities, it was reported that urns filled with Roman coins were found at Sutton Bonington and that they were 'sold for as much as five guineas each'. One other interesting aspect of the Calverton hoards is that most of the coins were small-value British copies of official Imperial coinage from the late 3rd century. The need to manufacture small coins for everyday purchases perhaps reflected the shortage of official currency flowing into the province, which in turn reflected larger problems within the Empire. A hoard found in Calverton therefore provides another connection between Rome and a tiny part of the Empire in its furthest north west territory that would later be called Nottinghamshire.

Although hiding your coin hoard within a single vessel seems to have been the norm for most hoarders, some used two containers. Such was the case with the hoard of 186 coins found in Forest Fields, Nottingham, in 1910. The Berridge Road hoard, so called, was recovered by workers at the junction of Lesley Road and Berridge Road, near the now long-gone Apollo Cinema. This hoard was in a small barrel-shaped pot, itself within a 'grey globular pot', and included 19 silver coins. The hoard's dates ranged from the reign of Emperor Vespasian to Marcus Aurelius. Two other matters stand out about this hoard. Firstly, it is one of the very few to have been recovered from anywhere in Nottingham itself. Secondly, the find record gives details about the era in

A worn coin, from the Calverton II hoard, minted in Rome, showing a faded profile of Emperor Claudius II, called Gothicus, who reigned 268–270. A barbarian-born soldier who became emperor and fought the Goths with considerable success, hence the name.

which the hoard was discovered. So, we learn that the coins were found when this part of inner-city Nottingham still had barley fields growing there. That was certainly some time ago.

Two brass *sestertii* from the Berridge Road hoard. Both are from the reign of Antoninus Pius and were minted in Rome. The reverse of the coin on the right shows the figure of the god Mars; that on the left reads 'Pax Aug' or Pax Augusta (peace of the Emperor).

The circumstance of the discovery in Forest Fields was the building of new roads. In other cases the unearthing of hoards has been caused by gravel extraction, an activity that continues along the Trent today. This was how a hoard of 289 copper coins was found near Thurgarton in 1949 and another 1,347 mixed coins were unearthed at Besthorpe, near Collingham, in 1964. The latter coins were described as being 'crammed into a pot, evidently used as a money box'. Both hoards contained rarities, the Besthorpe hoard being notable for its inclusion of many 4th century coin imitations. These imitations had actually been stamped on top of earlier coins, but the stamping work was so poor that the lettering of the earlier coins was clearer than the later lettering. The other hoard, near Thurgarton (the location has also been described as Hoveringham), included 40 coins produced in London during the brief reign of Carausias, a rebel admiral who declared himself Emperor in Britain and northern Gaul in 286 or 287. Carausias' London mint, the first Roman mint in Britain, helped him mount a propaganda campaign by producing coins extolling virtues such as 'The Genius of Britannia'. The mint ultimately outlived Carausias, who was murdered by his finance minister Allectus. Incidentally, another hoard of 280 coins found on a farm at Thurgarton in the 1950s was thought to have been buried during turmoil connected with the subsequent usurpation of Allectus... . you could go on. In effect, with coins spanning the centuries from the Roman Republic to the early 5th century, you could argue that the story of the Roman occupation of Britain can be tracked through the coins unearthed in Nottinghamshire. Which brings us back to the six million *denarii* question: why did people in Roman Nottinghamshire bury their money, and then not come back to get it?

Reverse view of a Roman Republican coin found in Nottinghamshire showing a spear-throwing charioteer and two horses. This coin became separated from its collection at some point and there is probably no way now of telling who found it, where or when.

As the theorising attached to the hoard at Thurgarton suggests, it is commonly thought that coins were buried or hidden during times of turmoil or insecurity. After all, if anyone today felt obliged to literally hide money away there would usually have be a *very* good reason for them not to recover it. But although nobody knows why people failed to recover their hoards of coins, we can surmise that the single biggest reason may not have been the owners' violent deaths due to war, as is often supposed. Other reasons could have included plain bad memory, change of land ownership, a desire to evade tax, moving away from an area (especially for soldiers) and, yes, a wariness about coming back to an area due to a risk of conflict. It all depended on who was doing the hoard burying, and when.

That said, a 'top down' reading of the Roman Britain narrative suggests there were times when people may have had ample reasons to feel they were living in uncertain times. One analysis of coin hoards in neighbouring Leicestershire, for example, has shown that five of 24 coin hoards were buried in the period 270–282.[4] Suggested reasons why hoarders may have felt compelled to hide their coins in the late 3rd century include (and I paraphrase): raids by Saxon pirates along England's east coast; internal rebellion within Britain and within the larger western Empire; and the 3rd century reform of the currency by the Emperor Aurelian. This last move was unpopular with the British who preferred to hoard their old coins rather than exchange them for new coins at a lower value. So it was argued. Is there any pattern to the Nottinghamshire hoards? Analysis is difficult because many of the sources that make up the HER entries are vague, but a far from scientific reading of coin dates suggests that nine of the recorded hoards — just under a third — date from the late 3rd century. This is a high proportion that suggests local people may have felt they had good reason to hide their coins at this time.

One significant Nottinghamshire hoard that was hidden in this period was the one of 3,436 coins, all produced between 253 and 282. The hoard was discovered at Little Morton, near Babworth, in 1988, and subsequently generously donated to Bassetlaw Museum by the landowners, Robert and Lorna Howard. Unlike some earlier hoards found in Nottinghamshire, this one was subjected to a full battery of analysis, including fieldwalking over the land by members of Retford and District Historical and Archaeological Society. This was pertinent since the hoard was found within a field enclosure/ditch system, probably part of a farm, that had been identified from the air by Derrick Riley in 1975. The dates of the coins, which contained many 'irregular' copies, perhaps minted locally, suggested they had been buried at the end of the breakaway Gallic Empire period when Aurelean's currency reform had been initiated. The conclusion was that the owner had buried the now valueless coins in the hope that they would one day be legal tender again.

Another suggested reason for hoarding is that hoards commonly acted as simple savings accounts, with coins added to or withdrawn as needed. Although early forms of banks existed in the Roman era, extending loans to merchants and property owners, savings accounts were a distant invention and burying wealth may have been a normal activity for those people who could afford to accumulate cash. Since most British hoards are found buried away from Roman urban areas, savers and other hoarders, such as tax-evaders, also seem to have had an understandable preference for burying their wealth in the countryside. Certainly no coin hoards in the Nottinghamshire

HER appear to have been found in Romano–British towns or villages, although two hoards were unearthed near villa sites. These were 40 coins found at the Thurgarton villa (undated, but this was presumably in the 1950s when the excavation started) and 75 late 4th century coins found 100 metres from the Mansfield Woodhouse villa in 1983. Another two finds, one of eight coins, one of 600 coins, were found near Bawtry and Scaftworth — site of the Roman fortlet — in the 19th century. One other possible reason for hoarding was highlighted by the finding of Britain's second largest coin hoard, near Frome, in Somerset, in April 2010. The hoard of 52,300 3rd and early 4th century coins was found (by a metal detectorist) in a large pot buried upright underground. With the cash weighing 160kg, the pot must have been too heavy to take away. This led to the suggestion that the money deposited in the pot may have represented religious offerings by a community, whose members added coins over time and had no intention of spending them.

Finally, as has been noted in other literature on the subject, every coin hoard found today is a failed hoard; failed, because the hoarder intended it to remain hidden. And as revealing as hoards may be about the times in which they were buried, and the times in which they were found, they tell us little about how widespread coin hoarding may have been in Roman Nottinghamshire. While we have a general idea of how many hoards have been found, and when some of them were buried, we have no idea how many hoards were recovered by the owners who hid them away 1,600 to 2,000 years ago — or how many hoards remain to be discovered.

Silver coin of Emperor Hadrian, part of the Ollerton hoard.

Notes

1. *An Imperial Possession: Britain in the Roman Empire* — David Mattingly. Penguin Books, 2007.
2. Hoards of Roman Coins Found in Britain: And a Coin Survey of the Roman Province — H. Mattingly. *The Journal of Roman Studies* 22, Part 1, 1932.
3. A Roman Coin Forgery from Nottinghamshire — A.C. Alvey. *Transactions of the Thoroton Society of Nottinghamshire* 86, 1982.
4. A Survey of Romano-British Coin Hoards in Leicestershire — M.J. Winter. *Transactions of the Leicestershire Archaeological and Historical Society* 53, 1977-78.

Bibliography

Internet sources used in this book

Some documents relating to the archaeology and dualling of the A46 Fosse Way are in the public domain:

A46 Newark to Widmerpool Improvement Specification for Archaeological Evaluation at Margidunum Working Paper No: D105795/5/023 January 2005 — prepared for the Highways Agency by Balfour Beatty and Scott Wilson http://www.persona.uk.com/A46newark/HA_docs/disposit_docs/ DD401-DD452/DD414. pdf [accessed 24th January 2010]

A46 Newark to Widmerpool Improvement Specification for Stage 3 Geophysical Survey and Archaeological Evaluation Working Paper No: D105795/5/027 May 2005 — prepared for the Highways Agency by Balfour Beatty and Scott Wilson http://www.persona.uk.com/A46newark/HA_docs/disposit_docs/DD401-DD452/DD416.pdf [accessed 24th January 2010]

A46 Newark to Widmerpool: Wider Economic Benefits Final Report May 2007 — prepared for *emda* by Steer Davies Gleave http://www.emda.org.uk/uploaddocuments/A46NewarkWidmerpoolWiderEcImpactsFINALMay07.pdf [accessed 24th January 2010]

Documents relating to the planning application to build homes on the Southwell villa site could be read in electronic form via Newark and Sherwood District Council's website when I looked for them in July 2010. The main archaeological report is in volume 1 below while photographs are in volume 2

The Former Minster School Site, Church Street, Southwell, Nottinghamshire: Archaeological Evaluation Volume 1 Report Text and Figures. Report prepared by JWA Architects on behalf of their clients Caunton Properties Limited by M. Rowe, March 2010. Planning ref: 02/02225/FULM

The Former Minster School Site Church Street, Southwell, Nottinghamshire: Archaeological Evaluation Volume 2 Appendices

Other documents and articles sourced online:

Britain, or, a Chorographicall Description of the most flourishing Kingdomes, England, Scotland, and Ireland — William Camden (London: George Bishop and John Norton, 1610). Copyright 2004 by Dana F. Sutton. This text was transcribed by Professor Sutton, of the University of California, Irvine, from Philemon Holland's 1610 translation. Accessed via the internet at: http://www.visionofbritain.org.uk/text/contents_page.jsp?t_id=Camden

An Archaeological Resource Assessment of the First Millennium BC in Nottinghamshire — Mike Bishop. East Midlands Archaeological Research Framework, 2006.

http://www.le.ac.uk/archaeology/research/projects/eastmidsfw/pdfs/20nott1stmill.
pdf [accessed 17th September 2010)

An Archaeological Resource Assessment of Roman Nottinghamshire — Mike Bishop. East Midlands Archaeological Research Framework, 2006. http://www.le.ac.uk/archaeology/research/projects/eastmidsfw/pdfs/25nottrom.pdf [accessed 17th September 2010]

The Earthwork called Sawley Fort — E.O. Houldsworth. Archaeology in Leicestershire and Rutland 1963–1966. http://www.le.ac.uk/lahs/downloads/alrPagesfromvolumeXLI-6.pdf [accessed 14th February 2010]

English Heritage Ancient Monument notification for Scaftworth fort and a section of Roman Road 350m north west of Holly House Farm, Monument No. 29923 1953 Revised 24th July 1998 http://www.bassetlaw.gov.uk/pdf/Roman%20Fort%20Scaftworth.pdf [accessed 14th May 2010]

English Heritage Ancient Monument notification for Roman villa, Styrrup with Oldcotes, Monument No. M4750 http://www.bassetlaw.gov.uk/pdf/Roman%20Villa%20Styrrup%20Oldcotes.pdf [accessed 25th May 2010]

George F. Campion — Bernard W. Beilby. News for Winter 2004. http://www.thorotonsociety.org.uk/news/thornews_winter2004.htm [Accessed 23rd March 2010]

George F. Campion: Further memories of Campion from a Thoroton Society Member — Barry Waite. News for Spring 2005. http://www.thorotonsociety.org.uk/news/thornews_spring2005. htm [accessed 23rd March 2010]

List of Scheduled Ancient Monuments in Bassetlaw District. http://www.bassetlaw.gov.uk/services/environment_and_planning/planning/conservation_and_heritage/list_of_ancient_monuments.aspx [accessed 25th May 2010]

Flawford Excavation Site. http://flawford.org.uk/index.htm

A Roman villa at Carnarvon Primary School, Bingham — Bingham Heritage Trails Association. http://www.binghamheritage.org.uk/history/roman_carnarvon_school.htm [accessed 28 February 2010]

Printed journal articles and books

The Adventures of Peregrine Pickle — Tobias Smollett. Oxford University Press, 1983

Aerial Reconnaissance and Excavation at Littleborough-on-Trent, Notts — D.N. Riley, P.C. Buckland, J.S. Wade, M. Dearne, B.R. Hartley, K.F. Hartley, G. Kinsley, T. O' Connor, W.B. Clark and B. Dickinson. *Britannia* 26, 1995

Agricola — Tacitus. In: *On Britain and Germany*. Penguin Classics, 1964

Air Reconnaissance in Britain, 1958–1960 — J.K. St. Joseph. *The Journal of Roman Studies* 51, Parts 1 and 2, 1961

Air Reconnaissance in Roman Britain 1977–84 — G.S. Maxwell and D.R. Wilson. *Britannia* 18, 1987

Air Reconnaissance of Southern Britain — J.K. St. Joseph. *The Journal of Roman Studies* 43, 1953

Along the Roman Roads — G.M. Boumphrey. George Allen & Unwin, 1935

Along the Roman Roads of Britain — J.H.B. Peel. Book Club Associates, 1977

The Ancient and Modern Trent — Bernard Smith. In: *Memorials of Old Nottinghamshire*, edited by Everard L. Guilford. George Allen, 1912

Ancient Life and Placenames in Nottinghamshire, Derbyshire, Yorkshire, Lincolnshire and Leicestershire — Roy Peters. North Trent Publishing, 1991

The Anglo-Saxon Cemetery at Millgate, Newark-on-Trent, Nottinghamshire — A.G. Kinsley. Nottinghamshire Archaeology Monographs 2, 1989, Department of Classical and Archaeological Studies (Archaeology Section), University of Nottingham

Anglo-Saxon Poetry — translated by R.K. Gordon. Everyman's Library, 1976

The Annals — Tacitus. Oxford World's Classics, 2008

Annals of Nottinghamshire Vol. IV — Thomas Bailey. Simpkin, Marshall & Co. Undated

The Annual Biography and Obituary for the Year 1828 Vol. XII — Longman, Rees, Orme, Brown, and Green, 1828

The Antiquities of Nottinghamshire Vols I, II and III — Dr Robert Thoroton, edited and enlarged by John Throsby, originally published in 1790 and 1796, reprinted by EP Publishing Ltd in collaboration with Nottinghamshire County Library, 1972

Archaeological Evaluation of Cropmark Field-systems at Ramsdale,

Arnold, Nottingham — Daryl Garton, Mark Southgate and Ruth Leary with contributions by M.E. Wright and J. Brown. *Transactions of the Thoroton Society of Nottinghamshire* 103, 1999

The Archaeology of Britain — edited by John Hunter and Ian Ralston. Routledge, 2009

Archaeology of the Fosse Way, Vol. 2. Implications of the Proposed Dualling of the A46 Between Newark and Widmerpool — D. Knight and G. Kinsley. Trent and Peak Archaeological Trust Report, 1992

Archaeology in Nottinghamshire: Achievements and Prospects — R.M. Butler. *Transactions of the Thoroton Society of Nottinghamshire* 58, 1954

Art in Roman Britain — J.M.C. Toynbee. Phaidon Press for the Society for the Promotion of Roman Studies, 2nd edition 1963

Art and Society in Fourth-Century Britain: Villa Mosaics in Context — Sarah Scott. Oxford University School of Archaeology Monograph 53, 2000

Art and Society in Roman Britain — Jennifer Laing. Sutton Publishing, 1997

Besthorpe Quarry, Collingham, Nottinghamshire: a Multi-period Occupation Site — Robert Bourn, Jonathan R. Hunn and James Symonds. In: *Three Iron Age and Romano-British Rural Settlements on English Gravels: Excavations at Hatford (Oxfordshire), Besthorpe (Nottinghamshire) and Eardington (Shropshire) undertaken by Tempus Reparatum between 1991 and 1993* — edited by R.J. Zeepvat with contributions by Paul Booth, *et al.* British Archaeological Reports 312, 2000.

The Brigantes: From Clientage to Conquest — W.S. Hanson and D.B. Campbell. *Britannia* 17, 1986

Britannia — William Camden. Published in three volumes in the series Historical Cultures and Geography 1600–1750, edited and introduced by Robert Mayhew. Thoemmes Press, 2003

Britannia: A History of Roman Britain — Sheppard Frere. Pimlico, 1998

Britannia Romana or the Roman Antiquities of Britain — John Horsley. Frank Graham, 2nd edition, 1974

British Iron Age Coins in the British Museum — Richard Hobbs. British Museum Press, 1996

A Bronze Head of a Three-Horned Bull from Thorpe (Ad Pontem), Nottinghamshire — R.C. Alvey. *The Thoroton Society of Nottinghamshire* 83, 1979

A Bronze Skillet-Handle from Chester and other vessels from the British Isles — J.C. McPeake and C.N. Moore. *Britannia* 9, 1978

Broxtowe: The Thoroton Society of Nottinghamshire Excavation Section Third Annual Report for the Year 1938. The Thoroton Society of Nottinghamshire, 1939

The Broxtowe (Nottm.) Early Iron Age Settlement — F. Hind. Reprinted from the *Nottinghamshire Guardian*, 1940

The Buildings of England: Nottinghamshire — Nikolaus Pevsner. Penguin, 1951

Car-Colston — T.C. Blagg. *Transactions of the Thoroton Society of Nottinghamshire* 74, 1970

A Centenary History of Nottingham — edited by John Beckett. Manchester University Press, 1997

A Cheek-Piece from a Cavalry Helmet Found in Leicester — Patrick Clay. *Britannia* 15, 1984

A City within a City: Little Chester, Derby, AD80–AD2000 — Joan D'Arcy. Self-published?

Clifton, Grove Farm (SK 544 366) — Matthew Hurford. In: *Archaeology in Nottinghamshire, Transactions of the Thoroton Society of Nottinghamshire* 112, 2008

Coinage and Identity in Pre-conquest Britain: 50BC–AD50 — Jonathan Williams. In: *Coinage and Identity in the Roman Provinces,* edited by Christopher Howgego, Volker Heuchert and Andrew Burnett. Oxford University Press, 2005

Coinage in Roman Britain — Richard Reece. Seaby, 1987

The Coinage of Roman Britain — Richard Reece. Tempus, 2002

Coinage, Settlement and Society in the Late Iron Age of East Midlands Britain — Jeffrey May. *Proceedings of the XI International Numismatic Congress Extrait du Volume II*, 1993

Coins and Power in Late Iron Age Britain — John Creighton. Cambridge University Press, 2000

The Commandant's House at Margidunum — Felix Oswald. University College Nottingham, 1948

The Conquest of Gaul — Julius Caesar. Penguin Classics, 1974

The Conservation of Romano-British Painted Plaster — Norman Davey. *Britannia* 3, 1972

Convivial Spaces: Dining and Entertainment in the Roman Villa — Katherine M.D. Dunbabin. *Journal of Roman Archaeology* 9, 1996

The Coritani — Malcolm Todd. Alan Sutton, 1991

Crocolana: The Nottinghamshire Brough — T. Cecil S. Woolley. *Transactions of the Thoroton Society of Nottinghamshire* 10, 1906

Crop Yields of the Prehistoric Cereal Types Emmer and Spelt: the Worst Option — Peter J. Reynolds. *Prehistoire d'Agriculture:*

Nouvelles Approaches Experimentales et Ethnographiques. Monographie du CRA, 6. CNRS, 1992

The Cult of Totatis — Adam Daubney. In: *A Decade of Discovery: Proceedings of the Portable Antiquities Scheme Conference 2007*, edited by S. Worrell, K. Leahy, M. Lewis and J. Naylor. British Archaeological Reports (*forthcoming*)

A Curse Tablet from Nottinghamshire — Eric G. Turner. *The Journal of Roman Studies* 53, Parts 1 and 2, 1963

The Decline and Fall of Roman Britain — Neil Faulkner. Tempus, 2004

The Decline and Fall of the Roman Empire — Edward Gibbon. Everyman's Library, 1993

Documents Relating to the Manor and Soke of Newark-on-Trent — edited by M.W. Barley. *Thoroton Society Records Series* 16, 1956

Dorket Head in Nottinghamshire — James and Catherine Turner. Sherwood Archaeological Society, 1997

Dragonby: Report at an Iron Age and Romano-British Settlement in North Lincolnshire — Jeffrey May. Two volumes, Oxbow Monograph 61, 1996

Dunston's Clump and the Brickwork Plan Field System at Babworth, Nottinghamshire: Excavations 1981 — D. Garton. *Transactions of the Thoroton Society of Nottinghamshire* 91, 1987

Eagles over Britannia: the Roman Army in Britain — Guy de la Bédoyère. Tempus, 2003

The Early Course of the Fosse Way: Kneeton to East Stoke — Malcolm Todd. *Transactions of the Thoroton Society of Nottinghamshire* 70, 1966

Early Landscapes from the Air: Studies of Crop Marks in South Yorkshire and North Nottinghamshire — D.N. Riley with a contribution by John Samuels and Jeffrey May. Department of Prehistory and Archaeology, University of Sheffield, 1980

East Bridgford, Notts: the Story of an English Village — Rev. Arthur Du Boulay Hill. Oxford University Press, 1932.

East Carr, Mattersey (SK706885) — D. Garton, L. Elliott, A. Howard, C. Hunt, A. Kennett and T. Morris. In: *Fieldwork by Trent and Peak Archaeological Trust in Nottinghamshire 1995–6,* edited by Keith Challis. *Transactions of the Thoroton Society of Nottinghamshire* 101, 1997

East Carr, Mattersey (SK7088) — T. Morris and D. Garton. In: *Fieldwork by Trent and Peak Archaeological Trust in Nottinghamshire 1996–7,* edited by K. Challis. *Transactions of the Thoroton Society of Nottinghamshire* 102, 1998

East Midlands Archaeological Bulletin 1959 — edited by M.W. Barley. University of Nottingham Department of Extra-Mural Studies

East Midlands Archaeological Bulletin 1962 — edited by M.W. Barley. University of Nottingham Department of Extra-Mural Studies

East Midlands Archaeological Bulletin 1965 — edited by Jeffrey May. University of Nottingham Department of Extra-Mural Studies

East Midlands Archaeological Bulletin 1974 — edited by M.W. Barley. University of Nottingham Department of Adult Education

East Midlands Archaeological Bulletin 1978 — edited by Hazel Wheeler. East Midlands Committee of Field Archaeology

The East Midlands in the Early Middle Ages — Pauline Stafford. Leicester University Press, 1985

The Emerging Past: Air Photography and the Buried Landscape — Rowan Whimster. Royal Commission on the Historical Monuments of England, 1989

An Enamelled Skillet-Handle from Brough-on-Fosse and the Distribution of Similar Vessels — C.N. Moore. *Britannia* 9, 1978

England's Coastal Heritage: a Survey for English Heritage and the RCHME — edited by Michael Fulford, Timothy Champion and Antony Long. English Heritage Archaeological Report no. 15, 1997

The Ermine Street, or Old Roman Road: a Paper Read at the Lincoln Meeting, June 17th, 1868, by the venerable Archdeacon Trollope, M.A., FSA Published by the Lincoln Diocesan Architectural Society.

Excavation at Holme Pierrepont Quarry in 2002–2003: Preliminary Survey of a Multi-Period Palimpsest on the Trent Gravels — Graeme Guilbert. *Transactions of the Thoroton Society of Nottinghamshire* 110, 2006

Excavation of an Iron Age and Romano-British Settlement near Gonalston, Nottinghamshire — Lee Elliott and David Knight. *Transactions of the Thoroton Society of Nottinghamshire* 100, 1996

Excavation of an Iron Age Settlement at Gamston, Nottinghamshire — David Knight with contributions by C.S.M. Allen, E.M. Appleton, A.G. Brown, V. Fell, R.J. Firman, J. Henderson, R.S. Leary, B. Levitan, L. Moffett, C. Mortimer, A. Turner-Rugg, D.F. Williams and M.E. Wright. *Transactions of the Thoroton Society of Nottinghamshire* 96, 1992

Excavation of a Romano-British Field System at Lamb's Close, Kelham, Nottinghamshire — David Knight and Vicki Priest with contributions by C.O. Hunt and R.S.Leary. *Transactions of the Thoroton Society of Nottinghamshire* 102, 1998

Excavation on the Site of Flawford Church, Ruddington, Nottinghamshire — H.M. James. *Transactions of the Thoroton Society of Nottinghamshire* 98, 1994

Excavation on the Saxon-Norman Town Defences at Slaughter House Lane, Newark-on-Trent, Nottinghamshire — A.G. Kinsley with contributions by M. Beech, M. Canti, C. Mortimer, C. Drage, V. Fell, J. Greig, R. Sheppard, J. Wells, R. Woodland and M. Wright. *Transactions of the Thoroton Society of Nottinghamshire* 97, 1993

Excavation on the Site of the Roman Villa at Southwell, 1959 — C.M. Daniels. *Transactions of the Thoroton Society of Nottinghamshire* 70, 1966

Excavations at Ad Pontem, 1937–1938 — Adrian Oswald. *Transactions of the Thoroton Society of Nottinghamshire* 42, 1938

Excavations at Ad Pontem, Thorpe Parish, Notts — R.R. Inskeep. *Transactions of the Thoroton Society of Nottinghamshire* 69, 1965

Excavations at Breedon-on-the-Hill — J.S. Wacher. *Transactions of the Leicestershire Archaeological and Historical Society* 52, 1976–77

Excavations at Farnsfield Roman Camp, Nottinghamshire — Catherine J. Swarbrick and James Turner. Trans*actions of the Thoroton Society of Nottinghamshire* 86, 1982

Excavations at a Romano-British Cropmark Enclosure near Menagerie Wood, Worksop, Nottinghamshire — D. Watson, C.O. Hunt, R.D.S. Jenkinson and R.S. Leary. *Transactions of the Thoroton Society of Nottinghamshire* 92, 1988

Excavations on the Romano-British Settlement and Anglo-Saxon Cemetery at Broughton Lodge, Willoughby-on-the-Wolds, Nottinghamshire 1964–68 — M.J. Dean and A.G. Kinsley. Nottinghamshire Archaeological Monographs 4, Department of Classical and Archaeological Studies (Archaeology Section), University of Nottingham, 1993

The Excavation of Roman, Medieval, and Civil War Remains at Trent Lane, Newark, Nottinghamshire — Richard Cuttler and Eleanor Ramsey with contributions by Val Fryer, Matilda Holmes, Rachel Ives, Erica Macey Bracken, Simon Mortimer, Stephanie Ratkai and Jane Timby. *Transactions of the Thoroton Society of Nottinghamshire* 109, 2005

Excavations on a Traverse of Margidunum — Felix Oswald. University of Nottingham, 1952

Exhibition in Nottingham January 30/31, 1899 — *Transactions of the Thoroton Society of Nottinghamshire* 3, 1899

Felix Oswald 1866–1958: a Memoir and a List of his Works — Grace Simpson and Adrian Oswald. Pamphlet, publisher unknown.

The Fenland in Roman Times — edited by C.W. Philips. Royal Geographical Society research series no. 5, 1970

Field Survey at Hall Close, Car Colston, Nottinghamshire — Colm O'Brien. *Transactions of the Thoroton Society of Nottinghamshire* 81, 1977

The Finds of Roman Britain — Guy de la Bédoyère. Batsford, 1989

Food and Cooking in Roman Britain: History and Recipes — Jane Renfrew. English Heritage, 2003

Food in Roman Britain — Joan P. Alcock. Tempus, 2001

The Fosse Way in Nottinghamshire and Lincolnshire — Trevor Dann and Keith Train. BBC Radio Nottingham, 1976

Further Excavations of an Iron Age and Romano-British Settlement near Gonalston, Nottinghamshire — Lee Elliott and David Knight. *Transactions of the Thoroton Society of Nottinghamshire* 101, 1997

The Gods of Roman Britain — Miranda J. Green. Shire Archaeology 34, 2003

A Guide to Leicestershire Archaeology — Elizabeth Blank. Leicester Museums, 1970

A Guide to the Roman Remains in Britain — Roger J.A. Wilson. Constable, 3rd edition, 1996

Hayman Rooke, FSA: An Eighteenth Century Nottinghamshire Antiquary — A.G. Sherratt. *Transactions of the Thoroton Society of Nottinghamshire* 69, 1965

The Histories — Tacitus. Oxford World's Classics, 2008

The History and Antiquities of the Town of Newark in the County of Nottingham — William Dickinson. Longman, Hurst, Rees, Orme and Brown; Nichols and Sons; And Baldwin, Craddock and Joy, 1819

The History and Antiquities of the Town of Southwell — William Dickinson. 3rd edition published 1819. Republished in 1996 by Nottinghamshire County Council

The History of Collingham and its Neighbourhood — E.G. Wake, 1867. Republished in 1998 by Nottinghamshire County Council, Collingham Medical Centre and Collingham Parish Council

A History of the County of Nottingham, Vol. II: The Victoria History of the Counties of England, reprinted from the original edition of 1910 for the University of London Institute of Historical Research by Dawsons of Pall Mall, 1970

The History of the Countryside — Oliver Rackham. Phoenix Press, 2000

History, Directory and Gazeteer of the Town and County of Nottingham with a Variety of Commercial and Statistical Information — Francis and John White. John Burton, 1844

A History of the English Church and People — Bede, Penguin Classics, 1977

A History of the Later Roman Empire AD 284–641 — Stephen Mitchell. Blackwell Publishing, 2007

The History of Mansfield — W.H. Grover. Frank Murray, 1894. Republished by F.B and S. Payton, Mansfield

The History of Mansfield and it's [sic] Environs — William Harrod, 1801. Republished in 1986 by F.B. & S. Payton, Mansfield

History of Nottingham — Charles Deering M.D., 1751. Republished by S.R. Publishers Ltd, 1970.

History of Southwell — Richard P. Shilton. Published 1818, republished by Nottinghamshire Leisure Services, Nottingham, 1993

A Hoard of Roman Coins from Besthorpe — Alan Cotterill, H.B. Mattingly and Malcolm Todd. *Transactions of the Thoroton Society of Nottinghamshire* 69, 1965

Hoards of Roman Coins Found in Britain: And a Coin Survey of the Roman Province — H. Mattingly. *The Journal of Roman Studies* 22, Part 1, 1932

Holme Pierrepont — D.G. Bilton. *Nottinghamshire Countryside* 32, 1, 1971

How the Celts Came to Britain: Druids, Ancient Skulls and the Birth of Archaeology — Michael A. Morse. Tempus, 2005

An Imperial Possession: Britain in the Roman Empire — David Mattingly. Penguin Books, 2007

An Inscription Recently Found at Bordeaux — Paul Courteault. *The Journal of Roman Studies* 11, 1921

I Lived in a Village: Stories of Life and Folk in Nottinghamshire in General and Oxton in Particular — Tom Shipside. Privately published for the Woolston Book Co, Nottingham, 1956

'Interpretatio': Roman Word Power and the Celtic Gods — Jane Webster. *Britannia* 26, 1995

Iron Age and Roman Occupation in the West Bridge Area, Leicester: Excavations 1962–1971 — Patrick Clay and Richard Pollard. Leicestershire Archaeological Unit, 1994

Iron Age Britain — Barry Cunliffe. BT Batsford/English Heritage, 1995

Iron Age Communities in Britain: an Account of England, Scotland and Wales from the Seventh Century BC until the Roman Conquest — Barry Cunliffe. Routledge and Kegan Paul, 1974

An Iron Age and Romano-British Settlement at Aslockton, Nottinghamshire: Interim Report — Colin Palmer-Brown and David Knight. *Transactions of the Thoroton Society of Nottinghamshire* 97, 1993

Iron Age Hill Forts in Nottinghamshire — B.B. Simons. *Transactions of the Thoroton Society of Nottinghamshire* 67, 1963

Iron Age/Romano-British Features and a Fourth Century AD

Christian Lead Tank from Flawborough, Nottinghamshire — Lee Elliott and Steve Malone with contributions by Ruth Leary. *Transactions of the Thoroton Society of Nottinghamshire* 109, 2005

Iron Age and Roman Sites at Red Hill, Ratcliffe-on-Soar, Nottinghamshire: Excavations of E. Greenfield, 1963, and Previous Finds — S.M. Elsdon. *Transactions of the Thoroton Society of Nottinghamshire* 86, 1982

An Iron Age Settlement at Whatton, Nottinghamshire — Laurence Platt. *Transactions of the Thoroton Society of Nottinghamshire* 109, 2005

Invasion: the Roman Conquest of Britain — John Peddie. Guild Publishing, 1987

Itinerarium Curiosum, Or an Account of the Antiquitys and Remarkable Curiositys in Nature or Art, Observ'd in Travels thro' Great Britain — William Stukeley. Printed for the Author, 1724

The Jewish War — Josephus. Penguin Classics, 1981

John Leland's Itinerary: Travels in Tudor England — John Chandler. Allan Sutton, 1993

Land and Settlement in Nottinghamshire and Lowland Derbyshire: An Archaeological Review — Colm O'Brien. Trent Valley Archaeological Research Committee, undated

The Late Defences of Margidunum — R.M. Butler. *Transactions of the Thoroton Society of Nottinghamshire* 56, 1952

A Late Iron Age and Romano-British Settlement at Rampton, Nottinghamshire — M.W. Ponsford with contributions by R.C. Alvey, Justine Bayley, David Dawson, Donald Mackreth and Catherine Turner. *Transactions of the Thoroton Society of Nottinghamshire* 96, 1992

A Late Third-Century Coin Hoard from Little Morton, Babworth, Nottinghamshire — Malcolm J. Dolby, Jean Eccles, Daryl Garton, Ruth S. Leary and Gwladys Monteil. *Transactions of the Thoroton Society of Nottinghamshire* 113, 2009

Lead Coffin Found at Crocolana (Brough, Notts) — a note by Arthur Smith. *Transactions of the Thoroton Society of Nottinghamshire* 45, 1941

A Lead Tank Fragment from Brough, Notts. (Roman 'Crococolana') — Dorothy J. Watts. *Britannia* 26, 1995

Legionary Speed of March before the Battle with Boudicca — Herbert W. Benario. *Britannia* 17, 1986

Leicestershire Archaeology, the Present State of Knowledge Vol 1: to the End of the Roman Period — Peter Liddle. Leicestershire Museums, Art Galleries and Records Service Archaeological Report No. 4

Letters of Cicero — edited by L.P. Wilkinson. Hutchinson, 1966

The Letters of the Younger Pliny. Penguin Books, 1974

Life and Letters on the Roman Frontier: Vindolanda and its People — Alan K. Bowman. The British Museum Press, 2006

The Making of the English Landscape — W.G. Hoskins. Penguin Books, 1985

Margidunum — Felix Oswald. *Journal of Roman Studies* 31, 1941.

Margidunum — Rev. J. Standish. *Transactions of the Thoroton Society of Nottinghamshire* 12, 1908

Margidunum — a Roman Fortified Post on the Fosse Way: Excavations of 1910–11 — T. Davies Pryce. Reprinted from the *Journal of the British Archaeological Association*, December 1912. Printed at the Bedford Press, London, 1912.

Margidunum: an Account of the Excavations on the Site of the Roman Station on the Foss Way, near Bingham, Notts — Felix Oswald. City of Nottingham Art Museum, Nottingham Castle, 1927

Margidunum Roman Villa and Small Town — Ruth Leary and Steve Baker. Trent and Peak Archaeological Unit Report, 2004

Medieval England: Towns, Commerce and Crafts 1086–1348 — Edward Miller and John Hatcher. Pearson Education, 1995

Medieval Roads — Brian Paul Hindle. Shire Archaeology, 1982

The Mysteries of Mithras: a New Account of their Genesis — Roger Beck. *The Journal of Roman Studies* 88, 1998

The Name of Margidunum, Roman Settlement, Nottinghamshire — Andrew Breeze. *Transactions of the Thoroton Society of Nottinghamshire* 109, 2005

Natural History: a Selection — Pliny the Elder. Penguin Classics, 2004

New Light on a Suspected Roman Road between Ratcliffe-on-Soar and Leicester — Stephen J. Lycett. *Transactions of the Leicestershire Archaeological and Historical Society* 73, 1999

Newark's Archaeological Resource: a Report for Newark and Sherwood District Council — Gavin Kinsley. Trent and Peak Archaeological Trust, January 1989

Notes on the History of the Navigation of the River Trent — J.T. Evans. Trent Navigation Company, 1945

Notes on Some Romano-British Pigs of Lead — G. Clement Whittick. *The Journal of Roman Studies* 21, 1931

Nottinghamshire Archaeological Society Tenth Annual Report for the Year 1945

A Nottinghamshire Bibliography: Publications on Nottinghamshire

History before 1998 — Michael Brook. The Thoroton Society of Nottinghamshire in association with the Nottingham Civic Society, 2002

Nottinghamshire Heritage 1, 2, 1989

Nottinghamshire Maps of the 16th, 17th and 18th Centuries: Their Makers and Engravers — F. Arthur Wadsworth. *Transactions of the Thoroton Society of Nottinghamshire* 34, 1930

Old Sleaford Revisited: a Lincolnshire Settlement in Iron Age, Roman, Saxon and Medieval Times: Excavations 1882–1995 — Sheila M. Elsdon. Oxbow Monograph 78, Nottingham Studies in Archaeology 2, 1997

Ordnance Survey Maps: a Concise Guide for Historians — Richard Oliver. The Charles Close Society for the Study of Ordnance Survey Maps, 1993

The Origin of the Coritani — Felix Oswald. *The Antiquaries Journal* 21, 1941

Our Church's Story — Dorothy M. Shrimpton. Printed by John P. Norman Ltd, Nottingham. Date unknown

The Pelican History of Britain I: Roman Britain — Ian Richmond. Pelican, 1955

The Place-Names of Roman Britain — A.L.F. Rivet and Colin Smith. Book Club Associates, 1981

Plant Remains from a Roman Well at Bunny, Nottinghamshire — D.G. Wilson. *Transactions of the Thoroton Society of Nottinghamshire* 72, 1968

A Portrait of the River Trent — Peter Lord. Robert Hale, 1968

The Pottery of a Claudian Well — Felix Oswald. *The Journal of Roman Studies* 13, 1923

Prehistoric and Roman Mining in the Peak District: Present Knowledge and Future Research — John Barnatt. *The Bulletin of the Peak District Mines Historical Society* 14, 2, 1999

Rampton, Moor Pool Close. In: *Archaeology in Nottinghamshire, 1999. Transactions of the Thoroton Society of Nottinghamshire* 104, 2000

The Recent Excavations on the Site of the Roman Camp of Margidunum — Felix Oswald. City of Nottingham Art Museum, Nottingham Castle, 1911

Recent Work at Osmanthorpe, Nottinghamshire — M.C. Bishop, P.W.M. Freeman, M.V. Andrews, C.P. Barclay, K. Hartley, D.F. Mackreth, J. Roy, Simon J.N. Tomson and K.F. Hartley. *Britannia* 24, 1993

Redhill Iron Age and Romano-British Site, Nottinghamshire: a New Assessment — Alan Palfreyman and Susan Ebbins. *Transactions of the Thoroton Society of Nottinghamshire* 107, 2003

Religion in Late Roman Britain: Force of Change — Dorothy Watts. Routledge, 1998

'Resurrection Major': a Biography of Major Hayman Rooke (1723–1806), Soldier and Antiquarian — Pamela McInally. University of Sheffield dissertation

A Relief of a Romano-British Warrior-God — Malcolm Todd. *Britannia* 2, 1971

Religions of Rome — Mary Beard, John North and Simon Price. Cambridge University Press, 2009

A River Crossing — M.J. Jackson. *The Nottinghamshire Countryside* 29, 3

Roads in Roman Britain — Hugh Davies. Tempus, 2002

The Roads, Trackways and Footpaths of East Leake: the History and Origin of their Names — R. Owen Wood. East Leake and District Local History Group, 1991

The Roman Amphitheatre in Britain — Tony Wilmott. Tempus, 2008

Roman Britain in 1949 — R.P. Wright. *The Journal of Roman Studies* 40, 1950

Roman Britain in 1961 — R.P. Wright. *The Journal of Roman Studies* 52, Parts 1 and 2, 1962

Roman Britain in 1962 — R.P. Wright and D.R. Wilson. *The Journal of Roman Studies* 53, Parts 1 and 2, 1963

Roman Britain in 1963 — D.R. Wilson and R.P. Wright. *The Journal of Roman Studies* 54, Parts 1 and 2, 1964

Roman Britain in 1964 — D.R. Wilson and R.P. Wright. *The Journal of Roman Studies* 55, Parts 1 and 2, 1965

Roman Britain in 1973 — D.R. Wilson, R.P. Wright, M.W.C. Hassall, A.K. Bowman and J.D. Thomas. *Britannia* 5, 1974

Roman Britain in 1983 — S.S. Frere, M.W.C. Hassall and R.S.O. Tomlin. *Britannia* 15, 1984

Roman Britain in 1992: II Inscriptions — M.W.C. Hassall and R.S.O. Tomlin. *Britannia* 24, 1993

Roman Britain in 1999 — B.C. Burnham, L.J.F. Keppie, A.S. Esmonde Cleary, M.W.C. Hassall, R.S.O. Tomlin and Barry C. Burnham. *Britannia* 31, 2000

Roman Britain in 2001 — Barry C. Burnham, F. Hunter, A.P. Fitzpatrick, M.W.C. Hassall and R.S.O. Tomlin. *Britannia* 33, 2002

Roman Britain in 2002 — B.C. Burnham, F. Hunter, A.P. Fitzpatrick, M.W.C. Hassall and R.S.O. Tomlin. *Britannia* 34, 2003

Roman Britain in 2003 — Barry Burnham. *Britannia* 35, 2004

Roman Britain in 2006: Inscriptions — R. Tomlin and M. Hassall. *Britannia* 38, 2007

Roman Britain in 2009 — E.M Chapman, F. Hunter, P. Booth, P. Wilson, S. Worrell and R.S.O. Tomlin. *Britannia* 41, 2010

Roman Britain and the English Settlements — R.G. Collingwood and J.N.L. Myres. Oxford University Press, 1937

Roman Britain: a New History — Guy de la Bédoyère. Thames & Hudson, 2006

Roman Britain: a Sourcebook — S. Ireland. Routledge, 1996

Roman Britain from the Air — S.S. Frere and J.K. St Joseph. Cambridge University Press, 1983

A Roman Bronze from Thorpe (*Ad Pontem*) Nottinghamshire — R.C. Alvey. *Transactions of the Thoroton Society of Nottinghamshire* 84, 1980

A Roman Brooch from near Harlow Wood, Nottinghamshire — R.C. Alvey. *Transactions of the Thoroton Society of Nottinghamshire* 83, 1979

Roman Camps in England: the Field Archaeology — Royal Commission on the Historical Monuments of England. HMSO, 1995

A Roman Coin Forgery from Nottinghamshire — A.C. Alvey. *Transactions of the Thoroton Society of Nottinghamshire* 86, 1982

Roman Coinage in Britain — P.J. Casey. Shire Archaeology, 1980

Roman Coins — Richard Reece. Ernest Benn, 1970

A Roman Curse Tablet from Nottinghamshire — *Loughborough Archaeological Society Bulletin* 6, autumn 1963

Roman Defended Sites at Kirmington, S. Humberside and Farnsfield, Notts., Recently Found from the Air — D.N. Riley. *Britannia* 8, 1977

A Roman Field System at Redhill, Ratcliffe-on-Soar — Michael Dawson. *Transactions of the Thoroton Society of Nottinghamshire* 105, 2001

The Roman Fort at Scaftworth, near Bawtry — J.E. Bartlett and D.N. Riley. *Transactions of the Thoroton Society of Nottinghamshire* 62, 1958

A Roman Fortified Villa at Norton Disney, Lincs — Adrian Oswald M.A. and L.H.D. Buxton F.S.A. *The Antiquities Journal* 17, 1937

Roman Forts in Britain — Paul Bidwell. Tempus, 2007

The Roman Fosse Way at Brough, Nottinghamshire — M.C. Bishop. *Transactions of the Thoroton Society of Nottinghamshire* 84, 1980

The Roman Invasion of Britain — Graham Webster. Routledge, 1993

Roman Leicester, A corrigendum: for 'Coritani', Should We Now Read 'Corieltauvi'? — R.S.O. Tomlin. *Transactions of the Leicestershire Archaeological and Historical Society* 58, 1982–83

Roman Lincoln: Conquest, Colony and Capital — Michael J. Jones. Tempus, 2002

Roman Lincolnshire revised edition — J.B. Whitwell. The History of Lincolnshire Committee, 1992

Roman and Medieval Remains in Church Street, Southwell, Nottinghamshire — Lee Elliott. *Transactions of the Thoroton Society of Nottinghamshire* 108, 2004

The Roman Military Diet — R.W. Davies. *Britannia* 2, 1971

Roman Mosaics of Britain, Vol. 1: Northern Britain including the Midlands and East Anglia — David J. Neal and Stephen R. Cosh. Illuminati Publishers for the Society of Antiquaries of London, 2002

The Roman Pottery Industries of South Yorkshire: a Review — P.C. Buckland, J.R. Magilton and M.J. Dolby. *Britannia* 11, 1980

Roman Road and Settlement, Long Bennington, Lincolnshire — Yvonne Boutwood. *Britannia* 29, 1998

A Roman Road at Belle Eau Park, Bilsthorpe, Nottinghamshire — Keith Challis, Vicki Priest, Carol Allen and Gavin Kinsley. *Transactions of the Thoroton Society of Nottinghamshire* 106, 2002

Roman Roads — Raymond Chevallier. Batsford, 1976

Roman Roads in Britain — Thomas Codrington. The Sheldon Press, 1928

Roman Roads in Britain — Ivan D. Margary. Two volumes. Phoenix House, 1955 and 1957

The Roman Settlement at Margidunum: the Excavations of 1966–68 — Malcolm Todd. *Transactions of the Thoroton Society of Nottinghamshire* 73, 1969

The Roman Site at Red Hill: Ratcliffe-on-Soar, Nottinghamshire — Herbert O. Houldsworth. *Transactions of the Thoroton Society of Nottinghamshire* 67, 1963

The Roman Station of *Ad Pontem*, now East Stoke; its Origin, and the Derivation of its Name — Felix Oswald. *Transactions of the Thoroton Society of Nottinghamshire* 55, 1951

A Roman Surgical Forceps from near Littleborough and a Note on the Type — Ralph Jackson and Kevin Leahy. *Britannia* 21, 1990

The Roman Swithland Slate Industry — Alan McWhirr. *Transactions of the Leicestershire Archaeological and Historical Society* 62, 1988

The Roman Villa at Glebe Farm, Barton-in-Fabis, Nottinghamshire: Excavations 1933–1949 — F.H. Thompson. *Transactions of the Thoroton Society of Nottinghamshire* 55, 1951

The Roman Villa in Britain — edited by A.L.F. Rivet. Routledge & Kegan Paul, 1969

Roman Villas — David E. Johnston. Shire Archaeology, 2004

Roman York — Patrick Ottaway. Tempus, 2004

A Romano-British Brooch from Willoughby-on-the-Wolds — D.F. Mackreth. *Transactions of the Thoroton Society of Nottinghamshire* 70, 1966

Romano-British Coin Hoards — Richard Anthony Abdy. Shire Archaeology, 2002

A Romano-British Duck Beaker from Red Hill, Ratcliffe-on-Soar, Nottinghamshire — R.S. Leary. *Transactions of the Thoroton Society of Nottinghamshire* 100, 1996

Romano-British Face Pots and Head Pots — Gillian Braithwaite. *Britannia* 15, 1984

The Romano-British Landscape of the Sherwood Sandstone of Nottinghamshire: Fieldwalking the Brickwork-plan Field System — Daryl Garton with a major contribution by Ruth S. Leary and other contributions by Jane Cowgill, Ron J. Firman and Liz Wright. *Transactions of the Thoroton Society of Nottinghamshire* 112, 2008

Romano-British Life in North Nottinghamshire; Fresh Evidence from Raymoth Lane, Worksop — Colin Palmer-Brown and Will Munford. *Transactions of the Thoroton Society of Nottinghamshire* 108, 2004

A Romano-British Native Site at South Muskham — Hazel Wheeler. *Transactions of the Thoroton Society of Nottinghamshire* 72, 1968

The Romano-British Rural Settlement at Staunton, Nottinghamshire — Malcolm Todd. *Transactions of the Thoroton Society of Nottinghamshire* 79, 1975

A Romano-British Site at Bingham — A. Gregory. *Transactions of the Thoroton Society of Nottinghamshire* 73, 1969

Romano-British Villa at Thurgarton — Editor's Note. *Transactions of the Thoroton Society of Nottinghamshire* 65, 1961

Romano-British Villas from the Air — D.R. Wilson. *Britannia* 5, 1974

A Romano-British Wood-Lined Well at the Wild Goose Cottage, Lound, Nottinghamshire — Daryl Garton and Christopher R. Salisbury with contributions by Ron J. Firman, Ruth S. Leary and Richard Sheppard. *Transactions of the Thoroton Society of Nottinghamshire* 91, 1995

Salvage Excavation of a Romano-British Site at Chainbridge Lane, Lound, Nottinghamshire, 1985 — J. Eccles, P. Caldwell and K. Mincher. *Transactions of the Thoroton Society of Nottinghamshire* 92, 1989

Sanderson's Map: 20 Miles around Mansfield, reprinted in two parts.

Nottinghamshire County Council and Derbyshire County Council, 2001.

The Second Inscribed Tablet from the Roman Site at Red Hill, Ratcliffe-on-Trent, Nottinghamshire — B.C.J. Williams. *Loughborough Archaeological Journal* 7, autumn 1964

Slaves and Masters in the Roman Empire: a Study in Social Control — K.R. Bradley. Oxford University Press, 1987

The Small Towns of Roman Britain — Malcolm Todd. *Britannia* 1, 1970

Some Unrecorded Earthworks in Nottinghamshire — Adrian Oswald. *Transactions of the Thoroton Society of Nottinghamshire* 43, 1939

The Southwell Charter of 956 AD: an Exploration of its Boundaries — Philip Lyth. *Transactions of the Thoroton Society of Nottinghamshire* 86, 1982

Summer Excursion 1909 — The Rev. Dr. Scott-Moncrieff, Harry Gill, the Rev. A.W.B. Marshall, the Rev. George F. Twycross and T. Cecil Smith Woolley. *Transactions of the Thoroton Society of Nottinghamshire* 13, 1909

Southwell Pavement, Probably pre-Norman — Atwell M.Y. Baylay. *Transactions of the Thoroton Society of Nottinghamshire* 5, 1901

The Supply and Use of Money in the Roman World 200 BC to AD 300 — Christopher Howgego. *The Journal of Roman Studies* 82, 1992

A Survey of Romano-British Coin Hoards in Leicestershire — M.J. Winter. Transactions of the Leicestershire Archaeological and Historical Society 53, 1977–78

A Survey of Two Cropmark Sites in Lockington-Hemington Parish, Leicestershire — Patrick Clay. *Transactions of the Leicestershire Archaeological and Historical Society* 59, 1984–85

Sylloge of Coins of the British Isles: Coins of the Coritani — D.F. Allen. Published for the British Academy by the Oxford University Press, 1963

Temporary Camps at Calverton, Notts. — D.N. Riley. *Britannia* 14, 1983

Three Celtic Coins in Nottingham Castle Museum — D.F. Allen. *Transactions of the Thoroton Society of Nottinghamshire* 65, 1961

Three Dug-Out Canoes and a Wheel from Holme Pierrepont, Nottinghamshire — A.G. MacCormick, with contributions by J.H. Dickson, M. Ransom and R.C. Alvey. *Transactions of the Thoroton Society of Nottinghamshire* 72, 1968

Tile-Stamps of the Ninth Legion Found in Britain — R.P. Wright. *Britannia* 9, 1978

A Tour through the Whole Island of Great Britain — Daniel Defoe.

Penguin Classics, 1978

The Towns of Roman Britain — John Wacher. Batsford, 1978

Trentside: an Exhibition Curated by Nicholas Alfrey. The Djanogly Gallery, 2001

Trent Valley Landscapes: the Archaeology of 500,000 Years of Change — David Knight and Andy J. Howard. Heritage Marketing and Publications, 2004

Trent Valley Ware: a Roman Coarse Ware of the Middle and Lower Trent Valley — Malcolm Todd. *Transactions of the Thoroton Society of Nottinghamshire* 72, 1968

The Twelve Caesers — Suetonius. Penguin Classics, 1979

Two Beaded Torcs from Nottinghamshire — R.C. Alvey. *Transactions of the Thoroton Society of Nottinghamshire* 85, 1981

Two Hoards of Roman Coins from Calverton — H.B. Mattingly. *Transactions of the Thoroton Society of Nottinghamshire* 64, 1960

Two New Roman Military Stations in Mid-Nottinghamshire — D.N. Riley. *Britannia* 11, 1980

The Use of Coal in Roman Britain — Martin J. Dearne and Keith Branigan, FSA. *The Antiquaries Journal* 75, 1995

Vegetius: Epitome of Military Science — translated by N.P. Milner. Liverpool University Press, reprinted 2001

Walking Fields in South Muskham and its Implications for Romano-British Cropmark Landscapes in Nottinghamshire — Daryl Garton with contributions by Ruth Leary and Vicki Naylor. *Transactions of the Thoroton Society of Nottinghamshire* 106, 2002

Work at Margidunum — *Transactions of the Thoroton Society of Nottinghamshire* 26, 1922

Work of the Sherwood Archaeological Society 1960–2006: a Summary. Sherwood Archaeological Society

Newspaper cuttings, letters and archives

Another Find for Treasure Hunter. *Newark Advertiser*, 19th July 2010 http://www.newarkadvertiser.co.uk/news/view.asp? id=08edea55-e174-102d-9ecd-3d6f7910e241 [accessed 19th July 2010]

Bishop's Fears for Heritage. *Newark Advertiser*, 13th June 2008 http://www.newarkadvertiser.co.uk/news/view. asp?id=ee969efd-89ba-102b-b53b-c1a6f9edb7cf [accessed 30th June 2010]

Boy Finds a Second Roman Coffin. *Newark Advertiser*, 9th October 1971

Build in the Balance. *Newark Advertiser*, 23rd January 2009 http://www.newarkadvertiser.co.uk/news/view.asp?id= 479e2d90-39de-102c-bb9c-ce9ca152b7a0 [accessed 30th June 2010)

Debate Denied. *Newark Advertiser*, 12th September 2008 http://www.newarkadvertiser.co.uk/news/view.asp?id=e174643d- d156-102b-8b1e-16c8ad082291 [accessed 30th June 2010)

Dualling Details Shown to Public. *Newark Advertiser*, 1st March 2002

50 years Ago — Feb 2 1955. *Newark Advertiser* http://www. newarkadvertiser.co.uk/featurecontent/history/50-years/55feb. htm [accessed 4th December 2009]

History Group to Get Roman Well from A46. *Nottingham Evening Post*, 16th December 2009

John, 15, Finds Ancient Coffin. *Newark Advertiser*, 27th February 1971

Rare Finds at Bypass Dig. *Newark Advertiser* www.newarkadvertiser.co.uk/news/2002/2/8/story9.htm [accessed 4th December 2009]

Roman Well Found in A46 Works. *Nottingham Evening Post*, 21st September 2009

Scanners' Field Trip Ends in Court Date. *Newark Advertiser*, January 25, 2008 http://www.newarkadvertiser.co.uk/news/ view.asp?id=f59cdc95-1bc6-102b-8946-eb23ea313471 [accessed 3rd February 2010]

Skeletons Revealed by Excavation. *Nottinghamshire Guardian*, 10th October 1947

Thick Skull Amazes Nottm. Geologist. *Nottinghamshire Guardian*, 12th September 1947

Wildlife Trust in Complaints over A46 Habitat Loss. *Nottingham Evening Post*, 13th October 2009 http://www.thisisnottingham.co.uk/homenews/Wildlife-Trust-complaints-A46-habitat-loss/article-1412525-detail/article.html [accessed 25th January 2010]

Herbert O. Houldsworth's papers are in the Nottinghamshire

Archives, accession number 6830

T. Cecil Smith Woolley's obituary in the *Newark Advertiser* was printed on 5th February 1913 and is included within several boxes of family documents and diaries located in the Nottinghamshire Archives, accession number 6821

The sharp review of Ivan Margary's *Roman Roads in Britain, Vol. II, North of the Foss Way-Bristol Channel (Including Wales and Scotland)*, was published in *The Journal of Roman Studies* 48, 1958.

Illustrations

(Stone carving) University of Nottingham Museum 11

(Newspaper) Nottinghamshire Archives 18

(Helmet decoration) Newark and Sherwood District Council Museum Service (*photograph by author*) 19 and front cover

(Roundhouse) (*photograph by author)* 21

(Cromwell villa photo) Society for the Promotion of Roman Studies 23

(Gold coin) Bassetlaw Museum 28

(Claudius coin) Newark and Sherwood District Council Museum Service (*photograph by author*) 30

(Osmanthorpe map) Society for the Promotion of Roman Studies 31

(Adam Thompson) (*photograph by author*) 38

(Hand) (*photograph by author*) 40

(Tile in sand) (*photograph by author*) 41

(Wheel) Nottingham City Museums & Galleries 42

(Statue of Constantine) (*photograph by author*) 51

(Map of Margidunum) Original drawing by Trent & Peak Archaeology. Reproduced by permission of Bingham Heritage Trails Association 53

(Felix Oswald) University of Nottingham Museum 54

(Counters and face) University of Nottingham Museum *(photographs by author)* 55

(Sword and spear) University of Nottingham Museum 56

(Stone foundations) Highways Agency 63

(Skeleton) Highways Agency 63

(Road and excavation) Highways Agency 67

(Stone gods) University of Nottingham Museum 74

(3 × ToT rings) Drawn by and show by permission of Adam Daubney 76

(Attis) Bassetlaw Museum 77

(Mithraic altar) (*photograph by author*) 79

(Constantine coin) Nottingham City Museums & Galleries (*photograph by author*) 80

(Thorpe lead fragment) Newark and Sherwood District Council Museum Service (*photograph by author*) 82

(B/w Southwell drawing) Society for the Promotion of Roman Studies 85

(Grey head pot) Newark and Sherwood District Council Museum Service (*photograph by author*) 87

(Hunt Cup) Newark and Sherwood District Council Museum Service (*photograph by author*). 87

(Worksop coffin fragment) Bassetlaw Museum 89

(Two × jewellery) Nottingham City Museums & Galleries (*photograph by author*) 90

(Enamel box lid) University of Nottingham Museum (*photograph by author*) 90

(Bronze bracelet) Newark and Sherwood District Council Museum Service (*photograph by author*) 91

(Campion colour drawing) Nottinghamshire Archives 96

(Samian pottery with name) Newark and Sherwood District Council Museum Service (*photograph by author*) 98

(Notice board and signpost) *(photographs by author)* 115

(Stukeley pic) Nottingham City Council and www.picturethepast.org.uk 115

(Ad Pontem photograph) Cambridge University Air Photograph Library 132

(Map of Ad Pontem) The Thoroton Society of Nottinghamshire 133

(3 × coffins) Newark and Sherwood District Council Museum Service (*photograph by author*) 140

(Ear pick) Newark and Sherwood District Council Museum Service (*photograph by author*) 141

(Norton Disney horse statue) The Trustees of the British Museum 142

(Fosse Way fence) (*photograph by author*). 147

(Bridlepath) (*photograph by author*) 148

(EB sign) (*photograph by author*) 149

(Stukeley image) Nottingham City Council and www.picturethepast.org.uk 152

(Well) Highways Agency 153

(Longhedge Lane pics × 3) *(photographs by author)* 155–156

(Haughgate Hill) *(photograph by author)* 160

(Littleborough × 2) *(photographs by author)* 162

(Scaftworth fortlet) The Thoroton Society of Nottinghamshire 167

(Scaftworth map) Society for the Promotion of Roman Studies 168

(Southwell boundary map) The Thoroton Society of Nottinghamshire 170

(2 × Southwell rural boundary photos) photographs by author 172

(Camp Hill) *(photograph by author)* 172

(Map of Redhill) The Thoroton Society of Nottinghamshire 178

(Forts map) Society for the Promotion of Roman Studies 184

(Broxtowe pic) *(photograph by author)* 187

(Borstal) Nottinghamshire Archives 188

(Skillet) University of Nottingham Museum 189

(Map of Broxtowe fort) Nottinghamshire Archives 190

(Campion's drawing of pottery) Nottinghamshire Archives 192

(Campion newspaper pic) Nottinghamshire Archives 193

(Osmanthorpe map) Society for the Promotion of Roman Studies 194

(Calverton camps) Crown Copyright.NMR 197

(Farnsfield camp) Crown Copyright.NMR 199

(Gleadthorpe camp) Crown Copyright.NMR 201

(Gleadthorpe photo) *(photograph by author)* 202

(Holme camp) Crown Copyright.NMR 203

(Holme photo) *(photograph by author)* 204

(M/Woodhouse mosaic) The Society of Antiquaries 206

(M/W drawings) The Society of Antiquaries 209

(Colour Cupid painting) The Society for the Promotion of Roman Studies 212

(Roof tiles) Newark and Sherwood District Council (*photograph by author*) 214

(Mosaic) Newark and Sherwood District Council (*photograph by author*) 215

(Villa drawing) The Society of Antiquaries 220

(Villa model) Mansfield Museum (*photograph by author*) 224

(M/W drawing) The Society of Antiquaries 226

(Southwell map) University of Nottingham Museum 228

(Southwell plaque) *(photograph by author)* 230

(Southwell mosaics × 2) University of Nottingham Museum 230–231
(Graffiti) *(photograph by author)* in June 2010 233
(Colour mosaic) Nottingham City Council and www.picturethepast.org.uk 235
(Hut) Nottingham City Council and www.picturethepast.org.uk 236
(Fr Gerry White) *(photograph by author)* 240
(Car Colston) The Thoroton Society of Nottinghamshire. 242
(Thurgarton b/w photo) C.E. Coulthard and www.picturethepast.org.uk 243
(Sphinx) University of Nottingham Museum *(photograph by author)* 244
(Epperstone rural photo) *(photograph by author)* 245
(Cromwell b/w photo) Cambridge University Air Photograph Library 246
(Gladiator coins) Newark and Sherwood District Council Museum Service *(photographs by author)* 248
(Map) Map created by and shown by permission of Nottinghamshire County Council Historic Environment Record 251
(Trajan coin × 2) Nottingham City Museums & Galleries (*photograph by author*) 252
(Gothicus coin) Nottingham City Museums & Galleries (*photograph by author*) 254
(Berridge Road × 2) Nottingham City Museums & Galleries (*photograph by author*). 255
(Republican coin) Newark and Sherwood District Council Museum Service (*photograph by author*) 256
(Hadrian coin) Newark and Sherwood District Council Museum Service (*photograph by author*) 258

Index of People and Place Names

Adcobrovatus 135
Ad Pontem 16, 30, 64, 73, 74, 116, 124, 129–137, 139, 142, 148, 149, 154, 155, 168, 170, 171-174, 183, 184, 195, 196, 227
Agricola, Julius 17, 19, 31, 35, 36, 46, 50, 111
Aire, River 158
Alaric 102
Aldborough (North Yorkshire) 97, 117
Alchester (Oxfordshire) 182
Allectus 255
Allen, Carol 173
Allen, G.F. 20, 26, 27
Allen, G.W.G. 132
Alwyn Road 188
Ancaster (Lincolnshire)16, 76, 82, 97, 134, 139, 170, 174
Anglesey 32, 80, 135
Anstey (Leicestershire) 179
Antonine Itinerary 115, 116, 121, 126, 129, 137, 159
Antonine Wall 97, 113
Anubis 78
Apicius 101, 102
Archbishop's Palace (Southwell) 228
Armitage, Tim 176
Arnold 17, 24, 198
Ashmolean Museum 225
Aslockton 22, 46
Aspden, Peter 62
Aston, Mick 140
Attis 77
Aurelian, Emperor 253, 257
Aurelius, Marcus Emperor 248, 253
Aurelius, Marcus (freedman) 70
Avon, River 112
Axe, River 112
Babworth 45, 51, 97, 101, 250, 257
Bailey, Thomas 206
Baker, Steve 60, 61
Balderton 143
Balfour Beatty 154
Balkans 105
Bargate (Newark) 143
Barley, Maurice 147, 148. 243
Barlow, Alfred 162
Barnby Moor 45
Barrow-on-Soar (Leicestershire) 179
Bartlett, J.E. 168
Barton-in-Fabis 49, 84, 100, 124, 180, 209, 210, 216, 218, 234–238
Basire, James 221
Batavians 135
Bassetlaw 8
Bassetlaw Museum 77, 89
Bavaria 20
Bawtry 8, 17, 28, 45, 94, 95, 104, 110, 158, 159, 160, 167, 168, 174-175, 183, 200, 258
BBC 154
Beckett, Prof. John 48
Bede 104, 106
Bédoyère, Guy de la 9, 36
Belle Eau Park 173
Belper (Derbyshire) 95
Berridge Road 254, 255
Besthorpe 38, 39, 44, 46, 94, 96, 106, 164, 255
Bilsthorpe 170, 171, 173, 174
Bingham 62, 64, 65, 67, 124, 130, 149, 150, 209, 210
Bingham Heritage Trails Association 62, 154
Birley, Prof. Eric 66
Bishop, Mike 23, 44, 195
Blagg, T.C. 242, 243
Blue Boar Lane (Leicester) 86

Blyth 45, 174
Bordeaux 70, 76, 101
Borrowash (Derbyshire) 175
Boston (Lincolnshire) 25
Boudica, Queen 17, 18, 19, 29, 32, 33, 47, 57, 117
Boudiga 77
Boumphrey, G.M. 122, 215
Bowden, Dr Will 70, 232–234
Brackenhurst college 170
Bradmore 241
Breedon Hill (Leicestershire) 20, 23, 66
Breeze, Andrew 24
Bridgford Street 148, 149, 150
Brigantes 18, 25, 29, 30, 33, 50, 111, 112, 184, 192, 195
Bristol 37
Britannia (and Britannia Superior and Inferior) 7, 17, 50, 51, 70, 76, 102, 103, 110, 113, 168, 179, 255
Britannicus 9
British Museum 72, 92, 141, 176
Brocolitia 78, 79
Brookes, Canon 88
Brough (Crococolana) 16, 81, 82, 86, 87, 88, 89, 91, 93, 97, 98, 115, 116, 119, 137–142, 143, 144, 151, 152, 175, 209, 247
Brough-on-Humber (Petuaria) 86
Broughton Lodge 127, 128
Brown, Cornelius 96, 144
Broxtowe 16, 17, 48, 186, 187
Broxtowe fort 18, 30, 90, 96, 102, 112, 180, 183, 186–193, 194
Brucius 83
Buckley, Richard 105
Bunny 101
Burrow Fields 12
Burrows Road 149
Burrowhill 125
Burton Joyce 23, 24
Burton, Samuel 242
Butler R.M. 7, 8
Butser Ancient Farm (Hampshire) 94, 223
Buxton, Dr L.H.D. 214
Byron, Admiral Sir John 206
Byron, Lord 88
Byzantium 102

Cadiz 101
Caerleon (Gwent) 238
Caesar, Julius 9, 14, 15, 24–27, 36, 50, 75, 79, 91, 100, 249
Calenus, Gaius Julius 70
Caligula, Emperor 9
Calverton 17, 21, 22, 30, 84, 174, 183, 196, 197–199, 253, 254
Camden, William 64, 66, 125, 127, 162
Camp Hill 172, 195
Campion, George 96, 188, 189–191
Camulodunum 28, 32, 33, 47, 76, 117
Camulorix 73
Canada 223
Caracalla, Emperor 51
Caratacus 18, 29, 33
Caratius 83
Carausias, Emperor 255
Car Colston 62, 115, 124, 209, 210, 216, 242–243
Car Dyke 93
Carlisle 117, 159
Carlton-on-Trent 38
Carnarvon Primary School 62
Carsington (Derbyshire) 92
Cassidy, Rt. Rev. David 232
Castleford (West Yorkshire) 158
Castlegate (Newark) 143
Castle Hill 12, 64
Castor 19, 75, 89
Catterick (North Yorkshire) 97
Cattuvellauni 20, 24, 29
Caunton 75
Caunton Properties (Southwell) Ltd 232
Caucasus 136
Celatus 68, 73
Cerialis, Petillius 30, 34, 117
Civitas Corieltauvorum 8, 35, 105
Chainbridge Lane 46, 90, 100
Challis, Keith 173
Charnwood Forest (and slate) 22, 59, 179, 241

Chesterfield 148
Chesterfield Canal 160
Chesterton, G.K. 123
Chevallier, Raymond 120
Chile 206
Churchover (Warwickshire) 24
Church Street 229, 231
Church Wilne Reservoir 175
Cicero 91
Cirencester (Gloucestershire) 112, 113
Clarborough 87, 88
Clark, W.B. 166
Claudius (Emperor) 9, 14, 15, 20, 28, 29, 30, 32, 47, 50, 71, 76, 80, 113, 183
Claudius II (Emperor) 254
Clayworth 160
Clifton 48
Clumber 45
Codrington, Thomas 109, 110, 113, 152, 163, 174, 175
Colchester (Camulodunum) 28, 135
Collingham 17, 38, 87, 116, 119, 137, 138, 139, 146, 152, 163, 183, 255
Collingwood, R.G. 83, 110, 111, 112, 113, 114
Collyer Road 253
Colston Bassett 62
Columella 219
Commodus, Emperor 248
Combs Farm 23, 200
Constantine, Emperor 51, 57, 71, 80, 102, 105
Constantine III, Emperor 177
Constantinople 52, 102
Cooper, Richard 126
Corbridge (Northumberland) 97
Corieltauvi (and Coritani) 14, 16, 18, 19, 20, 24–29, 31, 32, 33, 34, 35, 47, 50, 51, 75, 88, 90, 111, 112, 118, 124, 192, 249
Cornelius, Quintus 68, 69
Cosh, Stephen R. 217
Cossons, Arthur 236
Cossons, Sir Neil 236
Costock 179
Cotgrave 110, 121
Cottam 158
Coulthard, C.E. 243
Court Hill 179
Coventry 109, 122
Crawford, OGS 132
Crewe Lane 173
Crococolana (Brough) 16, 19, 40, 49, 116, 124, 129, 137–142, 159, 204
Cromwell 22, 23, 38, 40, 143, 209, 210, 216, 217, 245–247
Crookdale Lane 253
Crosshill Tumulus 128
Crow Wood 24
Cuckoo Bush 179
Cupid 84, 85, 86, 89, 211, 212, 216, 229, 231
Cuttler, Richard 145
Cybele 77

Dacia (Romania) 135
Daily Telegraph 151, 232
Daniels, Charles 216, 217, 228–232
Danube, River 105, 116, 248
Darwin (family) 73
Daubney, Adam 75
Davies, Hugh 119, 120, 121
Dead Man's Grave 73
Dean, Malcolm 127, 128
Dean's Residence 228
Deering, Charles 48
Defoe, Daniel 109, 110,112
Denton (Lincolnshire) 211
Derby (Derventio) 8, 93, 173, 175–180, 183
Derbyshire Ware 95, 97
Dere Street 120, 182
Devon, River 145
Dickinson, William 129, 142, 169, 224, 227
Dio Cassius 19, 32
Diocletian, Emperor 105
Dignus, Canius 68, 72
Dispater 73
Domitian, Emperor 124
Don, River 44, 158
Doncaster (Danum) 17, 95, 110,

158, 159, 167, 198
Dorket Head 16, 24, 174, 198–199
Dorset 32
Dover Beck 197, 198
Dragonby (Lincolnshire) 21, 26, 97
Drakeholes 160
Draycott 175
Druids 79, 80, 135
Dunham-on-Trent 161
Dunston's Clump 45, 97, 101
Durham 208

East Bridgford 11, 12, 16, 55, 64, 116, 129, 131, 147, 149, 150
East Leake 176, 179
East Midlands 7, 8, 15, 27, 28, 29, 33, 35, 47, 48, 51, 68, 70, 71, 75, 86, 92, 103, 120, 123, 145
East Midlands Development Agency 153
East Stoke 16, 75, 130, 135, 136, 143, 209
Ebbins, Susan 177
Edingley 193, 195
Edwalton 241
Egypt 78
Elagabalus, Emperor 218
Elliott, Lee 229
Elston Hall 73
Elston 242
Eltavona 142, 143
English Heritage 236
English Partnerships 222
Epona 89
Epperstone (villa) 49, 84, 93, 97, 170, 172, 209, 211, 243–245
Ermine Street 15, 16, 143, 156, 158, 161, 163, 174
European Regional Development Fund 222
Everton 160
Exe, River 111
Exeter 110, 114

Farndon 116, 129, 131,136, 150, 153
Farnsfield 17, 23, 30, 92, 173, 174, 183, 184, 195, 196, 199–201, 202
Faulkner, Neil 35, 50
Faustina, Volusia 70
Fenland 70
Fenwick Close 188
Ferry Lane Farm 39, 164
Firsby Road 188
Firth of Forth 120
Fiskerton 136
Flavia Caesariensis 51
Flavinus, Lucius Sempronius 69
Flawborough 81
Flawford 49, 84, 106, 209, 210, 216, 217, 237, 239–241
Flawforth Lane 241
Flintham Hall 65
Flintham Park 147
Forest Fields 48, 254, 255
Forest of Dean 72
Fosse Dyke 68, 73, 93
Fosse Way (and A46) 16, 30, 34, 37, 40, 49, 53, 54, 56, 58, 59, 61, 62, 65, 71, 73, 95, 106, 109–157, 158, 159, 170, 174, 175, 179, 182, 204, 208, 237
Fowler, William 206, 221, 225
Fox Wood 24
Frere, Sheppard 112, 113, 134, 174
Frisians 135
Frome (Somerset) 258
Frontinus, Gaius Antistius 70, 77

Gainsborough (Lincolnshire) 164
Gallienus, Emperor 253
Gallic Empire 253, 257
Gamston 22, 41, 42
Gateford 22, 89
Garton, Daryl 94
Gaul (and Gauls) 9, 14, 15, 20, 25, 27, 40, 42, 75, 79, 97, 105, 116, 249, 255
Germania 74
Gibbon, Edward 80, 102, 103
Gleadthorpe 17, 30, 173, 183, 184, 196, 201–203
Glebe Farm 234, 236, 237
Gloucester 112
Gonalston 22, 41, 42, 43, 46, 164

Granby 88
Grange Farm 200
Graves, Robert 9
Great Casterton (Rutland) 49, 211
Great North Road 143, 159, 174, 175
Great Weldon (Northamptonshire) 211
Great Witcombe (Gloucestershire) 230
Great Woodchester (Gloucestershire) 211
Green, John 64
Greenfield, Ernest 177
Greet Valley 171,193, 195
Greetwell (Lincolnshire) 51
Griffin, Rev. H.J. 165
Gringley-on-the-Hill 75
Grove Farm 48
Grover, W.H. 222
Guadalquivir, River 101
Gunthorpe 131, 136, 149

Hadrian, Emperor 9, 17, 40, 251, 258
Hadrian's Wall 32, 47, 57, 66, 78, 79, 99, 104, 106, 113, 120, 135
Haigh, Brendan 232
Hagan, Victor W. 111
Halam 195
Hall Close 242, 243
Halloughton 170
Harlow Wood 91
Harrod, William 220, 224
Hart, John 140, 141
Harworth 45
Haughgate Hill 160
Haverfield, Francis 88
Hayton 17, 183
Heichelheim, Dr F.M. 128
Helius, Flavius 68, 70, 71
Herecura 73
Hexgrave Park 92
High Cross (Leicestershire) 78, 112, 113
Highways Agency 115, 145, 152, 153
Hill, Rev. Arthur Du Boulay 150
Hill, Henry 88
Hind, F. 189, 190
Historic Environment Record 250, 251, 252, 257
Hodsock Priory 45
Holbeck 170, 172
Hollinwood (Holly) Hill 198
Hollinwood Lane 174
Holme 17, 30, 38, 141, 183, 195, 196, 203–204
Holme Pierrepont 22, 41, 42, 209
Honorius, Emperor 102, 105
Hoon, Geoff MP 153
Horsley, John 127, 129, 137, 159
Hoskins, W.G. 37, 43, 106
Houldsworth, Herbert O. 176, 177, 191
Hoveringham 42, 255
Howard, Robert and Lorna 257
Hucknall 251
Humber, River and Estuary 20, 30, 111, 158, 160, 164, 200
Hungary (Pannonia) 69, 116

Iceni 18, 29, 32, 47
Idle, River 17, 44, 104, 136, 160, 167, 168
Ingenua, Flavia 70
Inskeep, R.R. 132, 133, 135
Isis 78, 79 Italy
14, 34, 40, 69, 116, 120, 218

James, Harry 242
Jerusalem 159
Jewry Wall 35, 78, 218
Jones, Mick 105
Joseph, Dr J.K. St 132, 134, 139, 174, 203, 245
Josephus 117, 118, 184
Judea 118
Julian, Emperor (Apostate) 80, 104, 168
Jupiter 71, 76
Jupiter Britannicus 129

Kean Construction 231, 232
Kegworth 179
Kelham 38
Keyworth 241

King Street 15
Kinsley, Gavin 145, 173
Kirkby-in-Ashfield 252, 253
Kirklington 172, 173, 193, 195, 224
Knaith (Lincolnshire) 95
Kneeton 147
Knight, David 42, 43
Knight, John 221
Kurdistan 78

Laing, Jennifer 83, 84
Lake District 62
Lamb Mr 251
Lamb's Close 38
Langar 209, 217
Langford 204
Langford Hall 151
Langold 221
Laurentum (Italy) 218
Laxton 209, 210
Lea (Lincolnshire) 95
Leary, Ruth 45, 60, 61
Leicester (Ratae) 8, 11,12, 14, 24, 26, 33, 35, 38, 58, 61, 68, 69, 70, 76, 77, 78, 79, 84, 86, 89, 95, 103, 105, 109, 110, 113, 115, 116, 118, 120, 124, 125, 135, 176, 179, 218
Leland, John 159, 162
Lenton (Lincolnshire) 73
Lenton Priory 191
Lesley Road 254
Lezoux 98
Linby 75, 76
Lindsey 22
Lincoln (Lindum) 12, 14, 15, 17, 34, 35, 38, 46, 50, 51, 58, 61, 69, 70, 71, 74, 76, 78, 82, 86, 87, 89, 93, 95, 97, 101, 105, 109, 110, 111, 112, 114, 115, 116, 117, 118, 121, 124, 143, 152, 158, 159, 160, 161, 166, 167, 168, 182, 194, 200, 247
Lindbridge Road 187
Lindfield Road 193
Littleborough (Segelocum) 8, 17, 43, 87, 88, 93, 96, 97, 106, 110, 121, 158–166, 177, 223
Little Chester 175, 183
Little Danethorpe Farm 141
Little London (Lincolnshire) 95
Little Morton 257
Lockington (Leicestershire) 22, 124, 180, 209, 217, 247
Lodge Farm 24, 146, 147
London (Londinium) 14, 15, 16, 17, 32, 78, 79, 88, 115, 118, 120, 159, 255
Long Bennington (Lincolnshire) 143, 174
Long Billington 126
Long Eaton 22, 68, 71, 175
Longhedge Lane 147, 155, 156
Longland Lane 199
Longthorpe (Cambridgeshire) 32, 117, 194
Long Whatton (Leicestershire) 179
Lound 43, 46, 90, 100
Lovely Grange 200
Lowdham 59, 60
Lowdham Road 149
Lower Kirklington Road 173
Low Holland Farm 161
Lowther Hill 200
Lucius 68
Lullingstone (Kent) 81, 230
Lunaris, Marcus Aurelius 68, 69, 70, 76, 101
Lutudarum 92
Lydney 72
Lyons (Lugdunum) 80, 116
Lyth, Philip 170, 173

Maccius of Lezoux 42
Macedonia 116
Mackreth, Don 190
Maglus 68, 76
Major Oak 224
Malaga 101
Malton (North Yorkshire) 117
Manor Farm 242
Manor Park Infants School 253
Mansfield (and museum) 75, 76, 91, 116, 220, 221, 222, 223, 224, 225, 227
Mansfield District Council 222

Mansfield Woodhouse 8, 34, 48, 49, 84, 148, 206–207, 209, 210, 211, 213, 216, 218, 219–225, 229, 234, 258
Marcellinus, Ammianus 104
Margary, Ivan D. 109, 110, 113, 117, 119, 143, 145, 150, 151, 158, 159, 160, 174, 176
Margidunum 7, 8, 11–13, 16, 19, 30, 34, 37, 38, 43, 46, 53–67, 74, 82, 84, 86, 87, 90, 91, 92, 93, 97, 100, 101, 104, 106, 107, 112, 113, 115, 116, 125, 127, 128, 131, 146, 147, 148, 149, 150, 153, 154, 155, 161, 179, 183, 184, 191, 198, 210, 216, 222, 242, 247
Marne 20
Mars 68, 74, 75, 83, 89
Marshall, Neil 117
Martin, H. 236
Martin, William 242
Marton (Lincolnshire) 161, 164
Masvetvs 40
Mattersey 45, 46
Mattingly, David 36, 38
Mattingly, Harold 84, 253
Maun, River 44
Maximus, Magnus 104
Maximus, Marcus Aurelius 70
May, Jeffrey 26
Maythorpe, HM Borstal Institute, 188
McInally, Pamela 225
Medbourne (Lincolnshire) 211
Meden, River 44, 202
Meering 97, 250
Mellor, S. 243
Menagerie Wood 43, 46, 92, 101
Menai Straits 135
Mercia 106, 123
Mercury 75
Mickleborough Hill 143
Miles, Frank 149
Miles, Mrs 64
Millgate 106, 143, 145
Minster School 227, 233
Misterton 17, 183
Mithras 77, 78, 80
Mons Pool Quarry 39, 40, 41, 96
Monty Python 233
Mosel, River 97

Nantosuelta 73, 83
Neal, David J. 217
Nene, River and Valley 24, 40, 87, 95, 97, 112
Neptune 72
Nero, Emperor 32, 33, 50, 137, 183
Nether Broughton 126
Nether Heyford (Northamptonshire) 211
Nettleham (Lincolnshire) 74, 77
Newark 16, 28, 38, 41, 64, 73, 91, 96, 106, 109, 115, 119, 122, 129, 135, 138, 139, 140, 142–145, 151, 152, 153, 170, 174, 203, 214, 215, 224, 245, 247, 251
Newark Advertiser 137, 139, 140, 141, 232
Newark and Sherwood District Council 88, 91, 139, 215
Newark Technical College 128
Newport Arch 124, 161
Newstead 89, 252, 253
Newton-on-Trent (Lincolnshire) 161, 183, 194
Newton Street 149, 150
Nicholls, S.J. 238, 239
Nijmegen 89, 117
Noble and Cary 159, 167
Norfolk Street Villa (Leicester) 86
Normanton-on-Trent 38
Northgate 91, 143, 144
North Hykeham (Lincolnshire) 95
North Leverton 77
North Muskham 38
Northfields 222
North Scaffold Lane 141, 152
North Thoresby (Lincolnshire) 101
North Wheatley 161
Northumberland 123, 186
Norton Disney (Lincolnshire) 19, 49, 93, 97, 104, 124, 141, 141, 153, 209, 213–215
Norwich 88

Nottingham 48, 175, 200, 254
Nottingham Brewhouse Yard Museum 176
Nottingham City Museums & Galleries 73, 122, 235
Nottingham Evening Post 150, 155, 215
Nottingham Journal 188
Nottinghamshire Archives 150
Nottinghamshire County Council 155, 227, 231, 237, 250
Nottinghamshire Guardian 129, 131, 188
Novantico, Marcus Ulpius 135

O'Brien, Colm 243
Octavian (Augustus) 50, 177
Oldcotes 8, 84, 209, 210, 217, 238–240
Old Ox 23, 200
Old Rufford Road 174
Old Sleaford 21, 26, 87
Old Winteringham (Lincolnshire) 117
Ollerton 17, 44, 45, 94, 174–175, 183, 198, 248, 258
Osberton Hall 88
Osmanthorpe 17, 31, 136, 170, 171, 172, 173, 183, 185, 193–196, 200
Oswald, Felix 19, 20, 53–67, 74, 86, 90, 92, 97, 100, 102, 104, 106, 112, 135, 136, 147, 148, 168, 191, 211
Oswald, Adrian 19, 49, 54, 104, 130, 133, 135, 141, 150, 170, 209, 213, 214, 236
Owthorpe 121
Oxford 122
Oxton 23, 170, 174, 197, 200

Palfreyman, Alan 177
Parisi 25
Parkinson, John 92
Paulinus, Suetonius 32
Peak District 92
Peddie, John 118
Peel, J.H.B. 151
Pegge, Rev. Samuel 224
Persia, 80, 105
Peterborough 32, 117
Pevsner, Nikolaus 12, 200
Pius, Emperor Antoninus 40, 255
Plautius, Aulus 15, 29, 111
Pleasley 219, 221
Plicque, Albert-Edward 66
Pliny the Elder 80, 82
Pliny the Younger 218, 219
Plumptre Street 48
Plumtree 240, 241
Pluto 73
Point Shallows 176
Pollux 19, 75, 89
Portable Antiquities Scheme 75, 251
Portland, Duke of 215
Portway 179
Postumus, Emperor 253
Potter Hill 152
Potter, Rev. S.P. 176
Priest, Vicki 173
Primus 68
Prosperine 73
Proxsimus, Quintus Neratius 74, 77
Pryce, T. Davies 54, 56, 65, 66
Protus, Gaius Julius 92
Ptolemy 14, 24, 35
Pudens, Titus Valerius 69

Quintus 91

Rackham, Oliver 110, 123, 168, 169, 175
RAF Newton (and Newton) 13, 61, 62, 124, 209, 210, 216
RAF Swinderby 119
Rainworth Water 224
Rampton 22, 43, 46, 164
Ramsey, Eleanor 145
Ranskill 45
Ratcliffe-on-Soar power station 175
Raymoth Lane 22, 46, 96
Redhill 32, 33, 68, 71, 72, 73, 75, 84, 87, 90, 92, 93, 124, 175–180, 209, 222, 237, 247, 249
Red Hill Farm 70, 176, 177

Regni 29
Retford 28, 45, 90, 166
Retford and District Historical and Archaeological Society 257
Revill, S. 244
Rhine, River 97, 135
Ribchester 89
Richardson, Maurice 251
Richborough (Kent) 118
Richmond, Sir Ian 117, 125
Rigonemetos, Mars 74, 77
Riley, Derrick 44, 45, 132, 168, 169, 186, 194, 195, 197, 198, 199, 202, 257
Robin Hood Way 203
Robinson, Tony 139
Roman Bank Lane 174
Romanstone Plantation 153
Rooke, Major Hayman 48, 198, 200, 206–207, 209, 211, 213, 216, 218, 219–226
Rossington Bridge (South Yorkshire) 95, 97, 175, 183
Rotherham 173
Royal Commission on the Historical Monuments of England 185, 202
Royal Engineers 118
Royal Flying Corps 132
Rubicon 112
Ruddington 239–241
Ruddington Local History Society 240, 242
Rufford 174
Rushcliffe 11, 22, 101, 240
Rushcliffe Boys' School 127
Ryknield Street 173

Sabinianus 69
Saliga, Lucius Licinius 69
Salt Way 175, 180
Salway, Peter 70
Samian ware 65, 66, 97, 98, 240
Sanderson's Map 176
Sapperton 48
Sarapis 79
Sarrivs 97
Saufeius, Gaius 69
Saveria 69
Sawley 176, 180
Saxon Shore 104
Scaftworth and fortlet 104, 160, 167–168, 169, 183, 250, 258
Scampton (Lincolnshire) 211
Scapula, Ostorius 15, 29, 111
Scotland 17, 31, 97, 182
Scratta Wood 22, 92
Segelocum 17, 106
Senecio, Aurelius 70
Servandus 68, 69
Severn, River 30, 111, 112
Severus, Emperor 50
Sewstern Lane 16, 143, 156
Shakespeare, William 164
Sheffield 239
Shelford 97
Shelton 209
Shepshed (Leicestershire) 179
Sherratt, Andrew 225
Sherwood Archaeological Society 23, 201
Sherwood Forest 224
Sherwood sandstone 44
Shilton, Richard 227
Shipside, Tom 200
Shrimpton, Rev. Canon A.C. 241
Shrimpton, Dorothy 241
Shropshire 186
Sibthorpe 209, 210
Silvanius 72
Simpson, Grace 66
Six Hills (Leicestershire) 175, 176
Sleaford (Lincolnshire) 163
Smith, Arthur 89, 140
Smith, David 211
Smollett, Tobias 102
Soar, River 32, 35, 72, 175, 177, 179
Society of Antiquaries 88, 219, 221, 225
Solway Firth 17
Somerset Levels 110
Somme 20, 186
South Muskham 38
South Shields (Tyne and Wear) 223
South Wheatley 161
Southwell (and Minster) 8, 17, 34,

49, 84–86, 106, 116, 129, 143, 169, 170, 171–173, 183, 193, 195, 207, 209–212, 216, 217, 227–234, 244, 251
Southwell Charter 170, 173
Southwell Community Archaeology Group 232, 234
Southwell Diocese 139
Southwell Town Council 232
Spain 40, 100, 101, 105, 116
Sparsholt (Hampshire) 223
Spence, Ursilla 155, 227
Stanford-on-Soar 75, 76, 209, 250
Staunton 46
St Albans (Veralumium) 32
St Helen's Catholic Church 238, 239
St Nicholas Church 165
St Peter's Church 240, 241
Street Way (East Bridgford) 149
Streetway (East Leake) 179
Stukeley, William 64, 87, 109, 119, 126, 127, 129, 130, 137, 138, 142, 152, 165
Sturton-le-Steeple 161
Styrrup 24
Sucellos 73, 83
Suetonius 9, 33, 71,100
Sutcliff, Rosemary 117
Sutton Bonington 254
Sutton-in-Ashfield 92
Sutton-on-Trent 33, 38
Swarbrick, Catherine J. 201
Syerston airfield 147, 155, 156
Syrians 135

Tacitus 15, 19, 24, 27, 29, 30, 34, 46, 47, 74, 111, 112, 117, 136
Tadcaster (North Yorkshire) 158
Tauros Trigaranus 79
Templeborough (South Yorkshire) 117, 173
Tetricus, Emperor 241, 253
Theodosius, Count 104, 168
Theodosius, Emperor 80
Theseus 238
Thistleton (Rutland) 143
Thompson, Adam 39, 40, 41, 218
Thompson, F.H. 236–237
Thorpe (Ad Pontem) 16, 49, 73, 79, 81, 82, 83, 87, 92, 93, 97, 116, 148, 150, 151
Thorpe-bar 129
Thoresby 45
Thoroton, Dr Robert 126, 161, 200, 221
Thoroton Society of Nottinghamshire 7, 81, 88, 143, 160, 188, 191, 225
Throsby, John 126, 129, 200, 221, 224, 225
Thrumpton 72
Thrussington (Leicestershire) 121
Thurgarton 49, 170, 172, 209, 216, 242, 243–245, 255, 256, 258
Thurgarton Beck 243, 244
Thurgarton Priory 92
Thurmaston (Leicestershire) 120
Till Bridge Lane (Lincolnshire) 161, 165
Time Team 76, 139
Titocuna 73
Toutates 75
Todd, Malcolm 24, 25, 29, 46, 53–67, 74, 88, 97, 104, 147, 148, 191, 245
Tomlin, R.S.O. 24
Torksey (Lincolnshire) 93
Toynbee, Jocelyn 73, 83, 88
Trajan, Emperor 252
Trenico 76
Trent, River and Valley 17, 22, 25, 30, 32, 33, 34, 37, 38, 40, 41, 43, 44, 51, 68, 71, 93, 95, 96, 111, 112, 122, 129, 130, 131, 135, 136, 142, 143, 148–150, 158, 159, 161–164, 166, 171, 173, 175–177, 183, 189, 191, 192, 194, 195, 198, 203, 204, 209, 210, 217, 237, 245, 246, 251, 255
Trent, Lane 144
Trent Navigation Company 163
Trent Valley Ware 97
Trentlock 175, 176
Trier 249
Trinovantes 47

Trisantona(m) (River Trent) 112, 164
Trollope, Archdeacon 163
Tuscany 138
Tutela 77
Turner, Catherine 198
Turner, James 198, 201
Turner, Prof. E.G. 72
Tyne, River 17

University of Cambridge 132
University of Durham 72, 166
University of Exeter 56
University of Leicester 36, 105
University of London 72
University of Oxford 225
University of Nottingham (and museum) 54, 56, 70, 81, 101, 218, 222, 232, 242
University of Salford 39
University of Sheffield 44, 163, 166, 222
Upton 143, 251

Vale of Belvoir 11, 46, 150, 242, 243
Valentinian, Emperor 104
Valerius, Gaius 69
Vegetius 186
Vernemetum 16, 71, 74, 75, 100, 103, 116, 119, 122, 123, 125–129, 179
Verucunda 68, 86
Vespasian, Emperor and legionary commander 33, 50, 118, 189, 193, 254
Vicar's Court 228, 230
Victorinus, Emperor 121, 253
Villa Farm 153
Villa Rustica 219, 220
Villa Urbana 219, 220, 221
Vindolanda (Northumberland) 32, 47, 66, 99, 223, 249
Vine Street 78, 105
Viridios 76
Volisios 24, 25

Waal, River 135
Wacher, John 150, 219
Wade, John 166, 222, 223
Wake, E.G. 119
Wales 111, 238
Walters, H.B. 130
Warsop 80, 201
Warwicks Brewery 91
Water Newton (Durobrivae) 15, 95, 211
Watling Street 120, 159, 163
Watson, Grahame 21, 22
Welbeck 45, 224
Welland, River 24
Wessex 123
Wessex Cotswold Archaeology 154
West Bridgford 22, 48, 191
West Burton 158
West Leake 176
Westminster 118
Whatton 22
Whinbush Lane 197
White, Father Gerry 239, 240
Widmerpool 145, 153, 154
William the Conqueror 37, 119
Willoughby Fields Farm 146, 147
Willoughby-on-the-Wolds 16, 71, 74, 106, 115, 116, 119, 122, 125–129, 146, 175, 209, 217
Willoughby Skeleton 128
Wilmhurst, B. Mr 166
Wilsford (Lincolnshire) 73
Wilson, Roger Prof. 11,12, 65, 72, 222, 223
Winchester (Hampshire) 223
Winterton (Lincolnshire) 221
Winthorpe 38, 146
Wintour, Rev. 234
Wirksworth (Derbyshire) 92
Wiseton Park 160
Witham, River 33, 93
Woodborough 24
Wood Lane 179
Woolley, T. Cecil Smith 87, 88, 98, 137, 138, 139, 159, 162, 165
Worksop 22, 43, 45, 46, 89, 95, 101, 238
Wroxeter (Shropshire) 120

Yonge, George Rt. Hon. 221

York (Eboracum) 17, 51, 52, 70, 76, 78, 101, 115, 116, 117, 120, 158, 160, 168, 182, 194
Yugoslavia 79

Afterword

Roman Nottinghamshire was first printed in May 2011 and was reprinted within just a few weeks. However, since first publication there have been several significant developments in the archaeology and physical landscape of Roman Nottinghamshire. Perhaps the most important issues have been the completion of the dualling of the A46 Fosse Way, new discoveries around *Margidunum* and later developments in the prolonged planning row centred on the large villa at Southwell. Work along the A46 alone has produced a massive amount of archaeology including evidence for prehistoric flint-making, Bronze Age burials, Iron Age settlements and previously unknown Roman buildings, roads and infant burials around *Margidunum*, the Roman town that straddled the Fosse Way. Although these finds are still being analysed, they immediately raise questions about the Roman landscape, not least whether there needs to be a rethink on *Margidunum*. Recent discoveries appear to have enhanced, rather than further diminished, the status of a place once thought of as a small straggling road-side town that travellers would have passed through on their way to the brighter lights of Roman Lincoln or Leicester. In the meantime, a long-running excavation of two Romano-British communities at Besthorpe has been completed and a previously unknown village has been found nearby at Langford Quarry.

Publication of *Roman Nottinghamshire* has also led many people who have been involved in local excavations to come forward and tell their stories. In summary, there is a lot of new information that needs to be incorporated into a revised edition of the book. This should be published in 2014 when the book I am currently working on, *Roman Derbyshire*, comes out. Until then, readers who feel they have information to contribute to the revised edition are welcome to contact me via Five Leaves Publications or the Roman Nottinghamshire blog http://romannottinghamshire.wordpress.com/.

Mark Patterson
November 2012